The Stitching Book

A step-by-step guide to surface stitching techniques

Patricia Bage

Jill Carter

Ruth Chamberlin

Kay Dennis

Clare Hanham

Jane Rainbow

Pat Trott

Lesley Wilkins

SEARCH PRESS

First published in Great Britain 2012

Search Press Limited
Wellwood, North Farm Road,
Tunbridge Wells, Kent TN2 3DR

Including material previously published
by Search Press as:

Beginner's Guide to Drawn Thread Embroidery
by Patricia Bage
Beginner's Guide to Hardanger by Jill Carter
Beginner's Guide to Goldwork by Ruth Chamberlin
Beginner's Guide to Stumpwork by Kay Dennis
Beginner's Guide to Silk Shading by Clare Hanham
Beginner's Guide to Crewel Embroidery
by Jane Rainbow
Beginner's Guide to Mountmellick Embroidery
by Pat Trott
Beginner's Guide to Blackwork by Lesley Wilkins

Printed in Malaysia

The Stitching Book

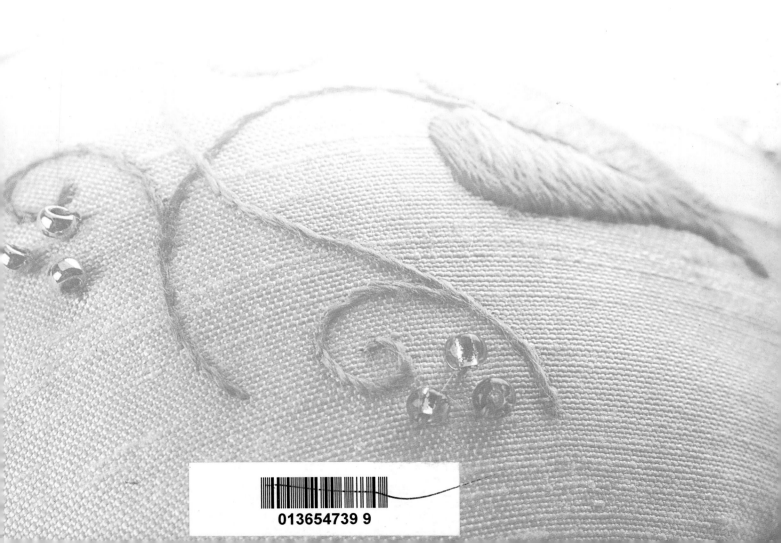

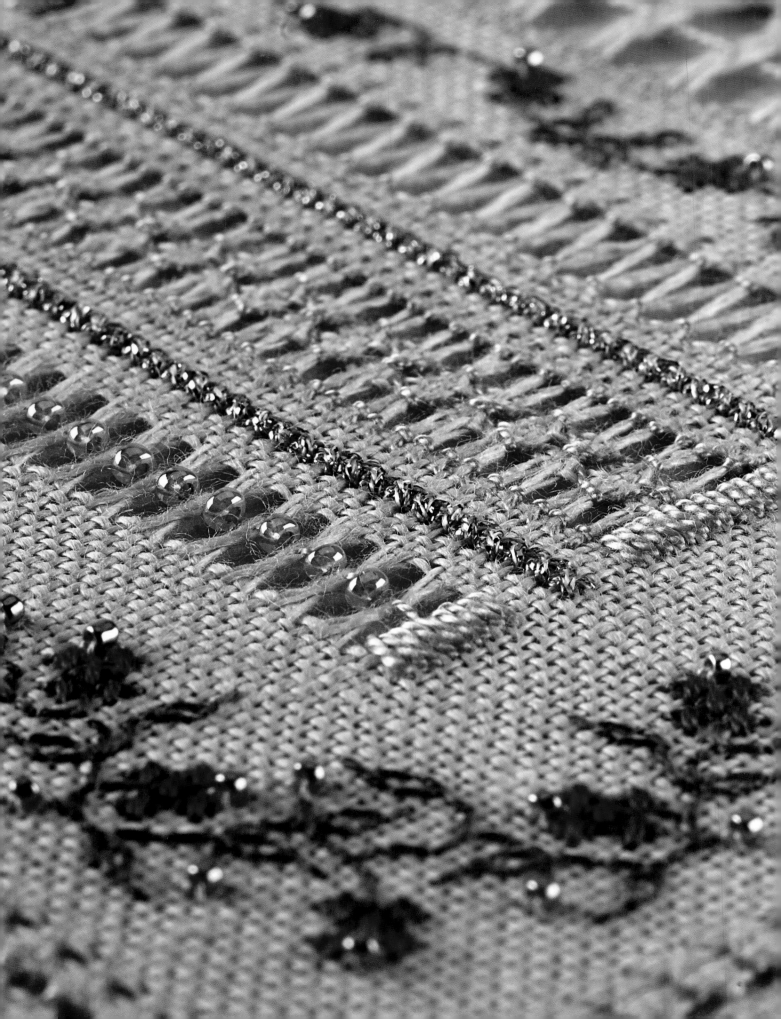

Acknowledgements

Thanks are due to the following organisations and individuals for their help with various sections of this book:

Zweigart in the USA for providing the linen fabric; Kreinik, USA for the silk and metallic threads; DMC, UK for the stranded and cotton perle; Wichelt Imports, Inc., USA for providing the Mill Hill beads and treasures; and Macleod Craft Marketing, UK for supplying the Caron Waterlilies silk threads used in the chapter on drawn thread embroidery.

The manufacturers of the computer program EasyGrapher Stitch Wiz, which was used to create the drawn thread embroidery stitch diagrams, and PremiumPlus 2000 with which the patterns for the drawn thread embroidery projects were drawn.

Linda Nelson, Melissa Campbell, Deborah Somerlot, Kris Herber and Ellen Brittain in the USA, Jennifer Lloyd in the UK, Debra Morris in Canada, and Gail Phillips and Marianne Wohlk in Australia for proofreading the drawn thread embroidery projects; Jenny Robinson, who completed the cushion on page 229 and who provided the instructions for it.

Siriol Clarry for producing the diagrams and charts for the chapter on Hardanger; and Alistair McMinn of Coats Craft UK, Cara Ackerman of DMC Creative World, Vartan and Sarah of Sew it All Ltd, Kreinik Manufacturing Co. Inc. and Craft Creations Ltd. for their support and generous contributions to the Hardanger projects.

Henry Allen for photographing the work on pages 250 and 269 and Angela Taylor for framing all of the work of Ruth Chamberlin.

Benton and Johnson, Kath Moore, Wendy at Mace and Nairn, Pearsalls, Perkins and Sons, Watts and Co., Mulberry Silks (Patricia Woods), Silk Route, BWH Designs of Whitby, Keith Lovell and the Art Shop, Oakham for their help and support and for supplying the materials used in the goldwork projects.

Publisher's note
All the step-by-step photographs in this book feature the authors demonstrating stitching techniques. No models have been used.

contents

Silk Shading 26

Crewel Embroidery 46

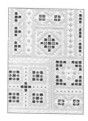

Introduction

Stitching simply means drawing a thread through fabric using a needle. In a practical sense it can be used to make clothes, accessories and fabric-based items for the home, but it can also be used decoratively, and it is this latter type of stitching, otherwise known as surface stitching or embroidery, that is the main focus of this book.

Embroidery is the art of embellishing or adorning by means of a needle and thread. Although modern sewing machines can produce a good range of embroidery stitches virtually at the 'push of a button', there is nothing more satisfying than producing a hand-worked piece of embroidery using methods that have been in existence for hundreds of years.

But despite its long history, there is nothing old-fashioned about traditional embroidery; combine it with modern threads, fabrics, designs and colour schemes and you can create a look that is both contemporary and timeless.

The aim of this book is to introduce you to several of the traditional forms of embroidery: the materials required, the stitches and techniques used and step-by-step projects with which to practise and consolidate them. Once you have acquired the basic skills, you can adapt them and move forwards with them, creating your own unique designs and placing them firmly in the twenty-first century. Either display them as framed pieces in their own right or use them to decorate clothes, accessories and items around the home – personalise your table linen, for example, brighten up a dull skirt or top, or create a special gift for a family member or close friend.

Embroidery has endured for many hundreds of years; however, this does not mean you should be afraid to experiment with it. Only by trying out new colour combinations, for example, and different types of fabrics and threads will you discover the joy of creativity and realise the potential of this exquisite art form.

A brief history

Early embroidery was mainly ecclesiastical and worked professionally. The Egyptian Copts of the fourth century, who were Christians, created embroideries showing saints whose robes and faces were shaded in long and short stitch, often within a circular design. These were mainly worked in silk but there are a few surviving that were worked in wool. In the thirteenth century, very fine embroidery with an emphasis on goldwork

Syon Cope

By kind permission of V&A Images/Victoria and Albert Museum.

The picture opposite is of the Syon Cope, made between 1300 and 1320 AD. The ground is a linen fabric and the whole of the background is covered in an underside couching. This technique involved laying silver gilt thread on the surface of the fabric and stitching over it with, in this case, a red and green silk thread. The thread was then pulled through the fabric, taking the loops to the underside, then the needle brought up at equal intervals to give an equal surface stitch. This method achieved a very malleable and serviceable texture, and when you look at this piece of work it is almost impossible to believe how such intricate work could be attained, particularly under what must have been very hard and difficult circumstances.

developed, but this was brought to a halt in the early fourteenth century by the Black Death, which led to a shortage in workers. Ecclesiastical embroidery was still in high demand, so people returned to quicker embroidery techniques, such as long and short stitch.

Embroidery became more domestic around the Tudor period and by the Stuart period long and short stitch was being used on a variety of styles of work. This work was often done by young girls as a sample of their skills, or by ladies of 'high birth' as a pastime.

The three-dimensional form of embroidery, stumpwork, became popular around this time. This was worked in silk and used a variety of different stitches including long and short stitch. The designs were normally biblical or showed royalty. The work was often made into beautiful caskets or mirror frames, many of which can be seen in museums.

Later, in the seventeenth century, crewel embroidery became popular, and long and short stitch was worked in the fine crewel wool that the technique was named after. Large leaves and pods inspired by the Indian 'tree of life' designs that had travelled across to Europe with silk imports were embroidered, sometimes entirely in long and short stitch. Large curtains and bed hangings in this style were made for great houses around England.

The eighteenth century saw a drop in the popularity of long and short stitch as canvas work became the vogue. In the nineteenth century, very fine silk shading was worked on to beautifully painted silk backgrounds. The designs were normally pastoral or biblical with figures whose clothes and drapery were shaded to show every fold. The hands and faces were finely painted, but the ground areas and any other main features were often worked in long and short stitch. This stitch is still done today as a part of various embroidery techniques and in a variety of different types of thread, as it has been throughout history.

Where to stitch

It is essential to have good light in which to stitch. If you are lucky enough to have time during the day, you can sit near a window, but if you can only grab an hour or two during the evenings, an anglepoise lamp fitted with a daylight bulb is a very good alternative to daylight. If you are right-handed, you should have your light source coming over your left shoulder so that, as you stitch, your right hand does not cast a shadow on the area you are stitching. Have your lamp on a small table on your left-hand side so that you can angle the light directly over your work. Of course, if you are left-handed, your light source will need to come from the right. If you sit facing a table, the light can come from the front, facing you.

It is also very useful to have all the threads, scissors, needles and other items needed in a box or bag near to hand.

The most important thing of all, however, is to be comfortable, so gather up all your materials, settle down and start stitching.

It's not just needles, threads and scissors that are useful for sewing — beads, ribbons, even a dab of fabric paint can be used to embellish your finished piece. Most people will have a small stash of these hidden away at home — seek them out and store them with the rest of your sewing kit.

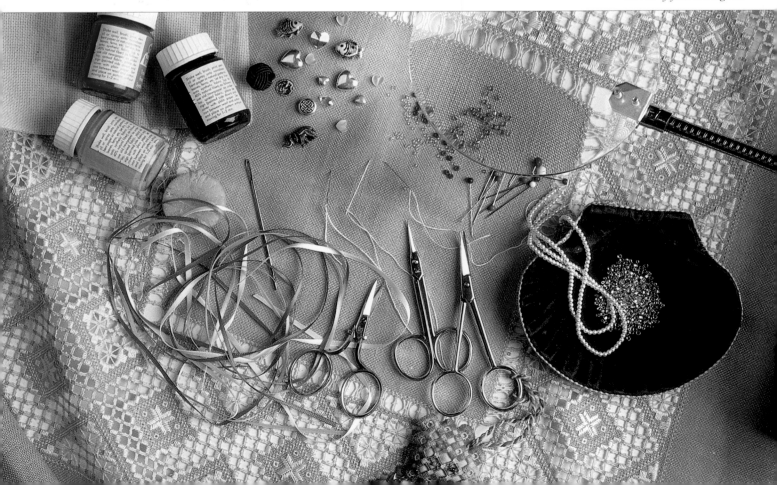

What to stitch

Many people feel they either cannot or do not want to design their own stitching projects. It really is important to understand that you do not have to be artistic to stitch – there are many wonderful kits on the market, and books packed with ideas and inspiration. However, if you do not want to work from a kit or follow someone else's pattern and want to be more creative, you can look for design ideas from many different sources. Train yourself to be observant. If you are good with a camera, you can take photographs of things that inspire you. There is so much around us that we don't really look at – the natural forms in our gardens, parks and open spaces; the buildings all around us (whether we live in the town or country); the fruit and vegetables we eat every day – all can be inspirational. Always have a sketchbook handy so that you can jot ideas down wherever you are. Even if you cannot draw easily, take a note of what interests you. The gathering of ideas gives you substance to work upon at a later date. Keeping a scrapbook can be very valuable too for collecting pictures of things that delight and inspire you – collect ideas from historical pieces, cuttings from magazines, greetings cards, wrapping paper, wallpaper and fabric.

When planning a design, you need to consider what size it should be. Think also about proportion. Remember that the space you leave out should complement the design – it is just as important as the design itself. It is also a good idea to decide upon what form the finished embroidery will take. As it is much cheaper to buy readymade picture frames, stools, cushion pads or whatever you wish to deocrate, this is the stage at which you need to decide the final measurements of your project.

The style of your design will, to some extent, depend on the type of embroidery you are undertaking. Mountmellick, silk shading, stumpwork and crewel work, for example, are traditionally associated with free-flowing floral designs and motifs based on nature, including birds, animals, leaves, berries, bees, butterflies and so on. Techniques

TIP ||||||||||||||||

Get into the habit of putting design ideas down in pencil and draw any shapes you delight in. The more drawing you do the more you learn to look, and with a better understanding of shapes the more your stitched design will become real and alive. It often helps to add colour to your drawings using watercolour paints or coloured pencils, but when it comes to designing, colour will be the last decision to be made.

Denim Bag
Clare Hanham

Use your designs to embellish bags, purses, hats, scarves and so on. This fun denim bag was embroidered with colourful butterflies embellished with small sequins, beads and metallic thread.

such as blackwork, Hardanger and drawn thread embroidery, which are worked on an evenweave fabric such as linen or cotton, work well with geometric designs. The Hardanger embroideries (see pages 136–167), for example, are based on Mediaeval tile designs; the drawn thread projects (pages 192–229) are inspired by traditional band samplers of the seventeenth century; and the blackwork embroideries are heavily influenced by those of the fifteenth, sixteenth and seventeenth centuries. By combining traditional stitches and techniques with contemporary fibres, threads and embellishments, you can put a modern twist on these beautiful and historical forms of embroidery.

You can often get your ideas flowing by working on a project. For example, you might choose a pile of leaves. Start with a worksheet and draw the pile of autumn leaves first; then draw the shadow the pile casts; then perhaps do another drawing of individual leaves – all very different shapes, with their varied outlines and patterns of veins. By this time you should really be understanding the shapes in front of you – how one line relates to another. Perhaps then draw one leaf beside another and one partly on top of another. Consider what shape is emerging on the page and whether the drawing (or by now the design) should lie flat on the page or whether the surface should become undulating. Now draw a square, an oblong or a circle and place the design that has emerged within one of these shapes, perhaps overlapping the edge of the chosen outline. This would give an entirely different effect, for the background of the shape then becomes important too.

As you will soon realise, your worksheet will be invaluable for exploring ideas. There are numerous possibilities, and you will find many ideas emerging. It is always exciting to work in this way for you can never tell what the outcome will be!

During the initial period of preparing a design, work only in black and white. Try hanging it on the wall in a spot you pass often, and each time look at it to check that you are truly happy with the proportions. When you are entirely happy with the composition, choose your colours and transfer the design on to the fabric (see pages 14–15). You are then ready to start stitching.

The design process

Butterflies are great fun to stitch because of the colours on their wings, and there are no difficult angle changes. They also give scope for inventing your own colour schemes. You can stitch imaginary butterflies, adding in glittery threads, beads and sequins.

In this example, the designer spent an afternoon chasing butterflies in a local butterfly house and got some great photographs of the more exotic species. She printed these out in black and white so that she could trace the basic shapes of the wings, bodies and different areas of colour, and then chose her own colours to stitch them in. The black and white pictures show where the shades change, so are really useful if you want to use different colours.

The butterfly in this silk shading project is a real specimen shown in its true colours, and the body has been slightly modified where the area is too small to stitch in too much detail.

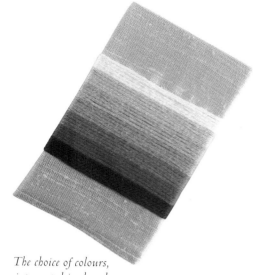

The choice of colours, interpreted in thread.

The photograph that provided the initial inspiration for the design.

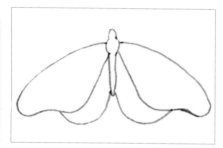

The outline for the butterfly project shown full size. As the antennae are stitched in a single stitch, it is best not to trace them on to the fabric, as covering the line with a single strand is very difficult.

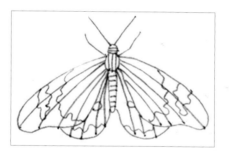

Pattern showing the direction of stitching.

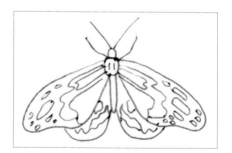

Pattern showing the areas of colour.

The finished embroidery, shown larger than actual size for clarity.

Transferring a design on to fabric

There are various ways of transferring your design on to a fabric base. The pounce method has been used for many years and is an excellent way of obtaining a perfect replica of your design, though many people now prefer to use either the light-box method or trace and stitch, both of which are described below. If you don't have a light box, attach the tracing of your design and the fabric to a window – the light will shine through and make the design line clearer!

The pounce method is ideal if no changes are to be made to the design. First, take a perfect tracing, then place it on a flat felt base and, with a fine needle (or 'pricker') held perfectly upright, prick around the entire shape making holes at regular (2mm or ⅛in) intervals. Place the pricking carefully in the right position on your fabric. Hold the tracing paper in position with your hand or pin the corners of the tracing with needles (which are less likely to mark the fabric than pins) and, with a felt roll, rub pounce powder all over the lines of the design. Remove the tracing paper carefully, making sure you don't smudge the pounced lines, then mix an even amount of watercolour paint on a palette and use a fine watercolour brush to paint the lines with a continuous stroke. Use black or white paint according to the background colour. Pounce powder is made in two colours – black and white – and is obtainable from art shops.

Light-box method

1 Begin by tracing your design on to tracing paper. Always take two tracings – one to transfer on to your background fabric and one to keep as a reference.

2 Fold your tracing in half horizontally and vertically to obtain the centre of your design.

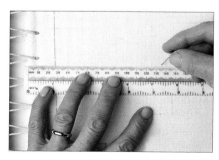

3 To find the centre of your background fabric, first lay a ruler squarely across the top half of the fabric and mark the centre point with a pin.

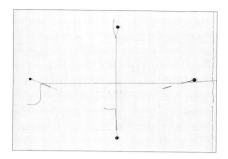

4 Tie a contrasting thread around the pin.

5 Follow the same procedure at the bottom of the fabric, securing the thread around the lower pin. Measure and mark a centre line across the width of the fabric in the same way. With a protractor, check that your two threads are perpendicular.

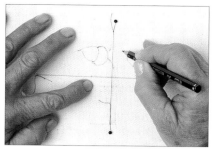

6 Attach your design to the back of the fabric using masking tape. Align the fold lines on the tracing with the threads marking the centre of the fabric. Working on a light box, trace over the design using an HB or B pencil or a marker pen.

Trace and stitch

This method involves using top stitching to mark the design. Some people are happy to retain the surface stitching and embroider over it. However, if you prefer, use a sharp-pointed pencil to draw a fine line by the stitches on to the fabric so that the impression is there. The stitches can then be removed.

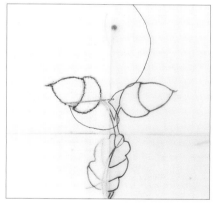

1 Place the tracing of the design on top of the fabric and align it with the centre lines as before. If you need to hold the tracing in position, pin the corners of the tracing using fine needles (these will not mark the fabric). Use a small backstitch to sew around the outline of the design using a no. 9 embroidery needle and ordinary sewing cotton. Use the same coloured thread as you intend to use for your embroidery so that you can sew over it if necessary.

2 When you have stitched around the whole design, carefully tear off the tracing leaving the surface stitching behind. Begin by tearing around the outside of the design and then remove the paper left within the shapes.

TIP ||||||||||||||||||

You can transfer your design on to the fabric either before or after you have secured it in a frame (see pages 16–20). If you choose to transfer the design after you have framed up, make sure that you have drawn out your design on paper before you begin. As well as being a reference for future work, this will enable you to determine the size of the frame you will need, and the size of the background fabric required.

Framing up

Securing your fabric in a frame keeps it taut and makes stitching easier. There are lots of different types of frame available, all of which require different ways of framing up. In the following sections you will be shown how to frame-up a hoop, a pin frame and a slate frame. The choice of frame depends on the type of fabric you are using and the size of the design. Whichever frame you choose, the most important thing is to ensure that the fabric ends up drum tight.

Preparing the fabric

Careful preparation of your fabric before placing it in a frame can make all the difference to the finished work. Iron the fabric carefully to remove all the creases and, if you are embroidering on to a fine fabric, back it with another stronger fabric such as calico or heavy cotton to help take the weight of the stitches. This will prevent the fabric from puckering around the stitching.

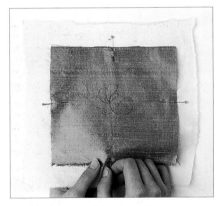

1 Pin your fabric on to a piece of backing fabric. Start with a pin on each side. Make sure that the two pieces are lying together on the grain.

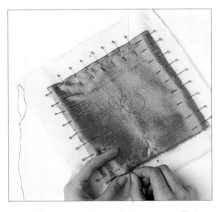

2 Pin outwards to the corners. This pushes any creases out. Pin with the pins horizontal to the fabric.

3 Stitch the two pieces of fabric together. This can be done in a variety of ways. One way is a long and short stitch, coming up into the main fabric and going down into the background fabric.

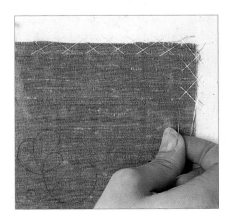

4 The other way is herringbone stitch. Again it is always best to start in the middle of an edge and stitch outwards. You can also use a sewing machine set on zigzag stitch.

TIP

Occasionally, it may be necessary to leave an extra long starting thread so as to be able to rethread this and then weave it into the back.

Embroidery hoop

You need to keep the fabric in the hoop (or ring) drum tight, so keep tightening it up as you work as it will loosen over time. Use a screwdriver to tighten the screw. The dumpy-handled type is good as it fits easily into your sewing kit. Be careful not to use one with the wrong size tip, as this will ruin the screw in your frame. You can wrap your ring frame in strips of calico or bias binding to help it grip the fabric, especially if you are working on a satin or silky fabric.

Loosen the screw and place one half of the ring underneath the fabric and the other on top. Push the two rings together and use a screwdriver to tighten the screw.

Pin frame

One of the many advantages of a pin frame is that it is quick and easy to attach and detach the embroidery to and from the frame – you can therefore use the same frame for more than one project. A pin frame is easily balanced in your arms or against a table, so it can be used without a special stand.

When you are pinning, pull the fabric taut and place the pins on the outside of the frame rather than on the top edge, and point them in towards the centre of the frame.

If you are working on fabric larger than the frame, pin up the area you want to embroider then roll up and pin the excess.

1 Place the fabric over the frame. Pin one corner, then the adjacent corners, then the fourth, diagonally opposite corner.

2 Pin the centre side. Continue until all the centre sides are pinned.

3 Pin halfway between the centre pin and corner pins.

4 Repeat, pinning halfway between two pins until the whole frame is pinned.

Slate frame

Slate frames are a traditional method of framing fabric ready for stitching that has been used for hundreds of years. They are particularly suitable for framing up large pieces of work. To determine the width of fabric you need, first measure the width of your design, including the space either side of it, and add 8cm (3in) for turnings (this will give you 4cm (1½in) each side for the slots in which you will place the string). To obtain the length of fabric needed, measure the depth of your design, again including the space above and below it, and add 2cm (¾in) for turnings. This will give you 1cm (approximately ½in) at the top and the bottom of the fabric.

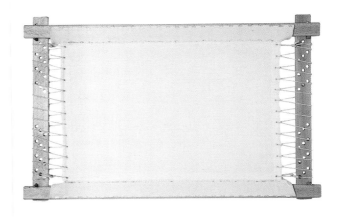

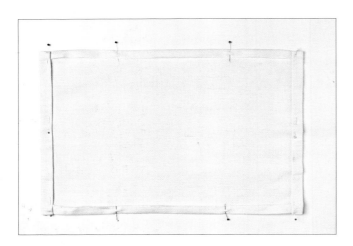

1 Cut out a piece of fabric on the grain to the required size. Fold the fabric piece in half lengthways on the grain and mark the centre at the top and bottom of the fabric with coloured thread. With the wrong side of the fabric facing, turn in the top and bottom edges of the fabric (on the grain) 1cm (½in) and pin this fold in place (pin inwards, as the picture shows: this contains the fabric better). Turn in each side 4cm (1½in) and fold twice: this double fold makes a slot for the string.

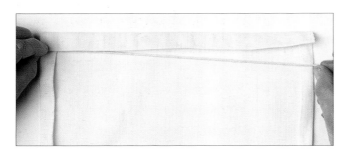

2 Open up each side seam and lay a length of string under the folds. This is to strengthen the sides when they are attached to the frame with string. Machine or backstitch the seams in place.

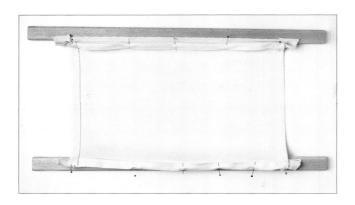

3 Mark the centre of the webbing on both slats with a coloured thread. Pin the top edge of the fabric to the webbing at their centre points. Make sure you pull the fabric slightly from the centre of the webbing so that you have an even, tight tension. Pin the fabric to both ends of the webbing, then pin in between at regular intervals. You will notice that there is 2cm (¾in) of spare webbing on both sides. This is because you need a gap between the edge of the fabric and the side of the vertical slat to enable you to pull your string firmly. Pin the bottom edge of the fabric to the webbing on the bottom slat in the same way.

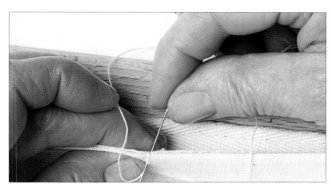

4 Oversew the fabric to the webbing at the centre point and then at both ends of the fabric (this is because the ends are particularly vulnerable when stringing the frame). Use a no. 8 needle and a strong thread.

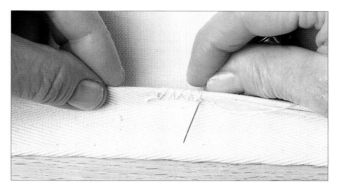

5 Return to the centre and attach the remaining fabric to the webbing using a herringbone stitch. Work to the end, then go to the other side and work a herringbone stitch to the centre. Repeat this process on the bottom webbing.

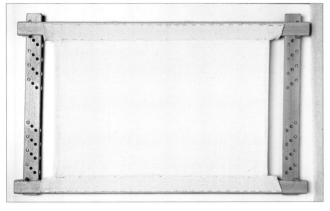

6 Slide in the vertical slats and secure them with the wooden pegs. Ensure the pegs are positioned in the same place on each side of the frame, and that the fabric is held tightly and evenly.

7 You now need to mark the positions of the holes for lacing. Make sure the string is tucked well into the seams while you are doing this. Using a pencil and ruler, make the first mark halfway across one of the side seams, just below the webbing. Make subsequent marks below this one at 2½cm (1in) intervals. Repeat along the other side seam.

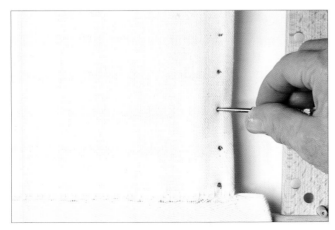

8 Make a hole through each pencil mark using a sharp point such as a stiletto. Be careful not to pierce the string that is tucked inside each seam.

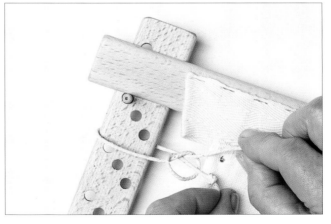

9 Cut off a length of string five times the depth of the linen and make a slip knot in one end. Attach the knotted end of the string around the top left-hand slat and pull up.

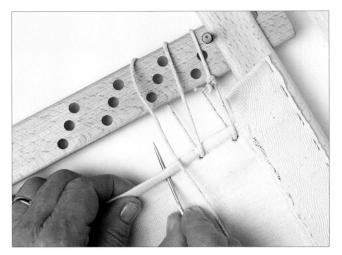

10 Using a large needle such as a tapestry needle, pass the string through the first hole in the linen, from front to back. Then take it behind and back over the slat and pass it through the next hole in the fabric.

11 Continue weaving the string firmly and evenly along the slat, making sure that the fabric is pulled straight and parallel to the slat. When the first side has been strung, leave it until the second side has been strung, then adjust the tension on both sides so that the spaces on either side of the frame between the linen and the slat are filled equally with string. When you are happy with the tension, wrap the string around the slat twice and secure with a slip knot. You should now have a lovely taut frame which is a delight to work on!

Working with a stand

Many people prefer to work on a frame which is being held in a stand. There are many stands available. A metal Lowery stand, like the one shown opposite, consists of a footplate that can slot under any chair you are sitting in to keep the stand stable, an adjustable pole so that your work is at the correct height, and an arm with a clamp on the end. The frame is held in the clamp by means of an adjustable screwplate. You can turn the frame round to enable you to stitch comfortably on any part of the embroidery. A lever on the arm allows you to rotate the frame to have your work at the correct angle for stitching and to loosen the arm so that you can turn the frame over to finish off and start new threads, without taking the frame off the stand.

A frame mounted in a Lowery stand, and an anglepoise lamp fitted with a daylight bulb, creates an ideal place to work.

Starting to stitch

Before you start stitching, it is essential to know how to thread a needle, and how to start and finish a thread neatly.

Threading a needle with cotton perle

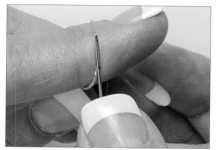

1 Wrap the thread around your forefinger and press firmly on it with the eye of a needle.

2 Rub the needle firmly up and down, drawing the thread up into a loop.

3 Pull the thread through the eye.

Threading a needle with metallic thread

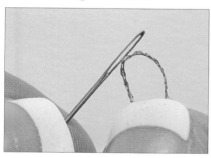

1 Make a loop in the thread.

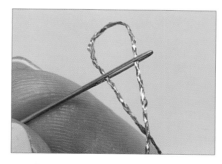

2 Push the loop through the eye of the needle.

3 Pass the needle through the loop.

4 Pull the thread tight to form a knot. This secures the needle on the thread and prevents the thread from slipping through the eye.

To start a thread ...

1 To tie a knot in the end of a thread, wrap the thread once around your forefinger.

2 Roll the thread towards you.

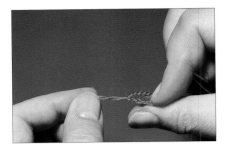

3 Tighten the knot.

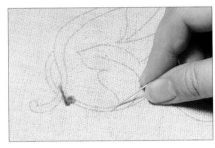

4 Place the knot approximately 2cm (¾in) from where you want the first stitch to be. Bring the needle up, making sure that the thread on the back is going across an area to be worked.

To finish ...

5 When you have finished your stitching, or are happy that the stitching you have done is secure, cut off the knot.

6 To finish off, turn the fabric over and weave the needle several times into the threads. Cut off the end.

TIP ||||||||||||||||||||||||||||||||

Occasionally, it may be necessary to leave an extra long starting thread so as to be able to rethread this and then weave it into the back of your work.

Mounting your work

When you have completed your embroidery, if you have decided to frame and display it, you will need to follow these basic guidelines. Use a white acid-free mounting board, available from good stationery or art shops. You will need to know the exact size of the picture frame before cutting the board, so it will fit nicely inside the frame.

1 Place the embroidery face down and cover it with a fine, dry cloth. Apply a warm iron gently and lightly so that the stitches are not flattened or distorted.

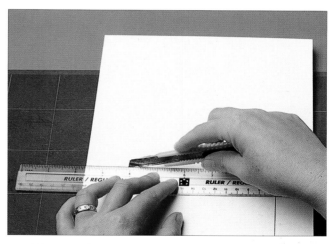

2 When you have decided how much of your embroidery you wish to frame, cut your mounting board to this measurement, using a craft knife and a cutting board.

3 Measure the board horizontally and vertically to find the centre. Push a needle through this centre point so that the point just comes through to the other side.

4 Measure the embroidery in the same way to find the centre point of the design, and push the eye of the needle on the mounting board through this point, so that the centre of the design is positioned accurately on the centre of the board.

5 When you are happy that the board is central, place pins through the fabric at the board's edges, sticking outwards so that the board can be turned over easily.

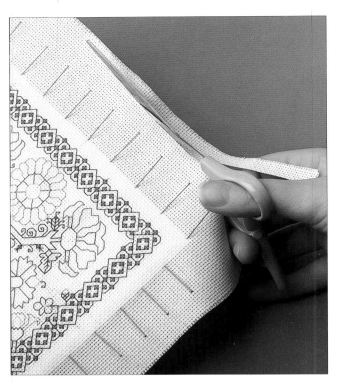

6 Trim the excess fabric to about 5cm (2in) all round and turn the embroidery over, face down.

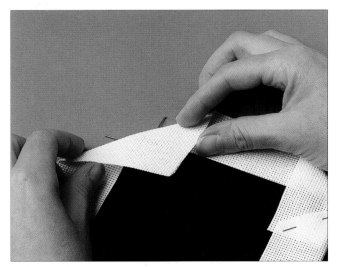

7 Mitre the corners, fold in the sides and pin them down.

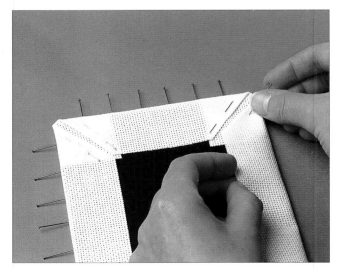

8 Sew the edges of the fabric together at each corner. Remove the pins.

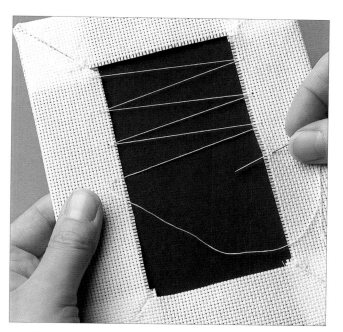

9 Fix the edges of the fabric in place with double-sided tape, or lace across the back using a strong thread.

10 Remove the pins and place the mount in the picture frame.

The mounted, framed embroidery.

SILK SHADING

The Climbing Leaves project, worked in autumnal shades (see page 38).

Silk was discovered in China over 46 centuries ago, making it one of the oldest fibres known to man. Its strength and sheen make it ideal for stitching, and embroidery worked in silk goes back many centuries; there are references to silk in the Old Testament.

The silk shading technique uses long and short stitch worked in silk or cotton thread. There are historical embroideries that appear to be shaded, but these are not always worked in long and short stitch – sometimes different coloured rows of split stitch worked tightly together were used to create a shaded effect.

Silk shading is very relaxing and satisfying to work, as once you get the hang of it, it can grow quickly and, with the right shades, look stunning. People are fascinated and inspired by the technique, and it really is achievable for any stitcher.

This chapter aims to take you through the basics of long and short stitch and on into projects, which can be used in many ways. Shading works well on many items, not just pictures for your walls, but for cards, pincushions, bags, purses, box lids and bookmarks, for example.

This antique piece of embroidery, mainly worked in long and short stitch, was among a bundle of fabrics and threads given to the author by Mrs Elizabeth Boswell. The flower head and the bud are particularly beautiful and show off the use of silk shading.

Materials

Fabric

Silk shading can be done on a variety of fabrics. Choose a plain fabric so that it does not distract from the stitching, however a slightly mottled cotton can give your work a more contemporary feel.

Fabrics can also be layered, so for sheen, use organza over a coloured background. Denim is also a great sturdy background fabric to work with. Silk dupion works well, as the slubs add texture to the fabric without distracting the eye from the stitching too much.

Unless you choose a very heavy fabric, it is always best to back it with a piece of calico or heavy cotton. However, if your calico is very rough, it may show through a pale fabric and slightly change the colour. Backing fabric helps to take the weight of the stitches and stops the fabric from puckering around the edge of the stitching. The projects in this chapter are all worked on silk dupion backed with calico.

When choosing the colour of your background fabric, place the threads you are going to use on to it. This will give you a good idea of how it will look. Check which colours are going to be at the edge of your design and are therefore going to be seen against the fabric.

Pale shades are the most natural choice for background fabric, but sometimes strong, dark-coloured fabrics work well as they can really throw the stitching forward. With darker fabrics, the background may show through between the stitches, so you have to be extra careful when you are stitching.

Try using complementary colours such as blue and orange, yellow and purple and red and green together.

Threads

Despite the name silk shading, you do not have to work in silk! Shading can be done in any thread. All the projects in this chapter are worked in normal stranded cotton embroidery threads, using one of the six strands. This may seem very fine, but it quickly builds up and gives a smoother overall look to the work.

TIP |||||||||||||||||||

When splitting your threads, hold them between your thumb and finger and pull one strand out upwards. The rest of the threads will ravel up underneath. If you try and pull a strand out sideways, it will twist itself up to the other strands and be harder to separate.

Needles and pins

The projects in this chapter are all stitched using no. 9 embroidery needles. These are sharp with a long eye, which is easier for threading. The needles that are called 'sharps' are also sharp, but have a smaller, rounder eye. You can use these, but they are harder to thread. The finer the needle you use for silk shading the better, as it will not make such large holes in the fabric, but obviously use something that you can thread!

Beware of old needles that have developed rusty patches and lost their coating, as they will be harder to work with. Also, if you have a needle that seems to be catching at the tip, get rid of it.

For silk shading it is best to have several needles, so that you can have all your colours threaded up in advance.

You will need dressmaker's pins to pin your backing fabric and fabric together before you start stitching.

Frames

It is essential to work silk shading in a tight frame, as if you do not, the length and the amount of stitches will pucker the fabric.

Wooden ring frames (see page 17) are great for getting the work really tight as you can tighten them using a screwdriver. They are available in a variety of sizes. Use one that leaves plenty of room around your design.

Seat frames are great to use, as by sitting on the base both your hands are left free for stitching.

Bigger designs may need to be worked in a slate frame (see page 18–20). These will also hold your work nice and tight, but they take longer to set up as you have to sew your fabric to the frame.

All the demonstrations and projects in this chapter were worked in ring frames except for the Dog Roses project, which was worked in a slate frame because of its size.

Ring frames in various sizes and a seat frame.

Beads

Seed beads, bugles and small sequins can be used to embellish and enhance your embroidery. Seed beads are used in the Climbing Leaves project on pages 38–39. Small sequins and beads set off the silk shading on the denim bag shown on page 12.

A selection of seed beads, bugles and small sequins.

Other materials

Light box This is used to help you trace designs on to fabric. They are available from good camera shops and craft suppliers in a variety of sizes.

Tracing paper You will need this to draw your design on, so that you can then trace it on to your fabric.

Black fine-line pen Trace your design on to the tracing paper with a black fine-line pen. This gives crisp, dark lines and should not leave marks on your fabric.

Low-tack tape or masking tape Tape your design to the light box (or a window) with either of these, as sticky tape will leave marks.

Pencil and coloured pencils You will need pencils for designing, and also for tracing the design on to your fabric and drawing on directional lines etc. A softer pencil is easiest to use, but if you are using pale threads, the graphite may come off on them. In this case use a coloured drawing pencil. Light blue is good with paler fabrics, and white or yellow for darker fabrics.

Shower cap This is great for slipping over a ring frame to keep the work clean while you are not stitching.

Screwdriver A screwdriver is essential for tightening your ring frame. Make sure you have the right size for your screw.

Scissors Small, sharp-pointed scissors are needed for cutting embroidery threads. Scissors with a slight curve on the tip are good for cutting threads close to the fabric. You will need larger dressmaker's scissors for cutting your fabric. Use separate scissors for paper.

Tweezers If you have tacked on your design (see page 15), tweezers are useful for removing bits of tissue paper left over when you tear off the tracing.

Thimbles You may need a thimble to protect your pushing fingers, especially if you are using very fine needles.

Iron Press your fabrics before you draw the design on. Check that your iron and ironing board are clean before you do so.

White tissue paper To keep your work clean as you stitch it, place a piece of tissue paper in between the two rings of your ring frame when you push it together. Then rip a small hole over the area you are working. You can also use tissue paper to wrap your work in when you are not working on it.

A light box, fine-line pen, tracing paper, white tissue paper, pencils, low-tack tape, scissors, thimbles, tweezers, a screwdriver and an iron.

Stitches

If you are already a stitcher, you will have developed your own techniques; however, these are the methods used by professional embroiderers – they may help you to produce even more beautiful work. If you have never stitched before, they are a great way to start!

Long and short stitch

Worked straight

Long and short stitch is great for filling big areas or delicately shading small areas. It can be worked with as many different shades as you like. If you have a range of colours, it works well to take every other colour, for example if you have shade numbers 1 to 6, you would use 2, 4 and 6 or 1, 3 and 5. However, this is just a guide and sometimes colours from other ranges have to be brought in.

One of the most common mistakes with this technique is to work regimented long, short, long, short stitches. This creates a striped effect instead of shading. The stitches only need to be slightly varied in length, so that a solid line is not formed. Longer stitches give a smoother overall look, so do not be afraid to stitch them long.

To guide you with direction and colours, you can draw on to your fabric with pencil. The stitches should overlap by a third, so divide the area you are stitching into as many colours as you have and draw lines on. Then make sure that your stitches are worked over these lines. This will allow for the next colour to come into it by a third without losing the amount of the first colour that you wanted.

Always work your shading in a single strand of thread, as this gives it a fine, smooth look. Using two threads may make it quicker to work but gives a lumpier, heavier look as the threads twist together.

Long and short stitch is meant to look as natural as possible, so relax when you do it, and do not worry too much about whether you are working each stitch in the right place. As with many techniques, it takes practice!

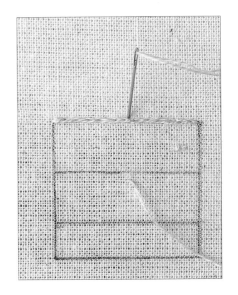

1 Draw a 2.5cm (1in) square on to the fabric and divide it into three equal sections. Select three thread shades to work with: a dark, medium and a light. With the lightest, work a split stitch edge (see page 37) across the top line of the square. To keep the correct angle for the area you are stitching, work your first stitch in the middle of the area as a guide. Come up into the fabric below the first line and go down over the split stitch edge.

TIP ||||||||||||||||||

Stitching from the middle to the left and then from the middle to the right helps to keep your stitching at the correct angle.

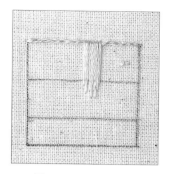

2 Work out towards one side. For each stitch, come up in the fabric and down over the split stitch edge. Each stitch should be a slightly different length from the one next to it, but none should fall short of the first pencil line. Work the stitches really close together so there are no gaps between them.

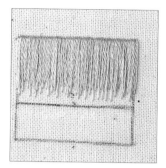

3 Go back to the centre and work in the same way, going out in the other direction. You may find this direction harder, one side is always easier! Remember to put lots of stitches in really close together.

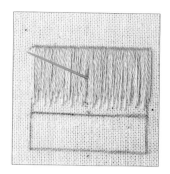

4 Cast on a single strand of your medium shade thread in the area below the stitching that you have just done. Bring the needle up a third of the way into the light stitches, in the middle as before. It does not matter if you split the light stitches.

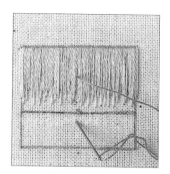

5 Take the stitch down below the next pencil line into the fabric. This is the opposite direction to the first row of stitches and all consecutive rows are worked in this way, up in the stitches and down into the fabric.

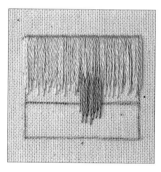

6 As with the light colour, stitch out to one side. This time you need to remember to stagger the length of the stitches at both ends.

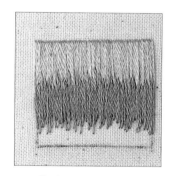

7 Go back to the middle and repeat as before, working out in the other direction. If you find that stitching this colour creates gaps in between the pale stitches above, this may be because the stitches of the first row were not packed in tightly enough.

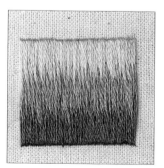

8 Using a single strand of your dark thread, work the bottom row. Come up into the middle row of stitches and go down over the pencil line at the bottom.

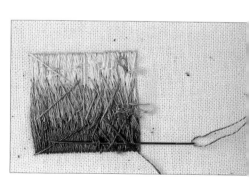

9 As you have no free space to cast off, turn your work over and weave the thread into the back.

Worked in a petal shape

As few shapes are perfectly square and straight, you need to learn how to vary the angle of your shading, so that you can stitch around different shapes. The main silk shading technique is the same, but you may need to add extra stitches, spread them out or tuck them in slightly.

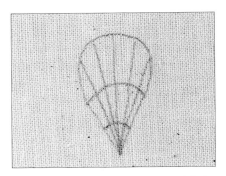

1 Draw a petal shape on your fabric and divide it into three sections, echoing the curve of the petal. Then draw direction lines to guide your stitches. Draw the central one in first so that it is vertical, then splay them out to either side from the bottom point. Select three shades of thread to work with, a dark, a medium and a light.

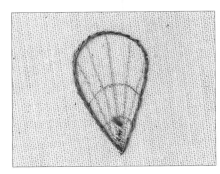

2 Using a single strand of the lightest colour, cast on in the shape with a knot and two small securing stitches. Split stitch all the way around the edge.

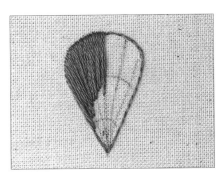

3 Bring the needle up just below the top pencil line in the middle and take it down over the split stitch edge. Work out to one side, varying the length of the stitches. Pack the stitches in tightly inside the petal, but spread them slightly as they go over the split stitch edge. Follow the directional pencil lines. All stitches should be angled towards the point at the bottom.

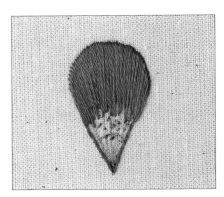

4 Work out to the second side in the same way. Remember to keep the stitches nice and long and vary the length at the bottom.

5 Work the medium shade out to either side from the middle, staggering the length at both ends. The stitches need to be splayed out when you bring them up into the light colour and tucked closer together as you take them down into the fabric over the second pencil line.

6 Using the dark thread, fill in the last little area. You will need fewer stitches, so place them carefully. As they are all going down towards one point, stop some of them slightly short so that it does not get too bulky at the point. Cast off by weaving into the back.

Stem stitch

Stem stitch can be used for stems and tendrils. It can be worked in a single strand of thread or in multiple strands for a thicker line.

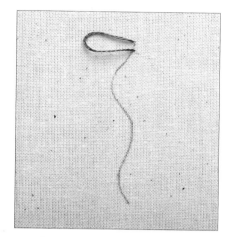

1 Cast on along the line you are going to stitch, or in any other area nearby that you are going to stitch over. Bring the needle up in the fabric and make a stitch, leaving a loop.

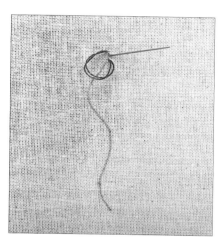

2 Bring the needle up halfway through the loop and pull the thread of the loop through.

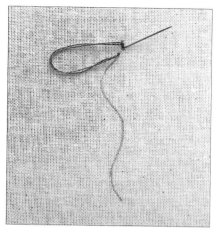

3 Take the needle forward making a second stitch, again leaving a loop of thread. Bring the needle back up halfway through the stitch, pulling the loop through.

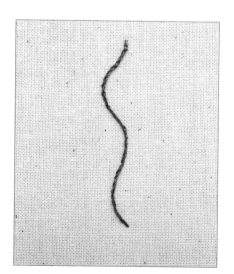

4 Continue stitching in this way, making sure that you always bring your needle up to the same side of the loop, so that you create a line of slanting stitches that are all slanting in the same direction.

This flower features long and short stitch worked in petal shapes and a stem stitch stalk.

Chain stitch

Chain stitch gives a thicker line than stem stitch and is also good for stems and tendrils.

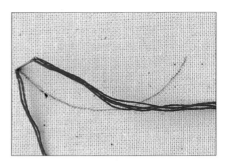

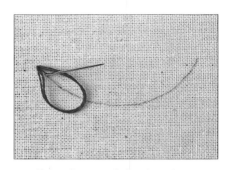

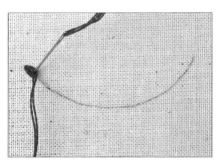

1   Cast on along the line you are going to stitch, or in any nearby area that will be stitched. Bring the needle up and, holding a loop out with your thumb, take the needle back down into the same hole.

2   Bring the needle back up into the loop and then pull the thread through, tightening the loop.

3   Take the needle down back into the same loop. The thread then creates a new loop for you to hold with your thumb. Bring the needle up ahead of itself on the line to hold this loop in place as you pull it through. Continue along the line.

The finished shape worked in chain stitch.

French knots

These can be used for pips, seeds and decoration. They look great when worked in groups and can be mixed with beads. The more strands of thread you use, the bigger the knots will be.

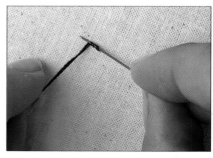

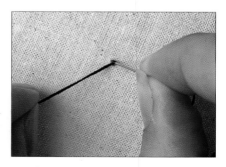

1   Bring the needle up. Holding the thread taut, wrap it twice around the tip of the needle.

2   Put the tip of the needle into the fabric and pull the thread tight, so that your little knot is formed before you pull the thread though.

3   Repeat to make multiple knots.

Split stitch

This is a very simple stitch, but makes an enormous difference to the quality of your finished piece. It can be used as a stitch on its own, but also as an outlining stitch underneath long and short stitch to help give a nice, crisp shape. Split stitch is worked around the outer edges of silk shading. You work the split stitch for each little area as you are going to stitch it.

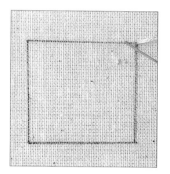

1 Having cast on, come up at the beginning of the line you wish to stitch. Make a small stitch, taking the needle forwards.

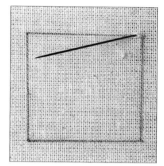

2 Take the needle back down beneath the fabric and bring it up halfway through your first stitch.

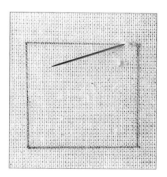

3 Make another stitch, again taking the needle forwards along the line and down through the fabric. Come up halfway through the stitch.

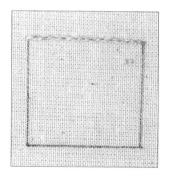

4 Work along the line in this way until it is complete.

Tulip
Clare Hanham

Tulips are wonderful to embroider as they have big, open petals, and not too many of them! They come in a variety of colours, so you can choose your favourite. The colours within tulips are quite varied, and can be dramatic, for instance, red tulips often have a yellow base and black streaks. However, pink tulips tend to be more subtle with cream and white areas. This gives lots of scope for shading. Begin by numbering the petals from 1 to 5, starting with the tiny part of the petal on the right, and stitch them in order using one strand of thread. First work split stitch around the petal and then start shading from the bottom upwards. Finally, work the stem in the same way.

TIP ||||||||||||||||||

You only need to split stitch around the outer edges as you work them. Any overlapping areas should be split stitched all the way round.

Climbing Leaves

This project has three quirky leaf shapes that are perfect for practising your shading. The angle of the stitches is very gentle and stays the same all the way down each side of each leaf. This allows you to concentrate on the blending of the colours. This sample is worked on a calico-backed silk in various lime greens, but why not use three of your favourite colours?

You will need

Off-white silk dupion,
  10 x 20cm (4 x 7⅞in)
Calico, bigger than your silk and to
  fit your ring frame
Stranded cottons:
  dark lime green
  medium lime green
  light lime green
  mustard
Nine gold seed beads
Pencil and tracing paper
Tacking thread
Pins
Needles: no. 9
Ring frame

The Climbing Leaves project, worked in autumnal shades.

The pattern for the Climbing Leaves project, shown full size.

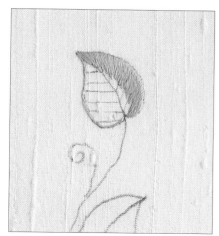

1 Trace the design and mount the background fabric on to calico (see page 16). Using one strand of the light lime green thread, work in stem stitch around the top leaf. Draw on pencil lines to guide you. The angle of the stitches should be at about 45° to the central stem. Work the lime green up one side of the leaf. Towards the tip of the leaf, fan the stitches out from one point. This is easier than trying to work tiny diagonal stitches and will give a much tidier effect. Remember to start in the middle of the leaf and stitch to the top, then return and work downwards.

2 Work the light green on the second side of the leaf. Fan the stitches out at the top to meet those from the other side. If necessary add a slightly longer stitch to define the tip of the leaf. Add in the medium lime green on to the first side. These should almost touch the central vein line in length. Work the second side of the leaf with the same colour.

3 Complete the first half with the dark lime green stitching down to the central vein. You can really exaggerate the long and short of the stitches here. As you are stitching in a smaller area, you will need fewer stitches, so take care where you place them.

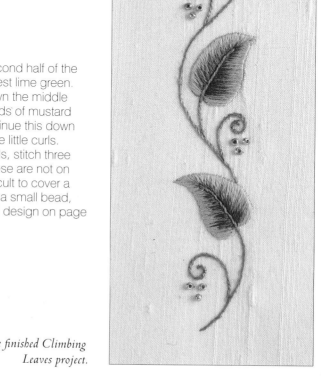

4 Complete the second half of the leaf with the darkest lime green. Add a stem stitch down the middle of the leaf in two strands of mustard coloured thread. Continue this down the stem, adding in the little curls. Under each of the curls, stitch three gold seed beads. These are not on the tracing as it is difficult to cover a pencil mark with such a small bead, so refer to the finished design on page 38 for placing.

The finished Climbing Leaves project.

Dog Roses

This project was inspired by dog roses growing in a hedgerow. These flowers are a great subject to embroider. Dog roses are ideal for shading as they have big, open petals and beautiful soft colours. They have been worked on a delicate green silk background to enhance the gentle colours in the shading. The whole design is worked in a single strand of thread.

You will need

Pale green silk dupion, at least 34 x 30cm (13½ x 11¾in)

Calico, bigger than your silk and to fit your ring frame

Stranded cottons:
   dark pink
   medium pink
   light pink
   white
   dark green
   medium green
   light green
   very light green
   soft yellow
   mustard

Pencil and tracing paper

Tacking thread and pins

Needles: no. 9

Ring frame

The pattern for the Dog Rose project, shown half size. This pattern shows the order of stitching for the main flower and the stitch direction for the whole design, though only the outline should be transferred to your fabric. The main rose on this design has five petals. You will see that this flower has two petals at the back, two in the middle and one at the front, with a turnover that is even further forward. Following the rule of working from the back forwards, the flower should be worked in that order. The leaves and stems of the design do not touch the rose or each other, so they can be worked in any order.

Main flower

1 Trace the design and mount the background fabric on to calico (see page 16). As this project is fairly large, it is best to tack the two fabrics together down and across the centre in addition to around the edges. This will stop the fabric from moving and should help avoid any puckering of the silk. Starting with the main rose, split stitch around the top edge of petal 1 in medium pink. Following the direction shown, start to shade the petal using the medium pink over the split stitch edge. Add in a few dark pink stitches along this edge and where it meets the petals on either side. Work on down the petal with light pink going into white at the flower centre. Remember to echo the outside shape of the petal with the shading. Finish the white neatly on the pencil line at the flower centre. Work petal 2 in the same way.

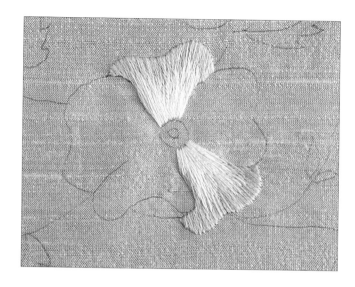

2 Petal 3 sits on top of petals 1 and 2, so it has a split stitch edge all the way around. Work the split stitch and start shading using pale pink. Add just a few flecks of medium pink, scattering them through the petal. Finish the petal in white, keeping the angle down the sides soft, so that although you are covering the split stitch edge, it is with an almost vertical stitch. This helps the petals blend together in the middle of the flower.

Petal 4 is worked with a split stitch edge from the point where it meets petal 5 around towards the base of petal 1 in light pink. Shade the right-hand side of the petal in light pink with flecks of medium pink, then into white. The left-hand side of the petal is a little darker with more medium pink down the edge where petal 5 overlaps.

3 Work a split stitch around petal 5 in light pink, but not the edge under the turnover. Shade the area just beneath the turnover with medium pink, working through light pink to a small amount of white towards the flower centre. Either side of the turnover, start shading in light pink and then white. Merge the areas together with a few medium pink stitches.

Split stitch all the way around the turnover in light pink. Working in small stitches, work the outer edge in medium pink, shading into light pink then finish the inside edge of the turnover (which is on top of the petal) in white.

Using the yellow, add in the filaments, varying their heights around the centre of the flower. Work the anthers on the ends of the filaments in French knots in mustard thread.

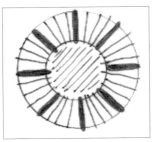

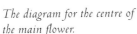

The diagram for the centre of the main flower.

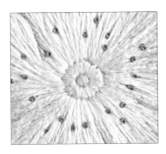

4 For the centre, work split stitch in a circle around the bottom of the petals using yellow, and then a second one a few millimetres inside this. To get a nice curve you will need to work really tiny stitches. Stitch up and over the split stitch edges all the way around the circle centre, keeping the stitches at the correct angle (see diagram on the left). You may find it helpful to put in a few guiding stitches first, to help you keep to the right angle. These are shown as darker lines on the diagram. Fill in the centre of the yellow circle with very light green stitches.

Leaves

There are four shades of green in this project. Some of the leaves are worked in the darker three shades, and some in the lighter three shades. Generally speaking, the leaves to the left of the stem are in the darker three, and those to the right are in the lighter three.

All the leaves are worked with the darkest of their colours on the outside edge, working into the paler shades in the middle. Split stitching can always be worked in the darkest colour of that leaf.

Because of the shape of the leaves, it is easiest to work each little point from its tip down one side, then take your needle back up to the tip and work down the other side. Repeat this with the next tip, so that the two then join up at the bottom. This is easier than trying to work up and down the tips in one go.

Repeat with the next two shades, working in the same way, echoing the outside shape of the leaf. The stitches should meet in the middle on the central line.

5 Work the leaf on the left of the stem in dark green, medium green and light green, as explained above.

6 Work the vein down the centre of the left-hand leaf in medium green in stem stitch. Then work the right-hand leaf in the same way, using medium green, light green and very light green. All the stems joining the flowers and leaves are worked in medium green and in stem stitch.

Half open flower 1

Half open flower 2

7 Work the base of the flower, split stitching in medium green. Start shading with dark green, coming from under the base of the petals. Continue into medium green to complete the shape. Add a highlight of light green low down on the left-hand side. Work the small leaf to the left, split stitching the spiky edge with medium green and shading, starting with dark green coming out from under the petal into medium green over the edge.

The small leaf to the right is shaded using dark, medium and light green. The dark is down the centre and light around the edges.

Work the back two petals first, split stitching and working mainly in light pink. Work down into white. Add a few flecks of medium pink in with the light pink on the outer edge.

Add filaments into the white area using yellow and work the anthers in French knots using mustard thread.

Split stitch around the edges of the turnover and stitch the top area in medium pink. Shade into dark pink where it meets the front petal. Work the front, right-hand petal with the turnover first. The main part of the petal is worked in light pink with flecks of medium pink at the bottom and white under the turnover. Split stitch around in light pink. The turnover is worked in mainly dark pink, with a few medium flecks on the edge over the main petal.

Split stitch all the way round the final petal using medium pink. The top edge is worked in light pink. Shade into white and then back into light pink. The base of the petal near the leaf is worked in medium pink. Add in a few flecks of dark pink.

8 The leaves of the second half-open flower are split stitched around in light green. They are then worked in medium green coming out from under the flower and shaded into light green, with just a fleck of very light green on the tips.

Start with the small section of petal just peeking through at the back. Split stitch the small curve on the outside of the petal. Work in light pink and white, with just a few flecks of medium pink.

Work the central back petal, split stitching all the way around the outer edge in light pink and shade mainly in light pink and white, with flecks of medium pink.

The petals to the right and left are worked next, using medium pink more heavily, as well as light pink and white. The turnover of the right-hand petal is worked in dark and medium pink.

The final front petal is split stitched all the way around in dark pink and shaded with all the pinks and a small amount of white at the bottom.

Bud

9 The pink of the bud is worked first with small amounts of light, medium and dark pink. Split stitch around the small green base of the bud in medium green and work with the three lighter shades of green. Start with the darkest coming from under the bud and down its sides. The smaller back sepal of the bud is also shaded using the three lighter shades of green with a sliver of the medium green down the outside edge and the very light green where it sits over the pink. The fine tendril is worked in stem stitch in light green.

The front sepal is split stitched all the way around in light green and worked in the same way as the back one with a sliver of medium on the outside edge and very light green next to the pink on the inside edge. The fine tendril is worked in stem stitch and in very light green. The small leaves on the main stem are worked in medium green.

Left: the finished Dog Rose project. If you do not fancy tackling such a large design, just work a small area of it. You could also use tracing paper to trace parts of it and rearrange them to form your own design.

Right: A selection of items stitched using silk shading.

CREWEL EMBROIDERY

Crewel embroidery is a type of surface stitching worked only in crewel wool, and it is the most traditional of English embroideries. Crewel wool is a two-ply worsted wool or yarn. As a result of being worked in wool, crewel embroidery is much thicker and heavier than other types of embroidery, and the stitching lies above the background fabric, not just on it. If a design is embroidered in any other thread, such as silk or cotton for example, it is called surface embroidery not crewel embroidery. However, exactly the same stitches and techniques are used. So, if you are not happy working with wool, feel free to work all the designs in this chapter in threads of your choice – but remember never to call your work crewel embroidery!

Crewel embroidery has been in existence for more than ten centuries and, generally, it becomes fashionable about every fifty years. It was especially popular during the mid-seventeenth century and is often referred to as Jacobean embroidery. The most famous early piece is the Bayeux Tapestry, in which pictorial panels depict the battle of 1066 between the Britons and Normans.

Many people find this type of embroidery easy. However, anyone who has worked only counted or canvas embroidery may find it a little more difficult to be 'free'. There is no counting involved. You dictate to the fabric rather than the fabric dictating to you. Hopefully, this chapter will help you to be a bold and free stitcher.

Paradise

Jane Rainbow

This colourful panel emphasises the joy of crewel embroidery, with its flowing design.
It incorporates all the stitches featured in this chapter.

Materials

Threads

There are various types of crewel wool on the market. They vary in thickness, texture, twist and hairiness! One of the most popular is a type known as Persian wool. It was originally spun especially for the Persian carpet repairers. It comes as three loosely wound two-ply strands, in 7.2m (8yd) skeins and 125g (4oz) hanks which equal approximately twenty-one skeins. There are hundreds of shades available in the Persian wool range and it has a natural lustre that gives an embroidery a silky appearance. All other wools tend to have a matt quality, and so they absorb light rather than reflect it.

The availability of wools varies considerably around the world. Brands or shade numbers of the threads have therefore not been specified; it is up to you to choose your own. Where quantities are given, these are in skeins and amount to 7.2m (8yd) of three strands, which is equivalent to 21.6m (24yd).

Persian crewel wool

English crewel wool

Fine English crewel wool

French crewel wool

Preparing your threads

When working with crewel wool, it is best to work with lengths no longer than 37cm (15in). However, Persian crewel wool is so strong, you can work with double this length. You can keep lengths of wool looped on a vacant embroidery hoop, a hole-punched piece of card, or a coat hanger. If there is more than one shade of a colour, keep these together and in order of darkness.

1 Remove the label and unravel the wool. Place the two ends together.

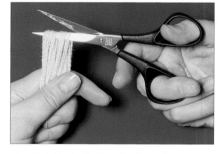

2 Fold in half, then half again, and continue until you have a satisfactory working length. Cut through all the loops to create separate lengths.

3 Loop the prepared skein of wool on to the frame.

4 To remove a single strand of wool, simply pull one from the loop of the knot.

Fabric

Crewel embroidery requires a furnishing-weight fabric rather than a dress-weight one. Ideally, the fabric should be made of fifty per cent linen. This has many advantages, one of which is that the fabric has spring. When you pull a thick needle through it, the hole springs open but it will also spring shut around the stitch. If you work on a pure cotton fabric that has no give, you will get sore fingers from pulling the needle through and holes at the base of the stitches. Fabric with an element of linen in it can also be stroked back into place around the stitches, where necessary. Finally, once you have finished stitching, the natural linen starches that are already in the fabric will come to life and crisp up the fabric during the stretching or blocking process.

Traditionally, crewel was worked on a hundred per cent linen twill, but this does not wear as well as linen and cotton union and is twice as costly and usually not as wide. Most linen union fabrics have ten or twelve per cent manmade fibre content, and the rest are made up equally of linen and cotton. They are available in a wide range of colours. If you are having problems finding them, ask in your local furnishing store for linen and cotton union fabrics.

Linen union fabrics are available in a range of colours, including blue, green, cream and gold. Threads (see page 48) should be chosen to work with your background colour to enhance the design.

When cutting the fabric, remember to allow enough turnings beyond the design for making up, and also allow for the embroidery frame you are using. Generally, add at least 12.5cm (5in) to your design area, but as you always need at least 52.5 x 32.5cm (21 x 13in) for the frame, this influences the final cutting.

Seal the raw edges of the fabric with either overlocking or blanket stitch, masking tape or seam binding. Iron out any creases using a hot steam iron before transferring the design on to the fabric.

Needles

Always use a no. 4 crewel needle. This has a long eye and a sharp point. You can also use a no. 20 tapestry needle for some stitches. If you have difficulty threading a crewel needle, try using a chenille needle – a no. 20 or 22 – this is similar to a tapestry needle, with a larger eye and sharp point.

From top to bottom: no. 4 crewel needle, no. 22 chenille needle, no. 20 tapestry needle.

Frames

It is essential to work crewel embroidery on a frame. It is very much easier to make good stitches if the fabric is held taut. If the frame is held or supported so that you have both hands free, this is better still.

Embroidery hoops or ring frames

These are available in different sizes, and in wood, plastic or metal. The deeper wooden ones are excellent for crewel embroidery – a 15cm (6in) frame (or smaller) if holding it in your hand. The hoop should only be held by the frame and your fingers should not push up on the fabric. It does not matter if you crush the embroidery in the hoop, it will all come back to shape during the stretching process.

If you are working on fabric that has a linen content, you will get a permanent hoop mark if you leave the material in the frame overnight! It is therefore imperative that you always remove an embroidery from a hoop or ring frame at the end of each session of stitching.

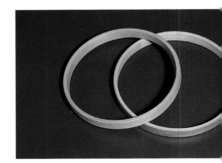

Embroidery hoop.

Pin frame

This type of frame is a copy of a medieval embroidery frame. The frame itself is made of wood. The wood is upholstered, and the work is attached to the padding with pins. You should pin on the outside of the upholstery, pointing the pins towards the centre. You will need to use a different thickness of pin depending on the weight of the canvas or fabric used: the finer the fabric, the finer the pin. The joy of this type of frame is that you can work on any size of embroidery. Simply pin the area you need to stitch over the frame. If the work is larger than the frame, unpin each section as it is worked, move on, re-pin and continue working. Should your work be smaller than the frame, attach scrap material to enlarge it to the required size. Another advantage of a pin frame is that you can leave the work on it for any period of time.

Pin frame.

Other items

Pens You will need a black felt-tip pen for tracing the design, and a water-erasable felt-tip pen for marking the design on to fabric.

Tracing paper This is used for transferring a design on to fabric.

Rule or tape measure This is used for measuring fabric and for positioning a design precisely.

Masking tape Use 2.5cm (1in) wide masking tape to cover the raw edges of fabric. Masking tape is also useful for securing a tracing to your surface when transferring a design on to fabric.

Scissors Large dressmaker's scissors are required for cutting fabric. Fine, sharp embroidery scissors should be used for cutting threads. You will also need paper-cutting scissors for cutting graph paper, paper for designs and tracing paper.

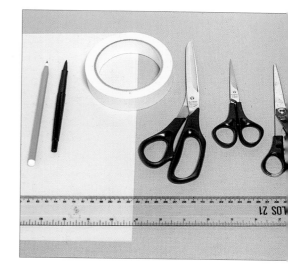

Stretching materials

Wooden board This should be at least 1.25cm (½in) thick. It is best not to use either a very hard or a very soft wood, as nails need to be inserted. Block board is ideal. Whatever board you use, it must be at least 5cm (2in) bigger than the fabric you want to stretch on it. If you are an embroidery addict, it is worth investing in a board at least 1m (40in) square.

2.5cm (1in) nails These are used to secure the fabric to the board.

Hammer Nails are hammered into the board and removed with a hammer. Choose a claw-type hammer if possible.

Graph paper This is used as a guide to ensure that the edges of the fabric are straight. It is essential for accurate stretching. Dressmaker's graph paper is excellent.

Mist sprayer A mist sprayer is an excellent way of ensuring that the fabric is dampened but not saturated with water.

Frames and stands

It is important to think about where and how you sit while embroidering. Try to ensure that you have good spinal support, and avoid spending hours crouched over a frame. Choose a frame that is adjustable to the height you need, so you are able to sit with your spine as straight as possible, for example a Lowery workstand. Also, take care of your eyes. Work with a magnifier if you need to, and with light directed on to your embroidery, but remember to look up and refocus your eyes often! If you are working with a hoop or ring frame, choose a 20cm (8in) seat or chair frame (shown on the right). This will allow you to sit in a comfortable chair, with the embroidery held in your lap, and work with both hands freely. This type of frame is also available with a clamp for a table, or freestanding on the floor.

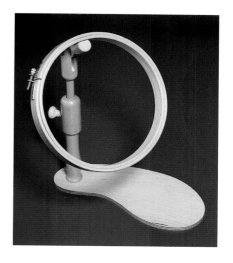

Stitches

This chapter contains only twelve crewel embroidery stitches. The three projects are all based on the same pattern (shown on the right) and have been worked using various stitches and colours. The final design (Les Sylphides) incorporates the stitches used in all three and uses yet another colour scheme. This will enable you to assess the different effects of colour and texture.

There are, of course, many more surface embroidery stitches. Hopefully, these designs will encourage further stitching. The number of different stitches used has deliberately been kept low to show how effective this type of embroidery can be.

Work your stitches from the outside in, from top to bottom, or as the sap flows back down to the roots. This helps the flow of the design. All the instructions that follow presume you have attached your starting thread appropriately (see page 22).

The pattern for the designs on pages 53, 57 and 62, reproduced three-quarters (75 per cent) actual size.

Giselle

This project introduces you to four stitches – stem stitch, chain stitch, split stitch and satin stitch. Once you have mastered the stitches, you will be able to work this flowing design.

Design size
12.5 x 21cm (5 x 8½in)

Colours
One skein each of two shades of pink and three shades of green
One strand of wool was used throughout.

Stitches
The calyx (base of the flower head) of each flower is worked in stem stitch – those on the larger flowers are in dark green and those on the smaller ones are in mid-green. The outline is worked first, then the rows are filled in with stem stitch. Each row is worked in the same direction.

The flowers and stems are worked in chain stitch – the larger flowers are in deep pink, the smaller ones are in pale pink and the stems are in dark green.

The leaves are worked using all three shades of green. Each leaf was outlined in split stitch first, then embroidered in satin stitch. The top left leaf has the top side worked in pale green and the lower side in mid-green. The remainder are in pale or mid-green, with the exception of the centre bottom leaf which is in dark green.

Stem stitch

This linear stitch is one that many people find easier to work in the hand and not on a frame. As crewel embroidery is a heavy form of stitching, it is important to have good fabric tension. The embroidery thread tension should be firm but not tight – each stitch should be neatly laid on to the fabric without gathering it, and the stitch should not wobble on the surface.

This demonstration shows a solid start, which would be suitable for the base of a leaf or flower. If you want to form a point, simply begin with a whole stitch rather than a half stitch.

When working parallel rows, make sure the twist of the rope formed by this stitch is identical in each row. Do not change the side that the wool is kept on part way along a row.

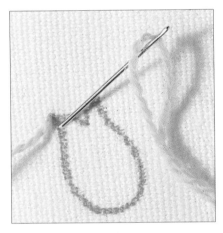

1 Work a half stitch.

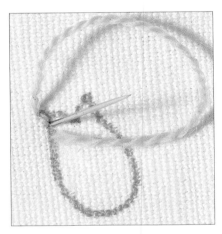

2 Bring the needle up at the beginning of the first half stitch.

TIP

Work a whole stitch to start, if you want to form a point (i.e. for a tendril). Then bring the needle up halfway between the first and second movements.

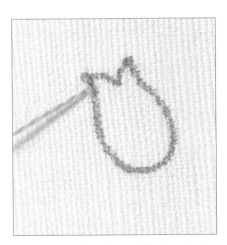

3 Pull the thread taut. Work a whole stitch and bring the needle up at the end of the first half stitch.

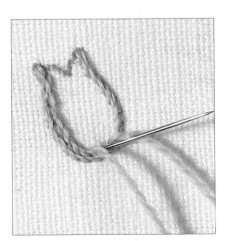

4 Repeat, working full stitches to complete the motif. Remember to keep the wool on the outside of the curve as you work.

TIP

Ideally, your stitching should be even. However, as curves become tighter, shorten your stitches so they do not fall over!

Chain stitch

This is another linear stitch, which again is often worked off a frame. It is best to work eight or nine stitches to 2.5cm (1in). Work all rows in the same direction.

This stitch has a pointed start and a blunt end, so consider this when planning where to begin.

If you are outlining a pointed petal in this stitch, step outside the loop when the point is complete, then come back up in the loop, change direction and continue.

The outlines of these hearts are worked in chain stitch.

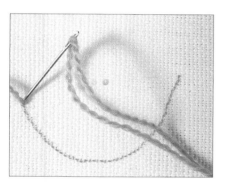

1 Come up at the point at which you want to start, then place the needle back down the same hole.

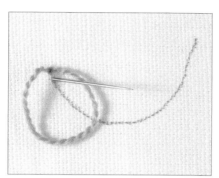

2 Come up about 3mm (⅛in) further along the design line, through the loop.

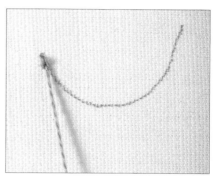

3 Pull the stitch taut, holding the thread horizontal to the fabric.

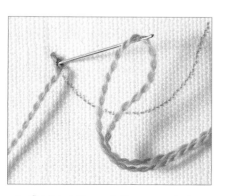

4 Go back through the same hole inside the loop to begin the next stitch (this makes the loop for the following stitch).

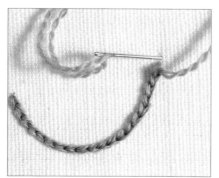

5 Repeat to outline the motif. To finish off, place the needle down outside the loop, making a small stitch to anchor the last link.

TIP ||||||||||||||||||

Should you need to join in a new thread whilst stitching chain stitch, leave the loop of the old thread on the front of the work, then attach the new thread and come up through the loop. Now tighten the old thread and finish it off, and continue with the new thread.

Split stitch

This is the last of the linear stitches, and it is frequently used to pad the edge of solid stitches: satin stitch, fly stitch and soft shading. In all the projects, you should work split stitch outlines around any area that is to be worked in these stitches. This stitch will not be seen when the piece is finished, so generous stitches may be worked where curves will allow.

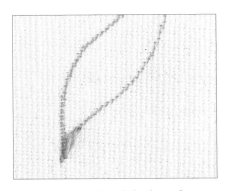

1 Work a straight stitch about 6mm (¼in) long to begin.

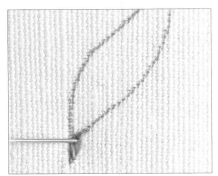

2 Bring the needle up a third of the way back along the straight stitch, to split the stitch.

3 Repeat, to outline the motif.

Satin stitch

Satin is the simplest stitch to work but probably the most difficult to get just right. Satin stitch is a collection of straight stitches tightly packed beside each other. Generally, work about nine stitches to 1cm (⅜in).

This stitch is most effective worked on an oblique angle. It is often helpful to mark direction lines with a water-erasable pen. Beware of having stitches at right angles to the design line.

You may find it easiest to start this stitch at the top of a curve or at a point, then to work either side of this.

The petals on the flower shown top right are worked in a split stitch outline, covered with satin stitch.

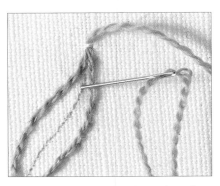

1 Outline in split stitch (see above). Work a straight stitch.

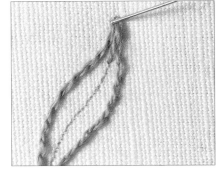

2 Bring the needle up as close as possible to the beginning of the first stitch.

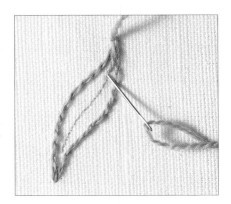

3 Take the needle down near the end of the first stitch.

4 Repeat, angling the stitches to reflect the contour of the design.

Coppelia

This section introduces you to five new stitches – fly stitch, buttonhole stitch, detached buttonhole stitch, spider's web stitch and French knots. Using these stitches together brings more texture to this flowing design.

Design size

12 x 21cm (5 x 8½in)

Colours

One skein each of three shades of blue
One skein each of three shades of green
One strand of wool was used throughout.

Stitches

The stems are worked in rows of dark green stem stitch and the leaves are worked in fly stitch using all shades of green. The calyxes are worked in dark green spider's web stitch.

The larger flowers use mid-blue buttonhole stitch on the outer edges of the petals, with dark blue detached buttonhole stitch edging. The long edges of the petals are in mid-blue stem stitch and the veins are made up of mid-blue French knots.

The smaller flowers are worked in pale blue buttonhole stitch, stem stitch and French knots. The detached buttonhole edging is in mid-blue.

Fly stitch

Fly stitch is a 'V' stitch. Worked as a solid stitch, it is a very effective way of working leaves, as the centre vein appears as you stitch.

Work this stitch as densely as you would satin stitch. Take care not to make too big a step on the edge or in the centre. In fact, these steps should all be the same size.

If a curved leaf is being worked, it may be necessary to add the odd straight stitch to bring the stitches round on the outside of the curve. It may also be necessary to complete with a little satin stitch.

Fly stitch is used to create the veined effect on these leaves.

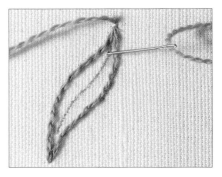

1 Outline the leaf with split stitch. Come up at the point of the leaf, outside the split stitch outline. Make a small straight stitch down the centre line, about 1cm (⅜in) long.

2 Bring the needle up almost beside the beginning of the first stitch, but slightly lower.

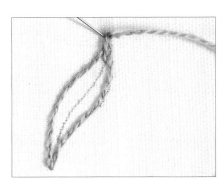

3 Take the needle down on the opposite side of the straight stitch.

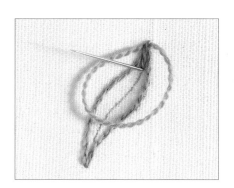

4 Come up at the bottom of the stitch, in the same hole, through the loop.

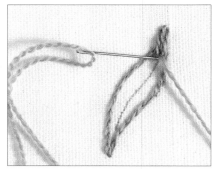

5 Pull the thread taut. Place the needle down at the end of the stitch, stepping below the loop, to make a very small stitch (as if you were finishing a chain stitch).

6 Repeat steps 2–5 to build up the stitches and fill in the motif.

Buttonhole stitch

If you are right-handed, stitch from left to right, and if left-handed, work from right to left. Keep good tension on the thread at all times and try to work the stitches close together so that no fabric shows between the stitches. When a point or end of a section is reached, finish off with a small stitch outside the loop. Then come back up inside the loop and continue as before. If you are using buttonhole stitch to add an edge to soft shading, alternate long and short stitches.

1 Work a straight stitch from the outside in, and bring the needle back up at the first hole.

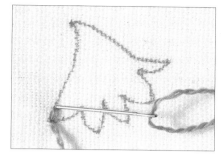

2 Take the needle down beside the end of the first stitch.

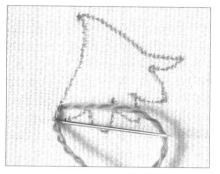

3 Bring the needle up inside the loop, in the design line, beside the first stitch.

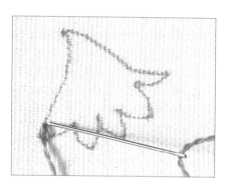

4 Pull the thread taut, keeping the thread level with the fabric. Place the needle down at the side of the beginning of the last stitch.

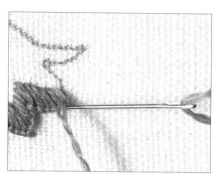

5 Repeat to outline the motif. To finish, take the needle outside the loop (see page 55, step 5).

Detached buttonhole stitch

This stitch puts a frill on to buttonhole stitch and adds a very effective texture. It is called 'detached' because you do not go through the fabric (except at the beginning or end of a row). When working more than one row, always work in the same direction.

1 Bring the needle up at the beginning of the buttonhole stitch. Pick up the loop at the edge of the buttonhole stitch.

2 Bring the needle up inside the loop. Pull the thread taut, keeping it level with the fabric.

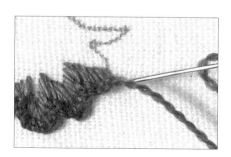

3 Repeat the stitch by stitching into every loop of the buttonhole stitch – this will build up a 'frill'. To finish off, place the needle on the outside of the stitching (see page 55, step 5).

Spider's web stitch

This stitch looks like rows of neat bullion knots (see page 65), but it is much more fun to work. Some rows will be shorter than others, depending on the design shape. The most common problem with this stitch is that not enough rows are worked. Try to ensure that the stitches are packed tightly into an area. Tension can also cause difficulties – it is best to work slightly looser than usual.

1 Work a central straight stitch in whatever direction required by the design.

2 Work parallel straight stitches approximately 2.5mm (1⁄10in) apart, or less, to fill in one side of the motif.

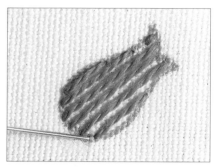

3 Work the other half of the motif. Bring the needle up on one side at the bottom of the motif.

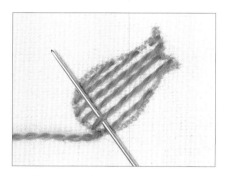

4 Rethread with a tapestry needle. Take the needle under the first straight stitch.

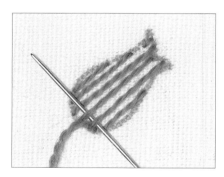

5 Take the needle back over the same straight stitch and under it and the next one.

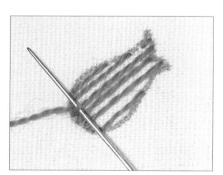

6 Repeat, to fill in a row. Remember that the rule is 'back over one and forward under two'. When you get to the end of the row, only wrap over and under one thread.

7 Take the needle back to the beginning of the row and repeat to fill in the motif. Always work in the same direction.

Berries look effective worked in circular spider's web stitch.

Circular spider's web stitch

Occasionally, you may want to work a circular area in spider's web stitch. To do this, you simply lay the straight stitches from the centre of the circle like the spokes of a wheel and then weave as you would normally, spiralling from the centre.

1 Work a circle of straight stitches. Bring your needle up as close to the centre as possible.

2 Take the needle back over the first stitch, then under it and the next two stitches.

3 Continue, spiralling the stitches round from the centre to complete the circle.

French knots

This is not a difficult stitch. If you want a bigger knot, thicken your thread but only wrap it once around the needle. When filling an area solidly with French knots, work around the edge first, then fill in.

1 Bring the thread to the surface. Pull the thread to the side and take the needle under the thread.

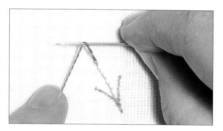

2 Wrap the thread once around the needle, with the needle pointing down.

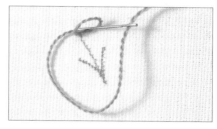

3 Place the needle back down, very close to, but not in, the same hole.

4 Pull the thread taut, taking the knot down on to the fabric.

5 Pull the needle down through the fabric to complete the knot.

6 Repeat to build up a series of French knots.

Sylvia

This section introduces you to three more stitches – laid filling, soft shading and bullion knots. When combined, they will produce a completely different effect from the basic design featured on page 53.

Design size
12.5 x 21cm (5 x 8½in)

Fabric size
Minimum 25 x 34cm (10 x 13½in)

Colours
One skein each of three shades of cream/yellow
One skein each of three shades of green
One strand of wool was used throughout.

Stitches
The stems, leaves and calyxes are outlined in green stem stitch.

The calyxes are worked in very close laid filling. The grid is mid-green, the tying stitch is dark green and the French knots are pale green.

The flowers are worked in soft shading using pale and mid-cream/yellow. The bullion knots that form the veins on the petals are in dark cream/yellow.

Laid filling

This very traditional crewel stitch is often referred to as 'noughts and crosses'. A grid of straight stitches is worked first. These should be very even, but the density of them will depend on the final effect required. Having worked in both directions and achieved beautiful, even squares, a small straight stitch or cross stitch is worked across the junction of threads to hold these in place, then a French knot is worked in each square. Generally, the area is then outlined in stem stitch.

Laid filling works well on leaves. This leaf was first covered with mid-green satin stitch, then the laid filling was worked in light green on top, with dark green tying cross stitches.

1 Work vertical rows of straight stitch.

2 Create a grid by working horizontal rows of straight stitch.

3 Bring the needle up in one of the corners of the grid and work a straight stitch over the junction of threads.

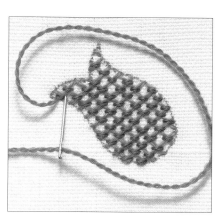

4 Repeat, to secure each junction.

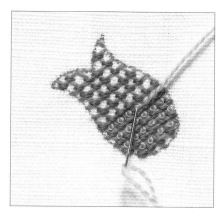

5 Work a French knot in each square (see page 61) to fill in the motif.

This colourful bird is worked in soft shading to add realism.

Soft shading

Soft shading is traditionally called long and short stitch, but 'long and short' sounds regimented, and this stitch should certainly not be that. The method shown here is the traditional method used by the exquisite Chinese embroiderers and The Royal School of Needlework, and it produces a truly blended effect.

Full and part stitches are worked to achieve soft shading. A part stitch is perhaps two thirds of the length of a long stitch. If the first row is worked thickly enough, it is possible to work the following rows openly so the colours bleed through each other.

Do not search for the ends of the shorter stitches, but come up where you would like to see a stitch. Remember that stitches can be overlapped to achieve curves.

It is perfectly acceptable to encroach into a previous colour or row, but you should not work these following rows densely.

There is plenty of opportunity to cheat with this stitch – like jumping back to a worked area and adding the odd stitch to achieve a better effect!

1 Outline the area in split stitch. Bring the needle up at the outside of the motif, at a point or top of a curve. Work a straight stitch, 1.25–2cm (½–¾in) in the direction required. Work a part stitch (two thirds the length of the straight stitch) alongside it.

2 Continue, alternating full and part stitches. Work them extremely close together, even overlapping, to make a solid edge.

3 When you have naturally completed an area, bring the needle back to an outside point, and continue working the stitch to fill in the rest of the motif.

4 Take a second colour, close in shade to the first. Take the needle up to split a stitch worked in the first colour, then down past the first colour embroidery to extend the motif.

5 Work straight stitches in the same direction as the first set to create subtle shading. These should not be as close together as the first set.

6 Take a third colour, close in shade to the second. Repeat stages 4 and 5 to fill in the motif.

Bullion knots

Embroidery is often considered one of the best therapies. However, this is not necessarily true when working this stitch!

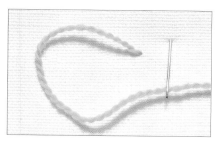

1 Work the needle up through the fabric, then down, leaving a large loop on the surface. The gap between the thread and the needle will determine the length of each stitch.

2 Bring the point of the needle back up at the start point. Wrap the wool several times clockwise around the needle.

3 Continue wrapping the thread around the needle, until you have a close set of coils the same length as the gap between the two stitch points.

4 Hold the coils with one hand, between thumb and forefinger.

5 With the other hand, gently ease the needle through the coils. Keep calm!

6 Lay the coils down on the fabric and stroke the stitch into place. Secure by taking the thread to the back.

Les Sylphides

Design size

37 x 21cm (15 x 8½in)

Colours

One skein of pale pink
Two skeins each of mid- and dark pink,
pale and dark green
Three skeins of mid-green
One strand of wool was
used throughout.

Stitches

Follow the instructions for the
individual carnation projects. Working
from left to right, embroider Giselle,
then Sylvia in the centre and Coppelia
on the right. The arrangement of the
shades of thread is as in the original
three panels, but where yellow and
blue are used, substitute pink.

An alternative suggestion:
You could work a bell-pull using five
repeats of the design stacked on top
of each other and touching. From
top to bottom use the designs in this
order: Giselle, Sylvia, Coppelia, Sylvia,
Giselle. The finished design size would
be 12.5 x 105cm (5 x 42½in).

Floral Symphony

Design size

25 x 39cm (10 x 15½in)

Colours

One skein each of three shades of
pink; three shades of coral; three
shades of blue; three shades of gold;
three shades of yellow; three shades
of fawn; three shades of turquoise;
pale green; dark olive green
Two skeins each of mid-green;
dark green; pale olive green;
mid-olive green
One strand of wool was used
throughout, except for eight areas of
French knots where two strands of
wool were used.

Stitches

All stems are worked in rows of fawn
stem stitch, and all leaves are worked
in fly stitch using all three shades of
green, turquoise and olive.

The small yellow flower on the
bottom left, and similar ones in the
top centre and far right, are worked in
mid-yellow and dark yellow satin stitch.
Their centres are made up of French
knots, with straight stitches to the
edge, in two steps in dark gold.

The larger flower in the bottom left-
hand corner has outer petals in soft
shading using all three shades of blue.
The middle area is worked in shaded
spider's web stitch using all three
shades of pink. Mid-pink is used for

the spokes. The heart of the
flower is in mid-gold and dark gold
bullion knots.

The small flowers to the right of this
are worked in pale yellow, mid-gold
and dark gold satin stitch. The calyxes
are in dark turquoise satin stitch.

The terracotta flower to the right of
this has petals worked in soft shading,
using all three shades of coral soft
shading. The inner area is filled with
French knots using pale yellow and all
three shades of gold; two strands of
wool were used for these. The calyxes
are in dark olive chain stitch.

Further to the right is a group of
blue flowers whose petals are worked
in satin stitch using all three shades of
blue. Their centres are filled with mid-
gold French knots using two strands
of wool. Their tiny leaves are worked in
pale and mid-olive fly stitch.

The flower on the far bottom right
has its centre worked in dark yellow
circular spider's web stitch. The petals
are worked in soft shading, using all
three shades of pink.

The small flowers above this are
in all three shades of gold and satin
stitch, with calyxes in dark turquoise
satin stitch.

The star flower to the left of these
has a centre of dark gold French
knots (one strand) surrounded by
mid-yellow satin stitch. The outer
parts of the petals are worked in
mid-coral buttonhole soft shading,
in which the outer edge of the soft
shading is worked in long and short
buttonhole stitch before continuing in
soft shading. A pale coral detached

buttonhole frill has then been added. The inner parts are filled with dark coral soft shading.

The central flower has petals worked in laid filling using all three shades of blue – mid for the grid, dark for the tying stitch and pale for the French knots. These petals are outlined in dark pink chain stitch. The inner petals are worked in mid-pink buttonhole stitch, with a pale pink detached buttonhole frill. The centre is worked in mid-pink and dark pink bullion knots and pale and dark pink French knots.

The flower on the far left has tiny leaves in mid-olive satin stitch. The petals are in mid-coral buttonhole stitch, with pale coral detached buttonhole frills. They are filled with dark coral French knots (one strand).

The small flowers at the top are similar to their counterparts below. The pink flowers are all worked in French knots (one strand) using pale coral and all three shades of pink.

The flower at the top right has a circular spider's web in the centre worked in mid-yellow, with a little dark yellow shading on the upper side. The petals are worked in all three shades of blue satin stitch.

Stretching

Before stretching your finished piece, you need to decide whether to wash it first. As crewel embroidery is made up of linen, cotton and wool, use the wool cycle on your washing machine with normal washing powder. Give it a good spin and then leave it to dry by a radiator. Then it is ready for stretching.

Stretching is one of the great exciting moments of crewel embroidery, as the starches from the linen bring sparkle back to the fabric.

1 Cover the board with dressmaker's graph paper. Secure in place with masking tape.

2 Remove any edge binding from the finished embroidery. Make sure the fabric is straight in line with a thread of the fabric. Place the embroidery right side up on top of the board. Line up one of the edges with a line on the graph paper.

3 Hammer in a nail every 2cm (¾in) along one of the sides. Repeat along an adjacent side. Try to work about 1.25cm (½in) from the raw edge of the fabric, keeping the edge of the fabric in line with a line on the graph paper. Note: pull firmly as you nail, so that the material is taut but not over-stretched.

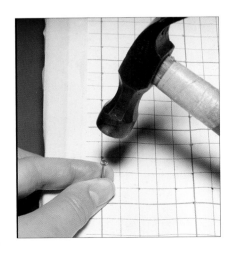

4 Turn the board around. Use the graph paper and the two completed sides as a guide to place holes along the other two sides, where you will eventually put the nails.

5 Pull out the fourth corner, diagonally opposite the first, so that it is square. Hammer in the corner nail, then two further nails to support the corner. If you cannot get the fourth corner square, remove the nails down the side, leaving the nails in the three corners. Now have another go!

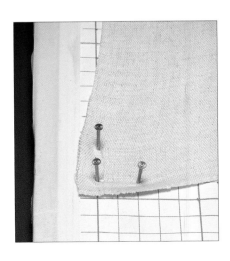

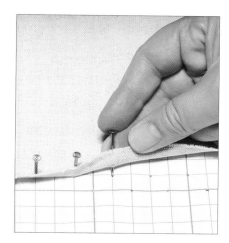

6 Gently push a nail through the fabric, then ease it into one of the holes made in step 4. Tap with a hammer to secure the nail. Repeat, to stretch the remaining two sides. The work should now be very square and firmly stretched.

7 Dampen the embroidery and fabric using a mist sprayer filled with water. Alternatively, use a wet sponge. Once you have stretched your piece, you can leave your graph paper in place, ready to stretch your next piece of embroidery. The graph paper in this demonstration has been used several times!

Stand the board somewhere warm to dry and, when dry, remove all the nails. You can stand the board up against a radiator to dry, place it in the airing cupboard or, if you are in a desperate hurry, a hair dryer is very useful. Do not leave the work wet and nailed out for too long as rust from the nails could damage the fabric. It has also been known for mould to grow on a finished piece. To avoid disappointment, as soon as the work is thoroughly dry, remove all the nails.

MOUNTMELLICK

Mountmellick embroidery employs many stitches and is an ideal introduction to embroidery, allowing you to concentrate on the stitches without having to worry about colour. Mountmellick is a form of white work and is always worked white on white. Its beauty is shown to advantage by the way the light falls on the sculptured stitchery.

Mountmellick embroidery was introduced to Ireland during the nineteenth century by Johanna Carter (c.1830), a member of the Society of Friends. It was developed in the town of Mountmellick in County Laois. The production of this technique was set up as a cottage industry to help the women of families affected by famine to earn some money. Readily available fabric and threads were used, and useful household items were made. The fabric available was stout cotton twill, which had a sheen, and is now called cotton sateen, or cotton satin jean. The thread used was a matte twisted cotton yarn. Designs were taken from nature, from looking at the surrounding countryside, and were mainly floral.

The Mountmellick technique is very bold and textured, and can be recognised by the following characteristics: it is always white on white; there are no drawn threads, open work spaces or eyelets; and it has contrast: smooth satin stitch against padded and knotted stitchery, and cotton satin fabric against the more matte cotton embroidery thread.

Mountmellick designs are fairly large scale, natural floral designs. There is often a buttonholed edge and a knitted fringe, which helps to carry the weight of the heavy embroidery to the edge of the design, and gives a feeling of balance.

This chapter contains a variety of designs, from small individual motifs to larger projects. The small motifs illustrate certain stitches and can be used on their own or combined on a larger item such as a cushion cover or table mat.

Convolvulus
Pat Trott

This convolvulus design is typical of traditional Mountmellick: it is white on white, and the contrast is provided by the matte cotton thread against the sheen of the fabric. Many different stitches are used to create the bold shapes, inspired by nature.

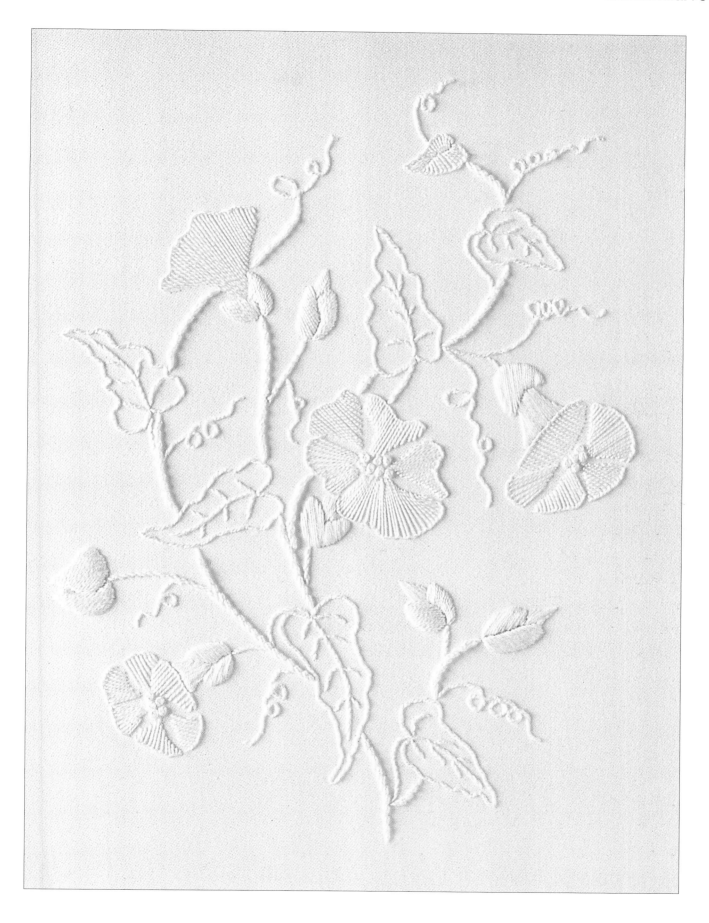

Materials

Fabric

Mountmellick embroidery requires a closely woven, heavy, cotton sateen fabric. It needs to be heavy enough to support the weight of the stitches, especially when working on a large project. This fabric can be obtained from specialist shops, but if you have difficulty, then buy a good quality heavy cotton. Fabrics you can use include white jean, drill, twill and cotton duck. You must not be able to see the weave of the fabric, as this will distract you when stitching.

A selection of threads and fabric suitable for Mountmellick embroidery. Matte thread should be used to contrast with fabric that has a sheen, or vice versa.

Prepare the fabric by pre-washing it before you transfer the design. This will remove any residual dressing and shrink the fabric. This is especially important if you are making an item that will require constant washing. When you have spent hours producing a beautiful work of art, it is heartbreaking if it shrinks in the first wash and the whole thing puckers.

Make sure you buy enough fabric to allow for mounting on to a frame while working, and also to leave enough room from the edge of your embroidery to the edge of the finished item. It is best not to embroider right up to the very edge of a piece of work – leave a little fabric between the finished embroidery and the buttonholed hem and knitted fringe.

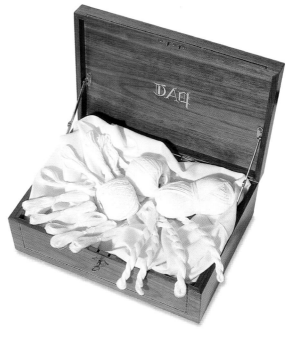

Threads

Traditionally, Mountmellick was worked with a matte cotton thread, but these days we have to use what we can get! It is important to have contrast in your work, so if you have managed to obtain a fabric with a slight sheen, then embroider with matte threads. If your fabric has no sheen, then you can afford to stitch with a mercerised thread that has a little sheen, for instance cotton perle. Suitable threads can include cotton perle, coton à broder, embroidery soft, craft cotton and some crochet cottons. Stranded cotton is not recommended for this particular technique, but a single, twisted thread.

Cotton perle comes in four thicknesses – 3, 5, 8 and 12. The thickest is 3 and 12 is the finest. This is a mercerised thread.

Coton à broder (in white) comes in six thicknesses – 12, 16, 20, 25, 30 and 35; 12 being the thickest and 35 being the finest. This is also a mercerised thread.

Embroidery soft comes in just one thickness and is a matte cotton.

Craft cotton is usually quite thick, and may be too thick for embroidery. You may use it occasionally if working on a large design, but it is best kept for knitting the fringe of a large project such as a bedspread or tablecloth.

Crochet cotton the larger balls of mercerised thread sold in knitting shops. Crochet cotton looks like cotton perle, but you should use a shorter length as it is not manufactured to stitch with and will become worn and fluffy when pulled through the fabric too many times. This comes in a variety of thicknesses; a no. 5 is quite good.

Purchase a variety of thicknesses of thread so that you have a lovely 'goody bag' to dip into. There is nothing more frustrating than not having the thread you need when you want to start embroidering.

Needles

The size of needle you use will depend on the thickness of the thread for the project you are working on. Choose a needle with a large enough eye that you can thread easily, either a chenille needle or a crewel needle. Chenille needles come in sizes 18 to 24 and have larger eyes than crewel needles, are slightly thicker and are ideal to stitch with when using a heavy duty cotton fabric, as they go through the fabric more easily when using a thick thread.

Crewel needles are finer, come in sizes 3 to 10 and are ideal when using a fine thread. Both types of needle have a sharp point. Again, gather a collection of sizes so that you have the correct size of needle for the thread you are using.

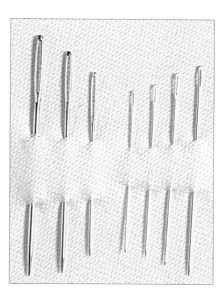

A selection of crewel and chenille needles suitable for Mountmellick embroidery. Choose a size with an eye large enough for the thickness of thread you have chosen.

Frames

Working on a frame keeps the fabric taut and leaves both hands free to work the stitches. You can sit at a table, with the frame propped between your lap and the table, but using a stand on which you can clamp the frame holds it very stable. There are many choices of stand available on the market, including a solid metal one with a clamp that can accommodate frames from small to large equally well. You can sit almost anywhere to use it, even in the sitting room with the rest of the family, as it just slots in under whatever chair you sit in.

Tambour or round frame

These are available in a variety of sizes, from 7.5cm (3in) to 30.5cm (12in), measured across the middle of the frame. The frame consists of two wooden rings that fit inside one another. The outer ring has an adjustable screw to enable you to tighten it around the inner ring to keep the fabric taut.

Slate frame

A slate frame has two rollers to which webbing is attached, and two side bars with a slot at both ends into which the rollers fit. These frames are made in various sizes, being measured along the length of the webbing. The fabric to be used must not be any wider than the webbing, but the length can be greater than the length of the side bars as the surplus fabric may be wound around the rollers.

Ideally, work on a frame large enough to show the whole design at once. If this is not possible, at least use a slate frame so that you can see the width of the design and can roll the fabric when the length of it is too long to fit on the frame.

Home-made frame

Wooden frames, made from lengths of soft wood, mitred at the corners and then glued and stapled together, can be made to the size you need.

Seat frame

It is an advantage to have both hands free when stitching, particularly when executing stitches such as French knots. A seat frame enables you to do this, as it has a flat 'foot' that can be placed under your leg to keep it steady while you are stitching. The seat frame is made up of two parts: a tambour frame fixed to a wooden rod, which is slotted into another hollow piece of wood and held in place with a screw.

Clockwise from the right: a seat frame; a large slate frame; a tambour frame with an adjustable screw and home-made square frames.

Other items

Scissors You need three pairs of scissors: dressmaking shears to cut the fabric, embroidery scissors to cut the thread, and paper scissors for cutting greaseproof paper, masking tape and sticky tape.

Bias binding Used to bind the inner ring of a tambour frame, to keep the fabric from slipping and to prevent the wood from marking it.

Crochet cotton Used to sew the fabric to the webbing on a slate frame, and to lace the sides of the fabric to the sides of the frame.

Masking tape or sticky tape Used to tape the design to a light source and to tape the fabric over the design ready to trace it.

Greaseproof paper This is used to trace your design on to, either from a book or from a copy.

Black pen This is used to trace the design on to the greaseproof paper. It needs to be a black pen, otherwise you will be unable to see the design through the fabric.

Water-soluble marker pen You will find this pen in most haberdashery shops. It is used to trace the design on to the fabric, and the blue marks it makes can be removed with cold water when the project is complete. Be careful not to buy an air-soluble pen, as the marks made disappear in air, often before you have time to finish a project. Do not iron the marks made with water-soluble pen, as heat will fix the lines. Also, test it on the edge of your fabric before you trace all the design. Just draw a small line on the edge of the fabric, then try to remove it by touching it with a paintbrush dipped in cold water. If it comes out easily, go ahead and trace the whole design.

Paintbrush and cold water When you have finished your embroidery, leave it stretched on the frame, and very carefully touch each design line with a clean paintbrush dipped in cold water. Magically, all the blue disappears and you are left with a lovely white embroidery.

Knitting needles For creating the knitted fringes that go round the edges of many Mountmellick embroideries (see pages 90–93).

Staple gun This is used to staple the fabric to the frame if you are using the home-made 'picture frame' type of frame described on page 76.

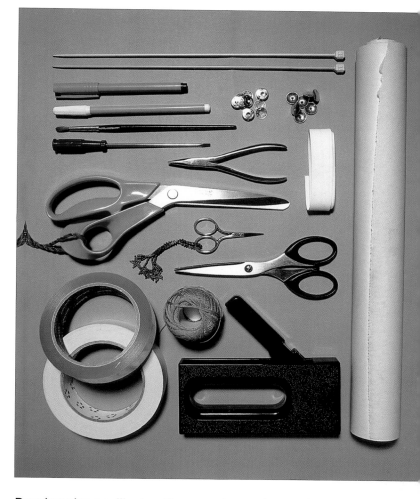

Drawing pins or silk pins These can be used to attach the fabric to a home-made frame if you do not have a staple gun.

Screwdriver This is used to loosen the staples and lift them out of the frame when you have finished the embroidery. Usually only one side of the staple comes out.

Pliers These are used to remove the staples from the frame after loosening them as above.

Tape measure This is used to measure the fabric before cutting. Allow enough room round the edge of the design to attach the fabric to the frame.

Stitches

This chapter contains thirteen stitches, which are shown step by step on pages 80–89. This sampler is a collection of thirteen motifs showing how the stitches can be used. From left to right along the rows, the motifs show:

Wheat Ears: detached chain stitch. Stems: stem stitch.

Dog rose Petals: padded satin stitch. Rose centre: French knots. Main stem: Mountmellick stitch. Stem on the leaf: stem stitch. Leaves: buttonhole stitch.

Acorn Stem: palestrina knot stitch. Leaves: split stitch. Acorns: padded satin stitch. Acorn cups: French knots.

Holly Stem: cable plait stitch. Berries: satin stitch. Leaves: coral knot stitch.

Blackberries Main stem and leaf veins: chain stitch. Small stem: stem stitch. Leaves: couching. Berries: French knots and detached chain stitch.

Shamrock Stem: stem stitch. Shamrock leaves: satin stitch. Tendrils: couching.

Elderberries Stems: stem stitch. Main stem, berries and leaves: buttonhole stitch.

Ivy Stem: Portuguese knotted stem stitch. Leaves: split stitch. Berries: buttonhole stitch.

Vine leaves Stem: cable plait stitch. Leaves and tendrils: couching. Leaf veins: stem stitch.

Catkins Main stem: satin stitch. Small stem: stem stitch. Catkins: French knots. Small leaves: detached chain stitch.

Long-stemmed blackberries Main stem: Mountmellick stitch. Small stems and leaf veins: stem stitch. Leaves: couching. Blackberries: French knots and detached chain.

Daisy Petals: satin stitch. Daisy centre: French knots. Stem: cable plait stitch. Leaf: buttonhole stitch.

Grapes on vine Main stem: cable plait stitch. Small stem: stem stitch. Tendril: couching. Grapes: outlined in split stitch, padded, then padded satin stitch.

Couching

You will find that not many of the 'line' stitches, such as stem or chain stitch, go round tight curves or sharp angles. Couching is therefore a very useful stitch for wavy, curly or jagged lines. It is also useful for holding down a thick thread on a line, enabling you to use a very thick thread that might not like being pulled through the fabric too many times. If you are couching the thread, you only need to pull it through at the beginning and end of the line.

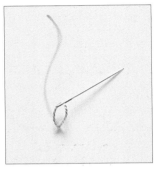  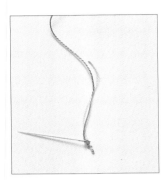 

1 Bring the thick thread (shown in blue) up through the fabric at the start of the design.

2 Bring the finer thread (shown in pink) up on one side of the thicker thread.

3 Take the needle down on the other side of the thicker thread and come up on the first side to start the second stitch.

4 A finished line of couching stitches. Threads in different colours are used here for clarity, but in Mountmellick, both threads would be white.

Split stitch

In this chapter, split stitch is used mainly to outline areas that are to be filled with satin or padded satin stitch. It makes a nice firm edge and will help to give a smooth, rounded effect to the petals. It can also be used on its own on wavy, curly or jagged lines in the same way as couching. The grapes on the vine shown below were all outlined in split stitch, then padded, then a final layer of satin stitch was added, completely covering the original split stitch outline.

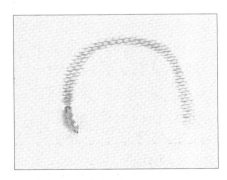 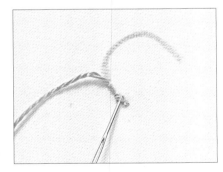 

1 Bring the thread up at the beginning of the design and go down with a straight stitch.

2 Come up a little further along the line. Take the needle back down near the end of the previous stitch to split it.

3 Repeat, to create a line of completed split stitches.

Chain stitch

As the name implies, this stitch looks like a chain. It is made up of small links, which are known as detached chain stitch when separate, but in chain stitch are linked together to form a chain. Chain stitch is a line stitch – it is principally used on lines, though it can be used in other ways. You work downwards from the top of the line to the bottom, towards yourself.

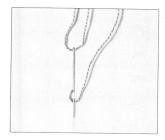

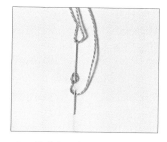

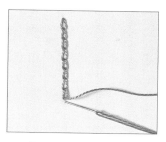

1 Come up from the back at the top of the design. Make an anticlockwise circle with the thread. Go back down the same hole. Come up a little way down the line, making sure the needle is inside the loop.

2 Pull the thread through to make a link. Go back down inside the first link in the same hole you came up in the previous step, and repeat.

3 To end the chain, take the needle down outside the last link.

4 For detached chain stitch, after making one chain link, go down outside the link.

Coral knot

This is another useful stitch for wavy, curly or jagged lines, especially if you make the knot on the points and angles of a jagged line, as on the holly leaves. You can space the knots very closely or far apart, depending on the thickness of thread, the design and the effect you want to achieve. Right-handers work from right to left, as shown here; left-handers from left to right.

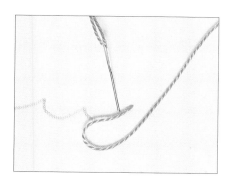

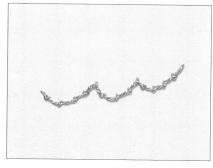

1 Come up on the right-hand side of the design. Lay the thread along the line of the design in the direction you are working, with the thread coming back towards you in an anticlockwise circle. Put the needle in above the thread, where you want your knot.

2 Pull the needle to the back and, before you have pulled all the thread through, bring the needle up again below the thread and level with the point where you went down. Make sure the needle comes up within the circle. Gently pull the thread up towards you, until it makes a knot.

3 Continue in the same way all along the line, spacing the knots where you want them.

Stem stitch

This is another line stitch, especially good for stems or branches. The finished effect should look like a rope. It is very effective on straight lines, but can also be used on curved lines. It works best on lines that curve from right to left. It does not work well on very tight curves or circles. Work from the bottom of a line up towards the top, away from yourself. The length of the stitches you make will depend on the thickness of the thread. When using a fine thread, make the stitches small, and when using a thicker thread, make them longer.

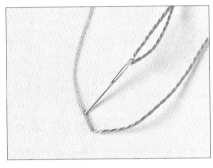

1 Come up at the bottom of the design. Keep the thread to the right of the line you're working on. Go down again a little way along the line.

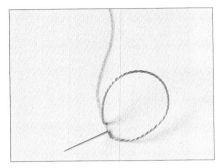

2 Come up again halfway between where you came up and where you went down, and pull through. Steps 1 and 2 apply only for the first stitch of the design.

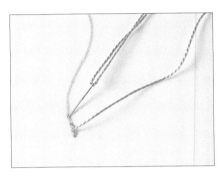

3 Keep the thread to the right of the line you're working on. Go down a little way above the top of the previous stitch.

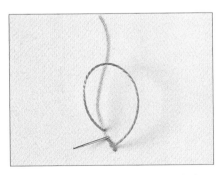

4 Come up through the same hole as the top of the previous stitch.

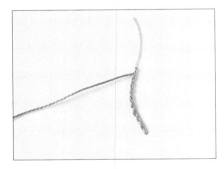

5 Continue, repeating steps 3 and 4.

The smaller stem of these catkins is worked in stem stitch.

Portuguese knotted stem stitch

This stitch can be used where you want a thick line; it is thicker than stem stitch. It can also be very useful where you need a more textured stem or branch. It is worked from the bottom of a line to the top, away from yourself. It looks a little complicated, but you soon get in a rhythm and this can be a very therapeutic, soothing stitch to do!

1 Come up at the bottom of the design. Go down a little way above it, keeping the thread to the right, and come up halfway between where you came up and went down (as for stem stitch).

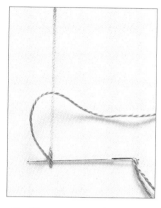

2 You now need to wrap this stitch twice. Keep the thread to the left. Form a clockwise loop and pass the needle from right to left under your first stitch, below the loop. That is wrap one.

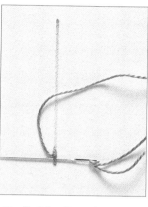

3 Pull the thread upwards to tighten the knot. Go round again and take the needle under the stitch, below the first wrap.

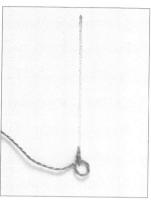

4 Make sure your second wrap is below the first. Pull the thread upwards to tighten the knot. (Steps 1 to 4 are for the first stitch only.)

5 Go down a little way above the top of the previous stitch. Come up just to the left-hand side and level with the top of the previous stitch. The bottom of the new stitch should overlap the top of the previous stitch.

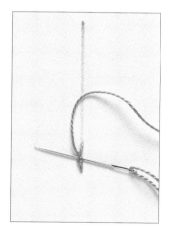

6 Pass your needle under the two overlapping stitches from right to left and pull taut. This makes wrap one.

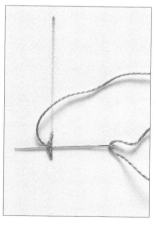

7 Pass the needle under the two overlapping stitches from right to left, and below the first wrap. Pull taut again.

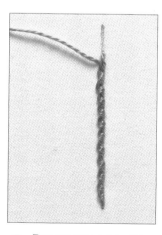

8 Repeat steps 5 to 7 to the end of the line. Then take the thread through to the back and finish off.

Satin stitch

The beauty of satin stitch lies in its simplicity: long, straight stitches lying next to one another with a smooth, even edge. However, the simpler a stitch, the easier it is to see mistakes, so great care must be taken with satin stitch. Take your time and do not rush! One of the ways to achieve a smooth edge is to outline the desired area in split stitch first. This gives you a line to work on. Another tip is to get the angle of the stitch right. Do not come up at the top or bottom of the petal, but about half or a third of the way up. Get your angle right, then work up to the top, then down to the bottom.

Dog Roses and Blackberries

Pat Trott

In this embroidery, satin stitch has been worked on the rose petals, buds and rosehips, and on the sepals at the bases of the flowers shown from the side. A single French knot has been added to the top of each rosehip and the centres of the flowers have been filled with French knots.

1 Outline in split stitch first. Start in the middle of the design. This helps you to set an angle for the stitches which you then follow throughout. Come up on the outside of the outline on one side of the design.

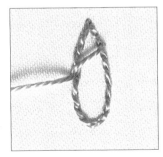

2 Hold the thread until you are happy with the angle the stitch will make, then go down on the opposite side of the design. Come up again on the first side, outside the outline as before.

3 Repeat along the design, making sure the stitches lie as close as possible to one another, and keep to the same angle.

4 Go back to the middle where you started, and fill in the rest of the design.

Padded satin stitch

Padded satin stitch gives a much higher relief than flat satin stitch. It is worked in the same way, but is padded first to give it height. This padding is worked inside the split stitch edge using the same threads as you use for stitching. Do not be tempted to use wadding or cotton wool – it will not work. When you have embroidered some of the stems and leaves in your design, you will have thread left in the needle that has been through the fabric a few times and got 'tired' and 'fluffy'. Use this to edge and pad some of the areas where you will be using padded satin stitch. This padding takes a long time and can be tedious if done all at once. Using the ends of the threads and doing it a bit at a time takes the tedium out of it. It feels really good to have most of the padding done so that you can use your newest threads to work the final layer.

1 After outlining the shape with split stitch, fill in the area with tiny straight stitches placed at random (seeding stitches).

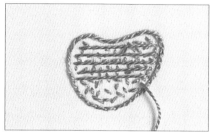

2 Cover the seeding stitches with long straight stitches, still within the outline.

3 Work the next layer of straight stitches at right angles to the first.

4 The last layer of straight padding stitches must be at right angles to the direction you want your final satin stitches to take.

5 Fill in with satin stitches, starting and finishing outside the outline, to cover it.

Padded satin stitch created the lovely, raised effect of the petals in this dog rose design.

French knots

French knots should look like a 'lady's bun hairstyle' – nice and round with a dimple in the middle. To achieve this effect, you should only wrap the thread round the needle once. To make knots of different sizes, you should use a thicker or a finer thread – rather than varying the number of wraps.

 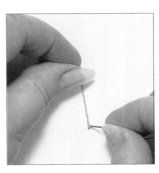  

1 Come up from the back where you want the knot to be. Hold the thread in your left hand. Put the needle on top of the thread and wrap the thread round it once.

2 Re-enter the fabric very close to where you came out. When the needle is halfway down, gently pull the thread taut.

3 Push the needle down and pull through to make a knot. The finished knot should look like a little circle with a dimple in the middle.

4 Work more French knots to create a cluster.

Buttonhole stitch

This stitch is used to edge your finished projects before adding the knitted fringe, but it can also be used as a stitch in its own right, mainly on leaves. It is worked from left to right. The leaves were worked up one side and down the other, sharing the middle line, thus creating a vein in the middle. The berries were worked in a circular way, the top of all the stitches sharing the same middle hole.

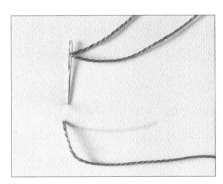 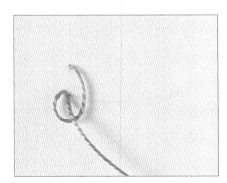 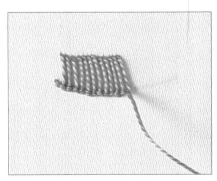

1 Come up on your design line. Go down the desired stitch length up from the line. The thread goes round in an anticlockwise circle.

2 Come up on the bottom line to the right of where you started, inside the anticlockwise loop. Pull through and pull taut so that the stitch lies flat on the fabric.

3 Repeat steps 1 and 2 to the end of the line. Finish off by going down to the right of your last stitch, on the design line.

Palestrina knot stitch

This is a lovely textured line stitch that can be used for stems and branches that need a 'knobbly' look. It is also known as double knot stitch. The knots look good when worked quite close together, but of course you can place them further apart if you like. This stitch works particularly well in a thick thread. It is worked from top to bottom, down the line towards yourself.

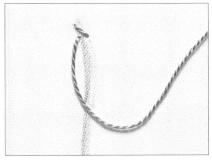

1 Work from top to bottom. Come out at the top of the line. Go down just below this point and to the right, to make a little diagonal stitch. Come up on the line again, below the first point. Keep the thread coming down towards you.

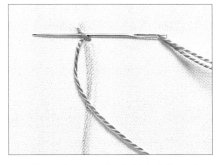

2 Pass the needle right to left under the diagonal stitch, to make a wrap.

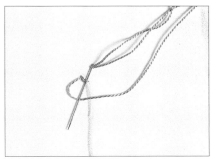

3 Make an anticlockwise circle with your thread and pass the needle top to bottom under the original diagonal stitch, below the wrap, making sure the thread is under the needle. Pull taut to make a knot.

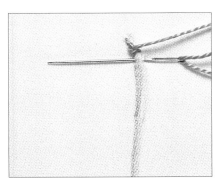

4 Keeping the thread up out of the way, go down to the right of the line, and come up on the line, to make another diagonal stitch.

5 Pull through and repeat steps 2, 3 and 4 to make a line of knots. Space them out as desired.

The stem of this oak leaf motif was worked in palestrina knot stitch.

Mountmellick stitch

Mountmellick is another line stitch but is wider than stem or chain, so it can be used on thick stems. It is a bold, raised stitch. One side of the stitch has a straight edge, the other has a little 'leg' that looks a little like a thorn, so this stitch can be used very well for the stems of roses or blackberries. It is worked from top to bottom down the line towards you.

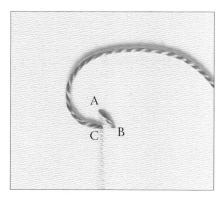

1 Come out at the top of the line (A). Make a diagonal stitch to the right and go down at (B). Come up back on the line below the starting point (C). Keep the thread out of the way at the top.

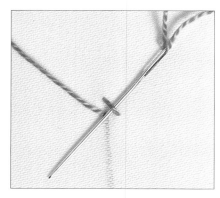

2 Pass the needle from top to bottom under the diagonal stitch, keeping the thread out of the way to the left of the needle.

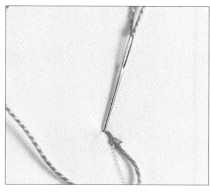

3 Now take the thread round in a clockwise direction. Go down the same hole you first came out of (A).

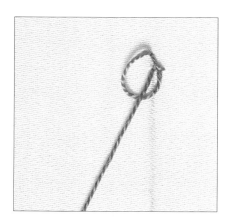

4 Come up through the second hole on the line (C). Make sure you are inside the loop of thread, and gently pull taut. This will form a triangle, with the straight edge on the left and the little 'leg' on the right.

5 Start the next stitch with a diagonal stitch (as in step 1) and repeat steps 2 and 3, as before, making sure that when you go down at A, it is inside the triangular stitch you have just made. (C of your first stitch becomes the A of your second stitch.) Come up at C of the second stitch, again making sure you are inside the clockwise circle of thread. You are now at step 4 of your second stitch. This C will now become A of your third stitch.

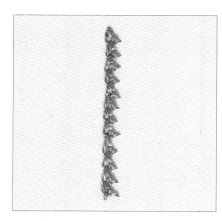

6 Continue down the line, and finish by going to the back just below the straight edge of the triangle.

TIP

With each stitch, you go in and out of A/C three times in total.

Cable plait stitch

This is a wide stitch useful for thick stems. It is made between two parallel lines that form a channel. Here it is used for the main, thick trunk of a vine. It can also be used around the edge of a project instead of buttonhole stitch. Let the stitch sit on the surface of the fabric; do not pull it too tightly or it will just fold up into the middle of the channel. This is a very pretty stitch and is another rhythmical, therapeutic stitch to work. It is worked from top to bottom down the channel towards yourself.

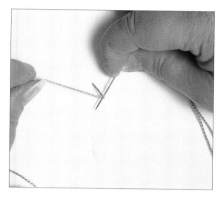

1 Come up on the left-hand line. Hold the thread in your left hand. Put the needle under the thread pointing towards 'eleven o'clock' and turn it anticlockwise towards you.

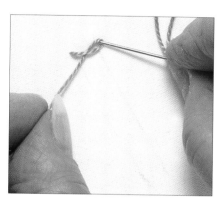

2 Continue twisting anticlockwise to make a loop where the exiting thread is on top of the long thread. Push the needle down on the right-hand line, inside the loop you have made.

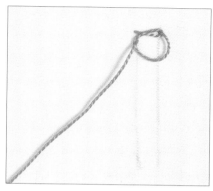

3 Push the needle up on the left-hand line. Make sure your thread is under your needle. Pull the thread taut round the needle. Pull the needle through to the front.

4 Pull the thread through, but do not pull too tight. The stitch should lie on the surface of the fabric.

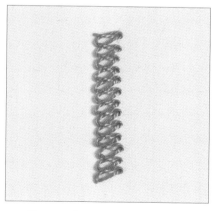

5 Repeat down between the two lines.

Cable plait stitch is ideal for thick stems like the one in this vine leaf design.

Knitted fringes

One of the main characteristics of Mountmellick work is the knitted fringe. It would be impossible to knit the length of fringe needed, especially on large items such as a tablecloth or bedspread, so the fringe is knitted sideways. It is knitted in multiples of three stitches, casting on enough stitches for the required width of fringe. There is nothing worse than a mean, sparse fringe – it needs to be full and weighty to look good – so it is knitted in multiples of thread simultaneously, usually three or four, from separate balls of yarn. The finer the thread you use, the more threads you need in the multiple. For the fringe shown below, cast on twelve stitches. You can use any number that is divisible by three.

Casting on

You can cast on in your usual way, but if you cast on with the one-needle method shown below, you can cast on using two needles held together as one. This will make the cast-on stitches a little looser, making it is easier to knit the first row.

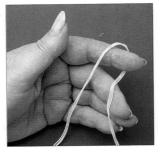

1 Take the three threads in your left hand as shown. The thread goes over the index finger and between the thumb and third finger.

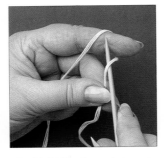

2 Hold the thread. Insert two needles under the thread as shown.

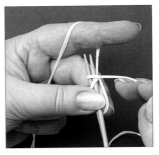

3 Hold the needles in your left hand and loop thread from the balls right to left, anticlockwise, round the needles.

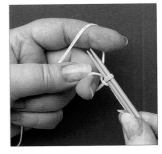

4 Pull the needles through the loop.

5 Pull the loop tight around the needles. Cast on twelve stitches in this way, and then pull out one of the needles ready to start knitting.

Knitting

6 Put the right-hand needle into the first loop on the left-hand needle.

7 Wind the thread right to left, anticlockwise, round the needle.

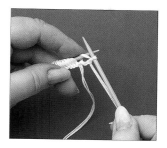

8 Pull the thread through the loop.

9 Slip the loop off the left-hand needle.

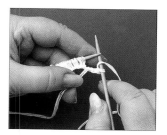

10 Make one by bringing the thread under the right-hand needle so that it is between the two needles.

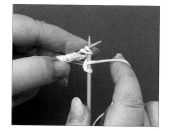

11 Knit two together: put the right-hand needle through two loops on the left-hand needle and repeat steps 7 to 9.

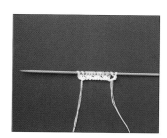

12 Repeat steps 6 to 11 to the end of the row.

13 Continue knitting rows until the knitted strip is long enough to edge your embroidery.

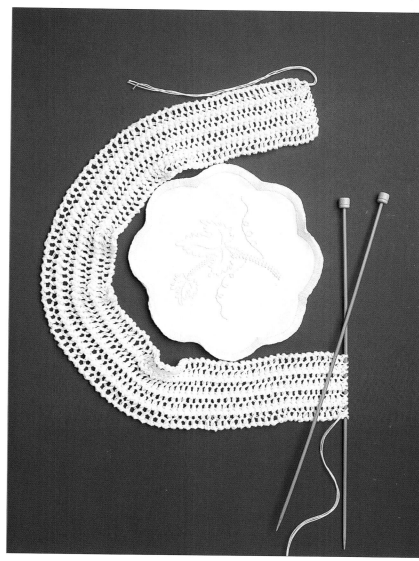

Casting off

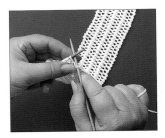

14 Knit one on to the right-hand needle.

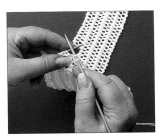

15 Knit a second stitch in the same way.

16 Put the left-hand needle through the first stitch.

17 Take the first stitch over the second and...

18 ...slip the stitch off the needle.

19 Continue until only five stitches are left on the left-hand needle. Cut off the thread.

20 Take the right-hand needle out, take the thread through the last stitch and pull tight.

21 Take the left-hand needle out of the last five stitches.

22 Unravel the edge with a needle. Pull out the first stitch.

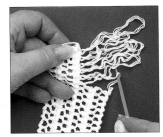

23 The fringe develops as more and more stitches are unravelled.

24 Stitch the fringe on to the finished piece.

A small mat with a vine leaf design. The buttonhole edge is completed, ready for the fringe to be sewn on to it.

The vine leaf mat with the knitted fringe sewn in place.

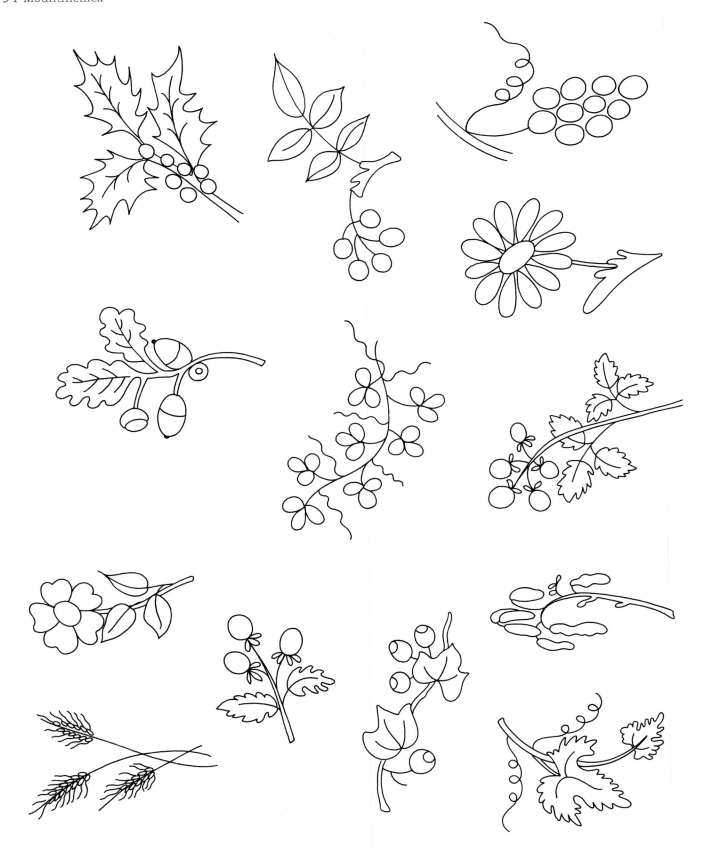

The patterns for the sampler on pages 78–79, reproduced three-quarters (75 per cent) actual size.

Poppies, Corn and Daisies

Pat Trott

The daisies have been worked with satin stitch. The outline under the satin stitch gives the petals a slightly raised effect, but it is not as pronounced as in padded satin stitch. The centres of the poppies and some of the daisies have been filled with French knots. The poppy petals have been created using buttonhole stitches.

STUMPWORK

Stumpwork dates from the seventeenth century and, traditionally, it is small, intricate and, sometimes, frustrating to make. But, once hooked, you will look at embroidery differently, and you may even find that flat needlework looks uninteresting by comparison.

Stumpwork is sometimes confused with the Elizabethan style of padded embroidery. Both types of work are raised, but the styles are completely different. The Elizabethan style generally has scrolled patterns in the form of coiling stems, with flowers and fruits, whereas the later stumpwork embroideries are more picturesque.

Stumpwork is currently enjoying a revival and is growing increasingly popular with embroiderers and lacemakers alike, who use both traditional materials and the extensive range of modern ones. A typical modern stumpwork embroidery contains flat, padded and freestanding embroidery, and slips (small pieces of needlework made on separate pieces of fabric).

Stumpwork is not as alarming as it might first appear. In this chapter there are projects that even someone new to embroidery can achieve with ease. You are guided, step by step, through how to make and use different types of padding, and the embroidery and needlelace stitches commonly used in stumpwork. When you get used to the stitches and techniques, try to develop your own ideas by experimenting with other modern materials. The real joy of this technique is designing and creating an original and unique embroidery that will be treasured for years to come.

Happy stitching!

Seahorse

Kay Dennis

The inspiration for this stumpwork picture came from a visit to a marine aquatic centre. The seahorse seemed to be motionless and oblivious to the hustle and bustle of the brightly coloured fish around him. The seahorse is worked in needlelace over a stuffed felt pad (see page 108). The fish are calico-covered interfacing slips, embroidered with satin stitch. The seaweed is cut from two layers of painted silk bonded together with iron-on interfacing.

Materials

Fabrics

A plain background fabric, strong enough to support the sometimes heavily padded and wired elements, should be used for stumpwork. A good quality, medium-weight calico is suitable for most projects, although silk with a backing of calico is also suitable. When setting up an embroidery project, allow sufficient fabric all round the design for mounting in a hoop and for final framing. Medium-weight calico is also ideal for use as the backing fabric in needlelace pads, and lightweight calico, which folds more easily, is best for making slips and stuffed pads.

Scissors

Always use sharp scissors. You will need a large pair for cutting fabrics, a general-purpose pair for cutting paper, wire, etc., and a small, very sharp pair for cutting threads.

Threads

There is a very wide range of threads that can be used in stumpwork – cotton, silk, metallic, synthetic and wool, all in hundreds of different colours and textures – each creating a different result. With experience you will be able to select the correct thread for the effect you want to achieve. Try to use the finest threads, 100/3 silks or one strand of six-stranded cotton. Space-dyed threads can be used to create interesting finishes; hand-dyed threads are preferable to machine-dyed ones as the latter can end up being too stripey.

Use a fine, strong crochet cotton no. 80 for needlelace cordonnets, in a colour to match that of the filling stitch thread. Only use sewing thread for work that is not going to be visible in the finished embroidery; for securing pads and for couching down the cordonnet threads.

Needles

Use the needle appropriate for the purpose. It should pass through the fabric easily, and it should have an eye large enough to take the thread comfortably, but not so big that the thread keeps falling out. You will regularly use three types of needle for stumpwork:

Crewel or embroidery needles for all embroidery stitches. They have long eyes and sharp points.

Sharps needles for all general sewing.

Ballpoint needles for making needlelace and for making stitches on top of each other.

Also use beading needles for adding decorative beads to your embroideries, and a large tapestry needle to help make cordonnets.

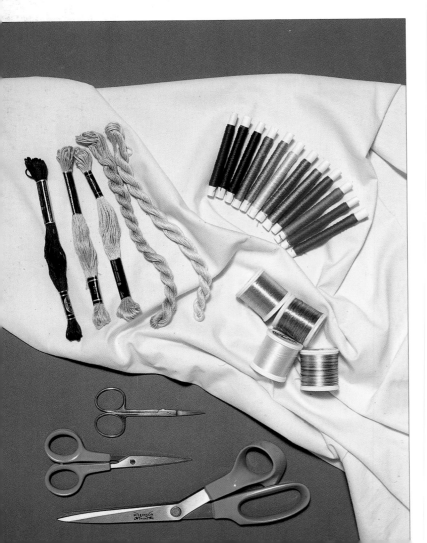

Crewel, ballpoint and sharps needles.

Padding

Interfacing This is a fabric stiffener available in different grades and thicknesses. Use a firm, heavyweight grade for raising flat surfaces and colour it with fabric paints.

Felt This comes in different thicknesses and grades, and in lots of colours. Use a smooth, thin felt in a colour that matches the embroidery threads for more rounded shapes. Pads can be made using layers of felt applied over each other, or by stuffing a single layer of felt with toy stuffing.

Toy stuffing Use a polyester toy stuffing, as it pulls out to almost single strands and can be pushed into the smallest of spaces. Kapok stuffing tends to be lumpy and it can be difficult to fill a space evenly. Quilters' wadding is not suitable for stumpwork.

Cotton moulds These are available from craft or hobby shops, and are ideal for making apples, oranges, etc. They should be painted before being covered with thread. Balsa wood is a good alternative to cotton moulds; it is a very soft wood that can be sculpted with a craft knife.

Beads Tiny beads or buttons can be used to decorate embroideries. Others can be wrapped in much the same way as cotton moulds.

Felt pens and pencils For sketching and for drawing paper patterns.

Fabric paint and brushes Use fabric paint to colour interfacing pads, cotton moulds and fabric slips before embroidering over them, and to paint the backgrounds for landscape designs. Use gold fabric paint to outline shapes on background fabrics before applying pads or stitches.

Acrylic paints Use these to colour wooden beads and other non-fabric items.

Dressmaker's pins For holding pads down on the background fabric before sewing them in place.

Tracing paper Used to transfer designs on to plain paper patterns.

Self-adhesive, transparent plastic This is ideal as the protective layer in needlelace pads.

Other equipment

Circular embroidery hoops are available in many sizes and are very easy to use. The background fabric is supported between two concentric rings, the outer one of which usually has a screwed clamp.

Slate frames are equally as good, especially for large embroideries, but you do have to stretch and sew the background fabric to the frame.

Silk frame and silk pins For stretching fabric before it is painted.

PVA glue To secure toy stuffing in open-ended felt pads and to secure silk thread when wrapping wire.

Thimble Especially useful when sewing through leather and similar materials.

Horsehair Used to strengthen the outlines of needlelace shapes that are to be freestanding.

Fine wire Incorporated in the top stitching of some pieces of needlelace to allow them to be bent into shape. Wrap paper-covered wire with silk thread to form flower stalks.

Cocktail sticks Use these to help fill felt pads with toy stuffing. They can also be used to create accessories for embroidery designs.

Stiletto This sharp, pointed tool is used for making small holes in fabric.

Tweezers Useful for intricate work and for removing small trimmings of thread.

Stitches

In this section, you will be shown the basic techniques of embroidered stumpwork. This sampler includes five projects and some small filler designs. Individual projects would make delightful embroideries on their own, and could be framed to make the perfect gift for someone special. The small designs could, for example, be used to decorate the lid of a box.

Each project is complete with step-by-step instructions to show you how to use different padding and raising techniques, and how to work the different stitches used to embroider it. Patterns are provided either with the projects or at the end of the chapter, on page 135.

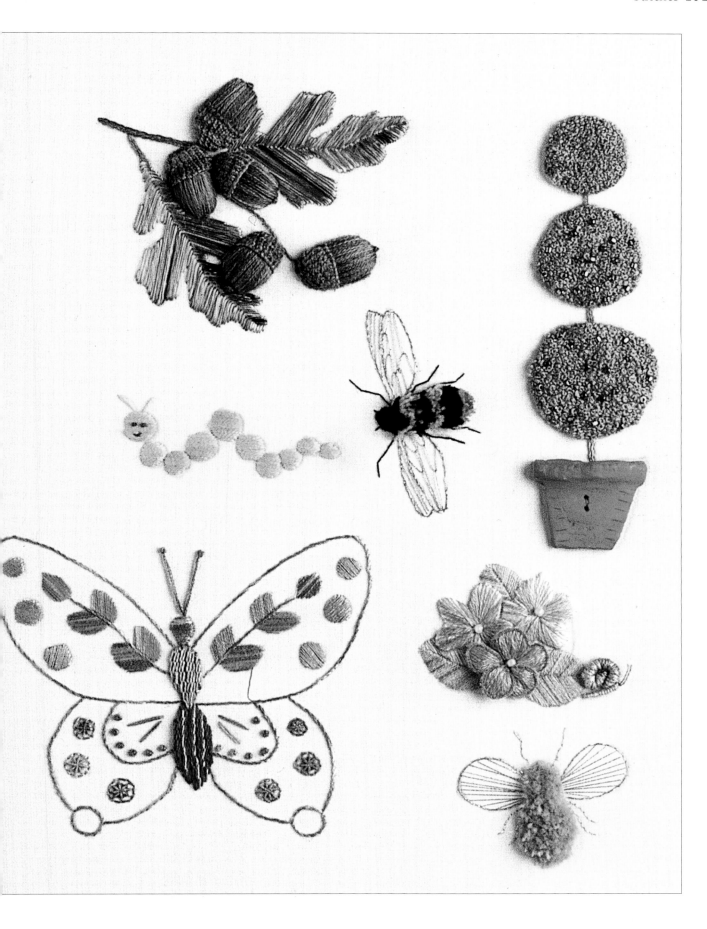

Flowing flowers

The padding used for the raised leaves and petals of this floral design are made from heavyweight interfacing. This is quite stiff, making it ideal for the crisp edges of leaves and petals. It also makes satin stitch easier to work as it helps guide the needle passing through the background fabric. You can paint the interfacing to match the thread colour so that the eye is not distracted by any white peeping through the stitches. Interfacing accepts fabric paint easily, but let it dry overnight before using it.

Satin stitch covers all the leaves and flowers, stem stitch is used for the flower stalks and Turkey knot stitch forms the raised body of the butterfly. The wings of the butterfly, which stand proud of the surface, are worked in long and short stitch over wire couched down on a separate piece of fabric.

You will need

- Medium-weight calico
- Fabric paint and brush
- Heavyweight interfacing
- Tracing paper and pencil
- Sewing thread
- Six-stranded cotton
- No. 7 embroidery needle
- Dressmaker's pins
- Fine wire
- Stiletto

Full-size pattern. Use gold fabric paint to transfer the outlines on to the background fabric. The wings of the butterfly stand proud of the surface, so do not transfer these. The lower petals, which are partly covered by the upper petals, are not padded, and the arrows on the upper petals indicate the direction of the satin stitches.

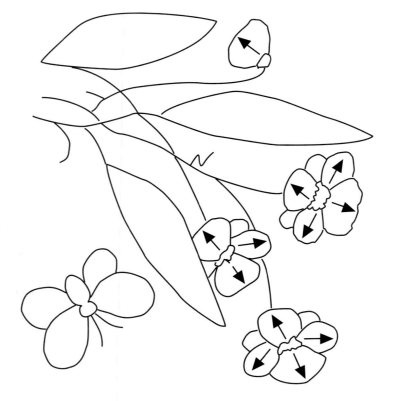

Preparing the padding

1 Transfer the outlines of the three leaves and the twelve petals shown here on to tracing paper, then cut out each shape. Keep the groups of petals together until you are ready to use them.

2 Use a green fabric paint to colour a piece of interfacing (the area must be large enough to cut out the three leaves).

3 Pin a tracing-paper leaf shape to the dry coloured interfacing, then cut out the shape.

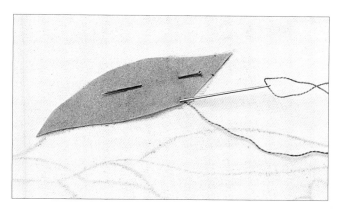

4 Pin the shape within its gold outline then, using a matching thread, stab stitch the leaf shape to the background fabric.

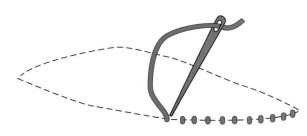

Stab stitch

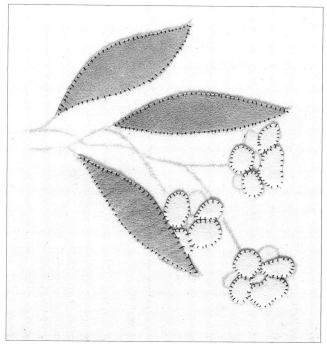

5 Cut out the other two leaves from the coloured interfacing, and the twelve petal shapes from white interfacing, then secure all the shapes to the background fabric.

Working the stalks

Stem stitch is used to work all the flower stalks. Use a no. 7 embroidery needle and one strand of six-stranded cotton thread. Work the longest stalks first, starting at the flower head or leaf end, then work the shorter stalks, blending them into the long ones.

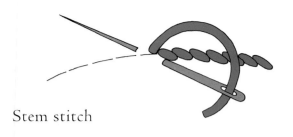

Stem stitch

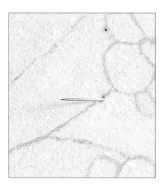

1 Bring the needle and thread up through the fabric approximately 6mm (¼in) from the start point of the stalk.

2 Take the needle down at the start point, then bring it back up again about 3mm (⅛in) beyond the first stitch.

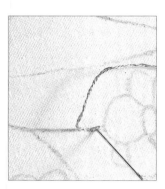

3 Now take the needle down through the fabric, approximately halfway along the first stitch.

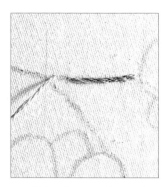

4 Bring the needle back up 3mm (⅛in) beyond the second stitch, then back down halfway along the second stitch. Continue working stitches until the stalk is complete.

Working the leaves and petals

The leaves and petals are all embroidered in satin stitch using a no. 7 embroidery needle and one strand of six-stranded cotton.

Make the first stitch across the middle of the shape, work out to one side, then go back to the middle and work the other side.

The lower petals on the diagram (see page 102) are not raised, and should be embroidered before working on the raised petals. Work the stitches from the centre of the flower outwards, generally in the direction of the arrows shown on the diagram.

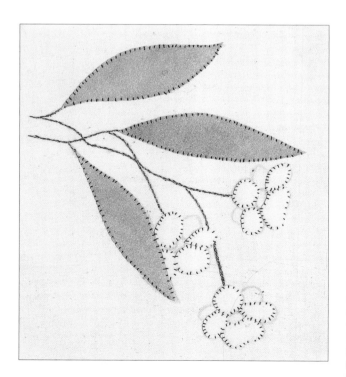

All stem-stitch stalks completed.

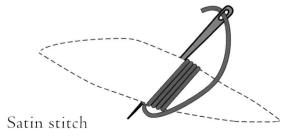

Satin stitch

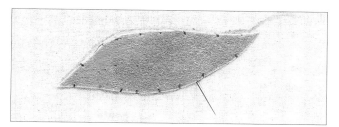

1 Bring the needle up through the fabric, one-third of the way along one side of the leaf shape.

2 Take the thread diagonally across the shape, hold it flat, then take the needle down through the fabric where the thread crosses the edge of the padding.

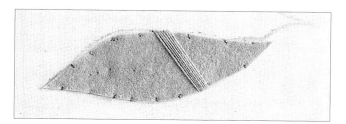

3 Bring the needle up at the right-hand side of the thread on the bottom edge of the padding, take it across the leaf, parallel to the first stitch, then back down through the fabric again. Continue working across the leaf shape.

4 When you have covered the right-hand side of the shape, work another series of satin stitches from the centre out to the left-hand side. Work the other leaves in a similar way. If worked carefully, satin stitch creates a wonderful sheen across the shape.

Working the butterfly

The body of the butterfly, which completes this project, is worked in Turkey knot stitch, using a no. 7 embroidery needle and two strands of six-stranded cotton. The resulting loops are trimmed off to create a fluffy raised area. The wings are worked on a separate piece of calico. Fine wire formers are couched on to the fabric, then the enclosed shapes are worked with long and short stitches. These stitches are worked with one strand of six-stranded cotton.

For clarity, the step-by-step photographs for making the wings do not include the embroidered body.

All satin stitches completed. Note that the centre of each flower head is filled with French knots (see page 112).

Full-size pattern.

The finished butterfly.

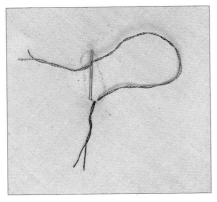

1 Starting at the bottom of the body, make the first knot leaving a short tail of thread on the surface.

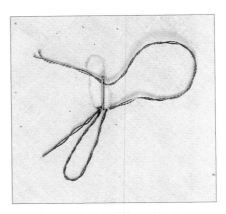

2 Tighten the knot, then, leaving a short loop on the surface, make another knot to one side.

3 Take the thread across the back of the fabric, then bring it up just above the first row of knots. Make another row of knots, then, repeating this step, work up the body shape.

4 Continue making rows of knots until the body shape is completely filled with knots.

5 Use a sharp pair of scissors to trim off the loops to create a rounded fluffy pile.

6 Transfer the outline of the four wings on to a piece of lightweight calico with gold fabric paint, leaving space for cutting out each wing. Cut lengths of fine wire to fit the contour of each wing. Allow for two 2.5cm (1in) tails to support the wings when they are sewn on to the body.

Turkey knot stitch

This stitch produces rows of secured loops which can then be trimmed to create a fluffy pile.

1. Insert the needle through the fabric at A, leaving a tail of thread on the surface. Bring the needle up at B, then down at C; pull the thread tight to make a small securing stitch.

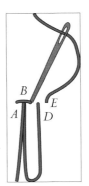

2. Bring the needle back up at A, then insert it at D, leaving a loop of thread on the surface. Bring the needle up at E, then down at B; again, pull the thread tight to make a securing stitch.

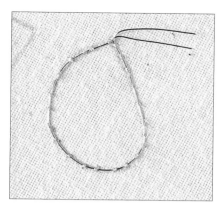

7 Couch the wire over the gold outlines.

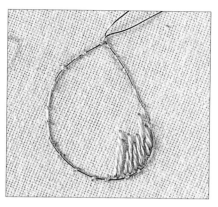

8 Starting at the outer edge of the wing shape, use one strand of six-stranded cotton and a no. 7 embroidery needle to make a series of long and short stitches alternately across the shape.

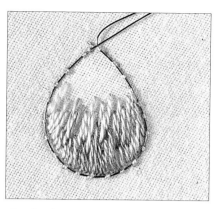

9 On the next and subsequent rows, bring the needle and thread up a short distance away from the first short stitch of the previous row, then take the thread through the end of this stitch and back into the background fabric.

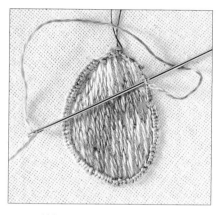

10 When the wing shape is completely filled with long and short stitch, work a hem of buttonhole stitches over the wire. Start at the base of the wing and work right round the shape. Do not cut off the excess thread as this is used to secure the wing to the body shape.

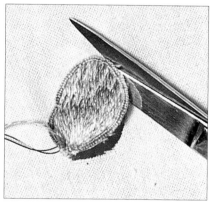

11 Cut round the outside edge, as close as possible to the buttonhole stitches.

12 Use a stiletto to make a small hole in the side of the body shape. Twist the wire tails together, then push them through the hole to the back of the fabric. Take the loose length of thread through the same hole.

Couching

Long and short stitch

Buttonhole stitch

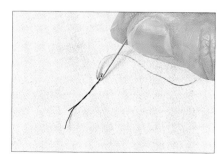

13 On the back of the fabric, fold the wire tail down the length of the body shape, then oversew it to secure it to the fabric. Repeat with the other three wings.

Acorns

Felt, padded out with toy stuffing, is used to create the rounded appearance of the acorns in this project. The stalks are embroidered in stem stitch (see page 104), the leaves and the basic acorn shapes are worked in satin stitch (see page 104), then the tip of each acorn is finished with a small French knot (see page 112). Finally, the acorn cups are worked in Ceylon stitch (see opposite), the texture of which is perfect for depicting the knobbly surface of the acorn cups.

You will need

Medium-weight calico
Felt
Thin suede
Tracing paper and pencil
Fabric paint and brush
Sewing thread
Six-stranded cotton
No. 7 embroidery needle

Stuffing the felt padding

Felt is a versatile padding material that can be stuffed to create rounded shapes for oversewing. Use a good quality fine felt, and select a colour that is compatible with the embroidery threads.

Cut the felt shapes so that they sit just inside the gold outline on the fabric. Stab stitches (see page 103) are used to secure the felt to the fabric; these should be very neat and as small as possible.

Take your time when stuffing the shapes; a smoother finish will be achieved by slowly building up the shape with small amounts of stuffing.

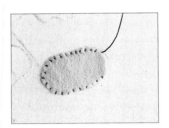

1 Stab stitch round the shape; bring the needle out of the fabric at an angle, then take it down through the edge of the felt. Leave a small gap.

2 Use a cocktail stick to push stuffing into the pouch. When you have achieved the required shape, close the gap with more stab stitches.

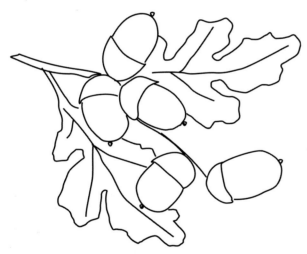

Full-size pattern. Use gold fabric paint to transfer all the outlines on to the background fabric.

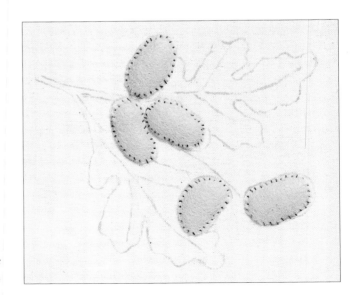

All padding stuffed and sewn on to the background fabric.

Working the acorns

Start the embroidery by using stem stitch and satin stitch to embroider the stalks and leaves respectively. Then, using a no. 7 embroidery needle and one strand of six-stranded cotton, cover the whole of each padded acorn shape with long satin stitches. Start in the middle of a shape, work across to one side, then go back and work the other side. Finish each acorn with a small French knot at the top. Now use the same needle and thread and Ceylon stitch to create the texture of the acorn cups as shown below.

1 Form the top edge of the cup with two satin stitches across the acorn, about halfway down the shape.

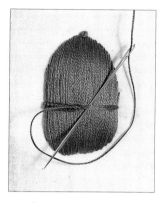

2 Bring the thread up at one side of the acorn, then work a row of slightly spaced buttonhole stitches over the two satin stitches.

Ceylon stitch

3 Take the thread down behind the acorn shape, bring it back up on the other side slightly below the last row, then work another row of stitches through the loops in the first row.

4 Repeat step 3 until the cup is complete.

The finished embroidery.

Poppy seed heads

Although these poppy seed heads are quite round in appearance, they are not as smooth as the acorns in the previous project. Felt is still used as the padding material, but, here, three layers of felt are sewn on top of each other.

The bulk of each seed head shape is covered with satin stitch (see page 104) and rows of stem stitch (see page 104) create the stalks. The textured top to each seed head is worked on a shaped piece of thin suede and consists of bullion knots (see opposite) worked from the tip of the seed head down to the points of the shape.

You will need

Medium-weight calico
Felt
Thin suede
Tracing paper and pencil
Fabric paint and brush
Sewing thread
Six-stranded cotton
No. 7 embroidery needle

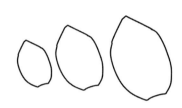

Felt shapes for the long seed head. Cut one set of these shapes.

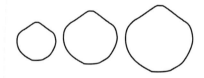

Felt shapes for the round seed heads. Cut two sets of these shapes.

Full-size pattern. Use gold fabric paint to transfer all the outlines of this pattern on to the background fabric.

Layering the felt padding

Layered felt is an ideal method of padding the shapes of these seed heads. Referring to the small diagram (above right), cut out sets of three, different-sized shapes for each seed head.

Then, starting with the smallest shape, use small, neat stab stitches (see page 103) to secure them on top of each other within the gold outlines on the background fabric.

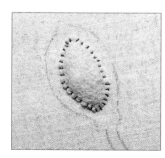

1 Use just four stab stitches to secure the smallest shape in the middle of the outline.

2 Overlay the second layer, secure it initially with four stitches, then stab stitch it all round.

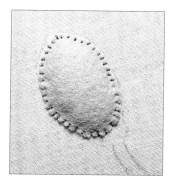
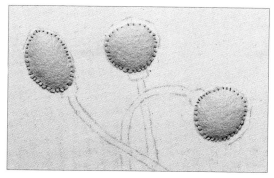

3 Stab stitch the third layer to complete the padding.

4 Work the other two seed head shapes in a similar manner.

Embroidering the design

Use a no. 7 embroidery needle and one strand of six-stranded cotton to work the stalks on the background fabric; make four or five rows of stem stitch, side by side.

Use long satin stitches to cover the seed heads, working from the top to the bottom of each shape. Work satin stitch across the join between the stalk and the seed head.

Draw the shapes for the tops of the seed heads on to a piece of thin suede. Work six bullion knots on each shape; start each stitch at the top centre of the shape and take it down to one of the points. Trim the shapes to size, then sew them over the top of the seed heads, leaving the bottom of each shape free.

The finished embroidery.

Bullion knot

Bullion knots are long, wrapped stitches, anchored at each end, that can be curled into shapes. The stitch is also known as worm stitch or caterpillar stitch — names which may suggest ideas for using it. Bullion knots can be made in any thickness of thread, but the thread must be smooth.

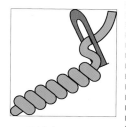

1. Bring the needle and thread up through the fabric at the top of the shape, insert the needle at one of the points of the shape, then bring it back up through the original hole.

2. Wrap the thread round the needle until the wrapping is long enough for the required stitch.

3. Pull the needle and thread through the wrapping.

4. Fold the wrapping back on itself, then take the thread down through the fabric at the other end of the stitch.

Topiary

In this project, only the short lengths of tree trunk, worked in stem stitch (see page 104), are embroidereded on the background fabric. The circles of foliage are slips, worked entirely in French knots on a separate piece of lightweight calico. These slips need little or no filling, as the surplus calico provides the stuffing. However, a more rounded effect can be achieved by adding toy stuffing.

Petite beads, to represent berries, are sewn on the completed mass of French knot foliage. Air-drying clay was used to make the flowerpot, but you can buy flowerpot buttons.

Making French knot slips

Paint the three circles on a separate piece of lightweight calico, leaving at least 2.5cm (1in) space between each for cutting out, then fill each circle with a mass of French knots.

You will need

Medium-weight calico
Lightweight calico
Tracing paper and pencil
Fabric paint and brush
Sewing thread
Six-stranded cotton
No. 7 embroidery needle
No.10 sharps or a beading needle
Petite beads
Air-drying clay or flowerpot button
Acrylic paint

French knot

The finished embroidery.

Full-size pattern. Use gold fabric paint to transfer all the outlines of this pattern on to the background fabric.

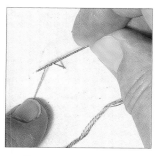

1 Bring the thread up through the fabric, hold the thread taut, then twist the needle round the thread twice.

2 Keeping the thread taut, take the needle back through the fabric just to the side of where the thread comes through it.

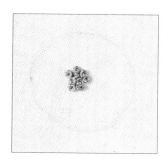

3 Release the thread when the needle has gone through the fabric. Pull the knot tight, then make more knots.

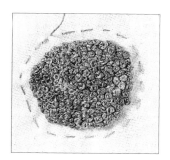

4 When the shape is full, work small running stitches approximately 6mm (¼in) away from the embroidery. Leave a tail of thread at one end.

5 Cut out the shape, 6mm (¼in) outside the running stitches, then pull the thread to draw the surplus calico up behind the embroidery.

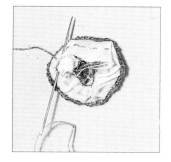

6 Flatten the shape, tucking in the surplus fabric, then secure the loose thread with a couple of stitches. Make the other two slips in the same way.

7 Roll out the clay, cut it into the flowerpot shape, then add a lip along the top edge. Use a pin to make two small holes in the middle of the pot. When the pot is dry, paint it with acrylics and leave it to dry again.

8 Use stab stitches (see page 103) to secure the slips over the painted shapes on the background fabric. Then, using a beading needle and a complementary colour of thread, randomly sew on the fine beads between the French knots.

Before sewing the three decorated slips to the background fabric, work the short lengths of the trunk in stem stitch (see page 104). Finally, when the paint is thoroughly dry, sew the flowerpot to the embroidery.

Butterfly

The three-dimensional effects of this butterfly design (see page 114) are all achieved with embroidery stitches; no extra padding is used. The outlines of the butterfly is worked in stem stitch (see page 104). Satin stitch, overlaid with raised stem stitch band, creates the body parts. The other decoration is worked with satin stitch (see page 104), padded satin stitch (see page 115), spider's web stitch (see page 115) and a few French knots (see page 112).

Stem stitch

Use stem stitch (see page 104) to work the outlines of the wings, the two half circles in the lower wings, the two small circles at the bottom of the wings and all the straight lines (see the diagram on the following page).

You will need

Medium-weight calico
Tracing paper and pencil
Fabric paint and brush
Six-stranded cotton
No. 7 embroidery needle

Full-size pattern. Use gold fabric paint to mark all the outlines on to the background fabric.

The finished embroidery.

Spider's web stitch

This stitch is used to embroider the three small circles in each of the lower wings. Contrasting colours have been used in the diagrams so that the stitches can be seen clearly. For the actual project, use one strand of six-stranded cotton in the same colour or complementary colours.

Raised stem stitch band

Work the two parts of the body separately, within each outlined shape. Use complementary colours for the satin stitch base and the straight stitch bars. For clarity, different colours have been used in the diagrams.

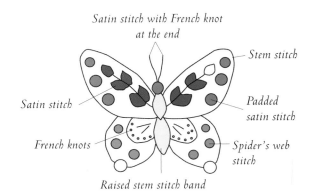

Satin stitch with French knot at the end

Stem stitch

Satin stitch

Padded satin stitch

French knots

Spider's web stitch

Raised stem stitch band

Diagram showing where the different stitches are used.

Raised stem stitch band

This stitch makes a solid, raised filling which can only be worked in straight rows, from either the top to the bottom or the bottom to the top. It can be worked in a single colour or as rows of different colours. The length of stem stitch can be varied by increasing or decreasing the distance between the straight stitch bars.

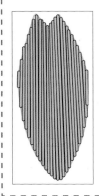

1. Using all six strands of cotton, fill each shape with satin stitches. If you want a more rounded body, sew more layers over the centre section.

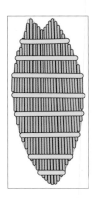

2. Next, using one strand of six-stranded cotton, sew a series of spaced straight stitch bars across the body.

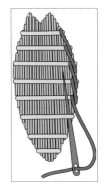

3. Finally, work stem stitches over the short straight stitches, making sure you do not pick up the stitches underneath.

Padded satin stitch

The three circles on each of the upper wings and the butterfly's head are worked with three layers of satin stitch. Each layer is sewn in a different direction on progressively larger circles. Again, for clarity, different colours are used on the diagrams for each layer. For the actual embroidery, use the same or a complementary colour of thread for each layer.

Other stitches

The lozenge shapes on the upper wing are worked in satin stitch (see page 104). The antennae are single, long straight stitches with tiny French knots (see page 112) on the end. More French knots complete the design on the lower wings.

Spider's web stitch

Spider's web stitch is worked on ribs of threads laid across a backstitched outline round the area to be embroidered.

   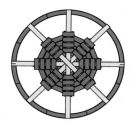

1. Referring to the coloured diagram on page 114, backstitch round the outlines of the shapes to be worked with spider's web stitch.

2. Now, bring the thread up at the edge of the shape, take it across the middle, then down through the opposite edge. Take the thread across the underside of the fabric and bring it back up to the front where you want the next rib to start. Make more ribs in a similar manner.

3. When all the ribs have been made, bring the thread up through the centre of the circle, just to the side of one of the ribs. Take the thread back over and under that rib, then under the next rib. Note that the thread does not pass through the fabric.

4. Take the thread back over and under this rib, then under the next. Continue working round the circle, taking the thread back over one rib then under two, until the desired portion of the circle has been filled. Fasten the thread on the underside of the fabric.

Padded satin stitch

 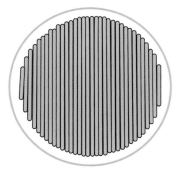 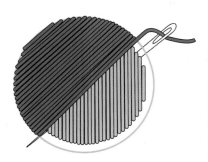

1. First, working an area 3mm (⅛in) inside the drawn circle, fill it with a layer of closely worked satin stitches (see page 104).

2. Now, working an area 1.5mm (¹⁄₁₆in) inside the drawn circle, sew a second layer of closely worked satin stitches at right angles to the first.

3. Finally, work a third layer of satin stitches at an angle of about 45° to the previous layer to cover the whole of the drawn area.

Needlelace

Needlelace is a technique that is well worth incorporating into stumpwork as it provides lots of textures that cannot be obtained with other embroidery stitches.

Small fragments of lace can be applied to the background fabric or over padded shapes. They can be stiffened with horsehair to make them stand proud of the surface, or with fine wire to allow them to be bent into freestanding shapes.

Needlelace is worked over a cordonnet (a strong cotton thread laid round the shape to be filled) which is temporarily couched on a needlelace pad with sewing thread. The needlelace pad consists of two or three layers of a backing material, a paper pattern and an overlay to protect the paper pattern from the needle. The filling stitches, which are all variations of detached buttonhole stitch, are all worked with 100/3 silk thread.

In this section, you will learn the basic principles of making a simple outline cordonnet (a leaf shape with a centre vein) and how to fill it with two types of filling stitch. You will then be guided, step by step, through the projects on this sampler, before moving on to more complex designs.

Leaf

Most needlelace shapes have simple outlines, where the cordonnet threads are joined on one side of the shape (see page 123). However, some shapes, such as this leaf with a centre vein, need careful planning to ensure they are able to support the finished needlelace. Here you will be shown how to make a needlelace pad and how to plan the cordonnet for the leaf. You will then learn two basic filling stitches.

Needlelace pad

You can make small needlelace pads to suit individual shapes or make them large enough to accommodate several pieces. If you use the latter method, it is best to complete all the shapes on the pad before releasing any of them. Make a sandwich of two or three layers of medium-weight calico, the paper pattern and a transparent, protective overlay.

Architect's linen can be used to protect your paper patterns, but self-adhesive plastic film, which is more readily available, is just as good. Tack all the layers together firmly.

Making a cordonnet

It is essential that cordonnets stay intact when the needlelace is released from the backing fabric, so joins must be kept to a minimum. Take time to plan the layout properly so that you can build a cordonnet from a continuous length of thread. Use the full-size pattern to estimate the length of thread required. Lay the thread along all the lines on the diagram including the central vein, double this length and add a short extra allowance. You will need 38cm (15in) of thread for this leaf.

The following steps show you how to build this particular shape, with its intersections at each end of the central vein.

You will need

Medium-weight calico
Paper pattern
Self-adhesive plastic film
No. 7 sharps needle
No. 10 ballpoint needle
No. 80 crochet thread
Sewing thread
100/3 silk thread

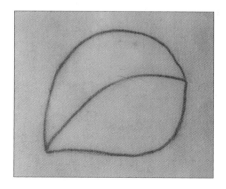

Needlelace pad for the leaf.

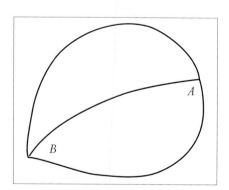

Full-size pattern for the leaf shape.

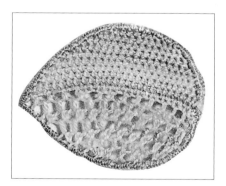

The completed needlelace leaf.

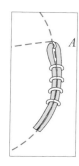

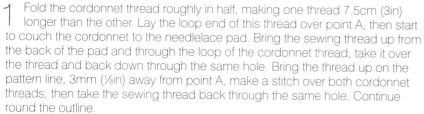

Make the couching stitches small, firm and neat — a poor foundation will result in a disappointing piece of lace. If the couching thread runs out before you have finished the cordonnet, take the thread to the back of the needlelace pad and secure it with three or four stitches, then start a new length.

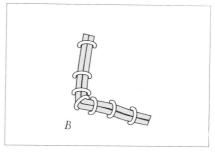

1 Fold the cordonnet thread roughly in half, making one thread 7.5cm (3in) longer than the other. Lay the loop end of this thread over point A, then start to couch the cordonnet to the needlelace pad. Bring the sewing thread up from the back of the pad and through the loop of the cordonnet thread, take it over the thread and back down through the same hole. Bring the thread up on the pattern line, 3mm (⅛in) away from point A, make a stitch over both cordonnet threads, then take the sewing thread back through the same hole. Continue round the outline.

2 When you reach point B, make an extra couching stitch at the point of the leaf (a sharp point is useful when making the filling stitches). Continue couching round the outer edge of the leaf back towards point A.

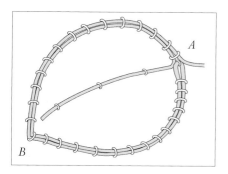

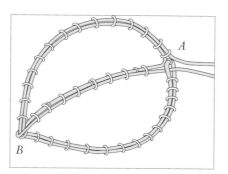

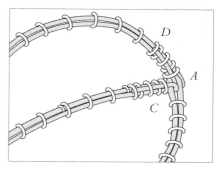

3 When you get back to point A, separate the cordonnet threads. Take the long one towards point B, couching it down in two or three places to hold it in position.

4 At point B, take the thread under and over the couched outline threads, lay it back down against the single thread, pass it through the original loop at point A, then couch down both threads to complete the vein.

5 At point A, fold the thread back on itself, then couch down a short length to point C. Use a large-eyed needle to pull the other thread through the original loop, fold it back to point D, then couch it down. Fasten off the couching thread on the back of the pad, then trim the excess threads.

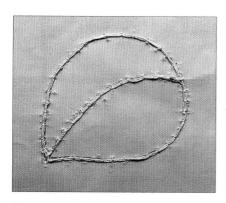

The finished cordonnet.

Filling stitches

One half of the leaf design is filled with single Brussels stitch, the other with corded single Brussels stitch. Both halves are worked from the central vein out to the edges. The filling stitches do not pass through the sandwiched layers of the needlelace pad, but are worked over and supported on the cordonnet threads.

Joins in the filling stitches can only be made at the end of each row, so you must ensure that you always have sufficient thread to work a full row of stitches. A good guide is to have at least three to four times the length of the space being worked.

Single Brussels stitch

Start this stitch with a row of buttonhole stitches across the cordonnet. The spacing of this foundation row of stitches governs the texture of the finished piece: use loose stitches for an open texture; tight ones for a dense texture. Subsequent rows of stitches are looped into those above.

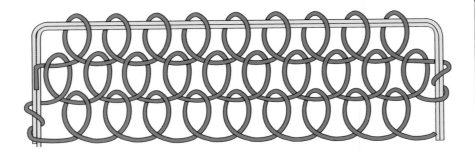

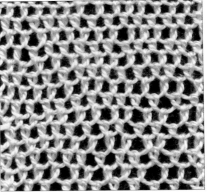

Single Brussels stitch.

Corded single Brussels stitch

This stitch is worked in much the same way as that above except that, at the end of each row of buttonhole stitches, the thread is laid back across the work as a 'cord', then the next row of stitches is worked round this cord and the loops in the previous row.

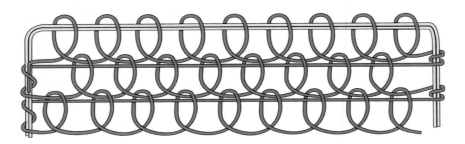

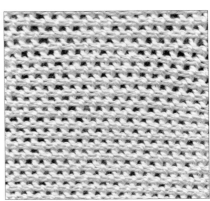

Corded single Brussels stitch.

Both of these examples have the same number of stitches in the row, but notice how the corded version has a more dense structure.

Double Brussels stitch

This is similar to single Brussels stitch, except that the first row of buttonhole stitches consists of spaced pairs of stitches — the space between each pair being the width of a pair of stitches. It is used to fill the flower petal (see page 125). On subsequent rows, pairs of stitches are worked over the loops between the pairs of stitches in the row above.

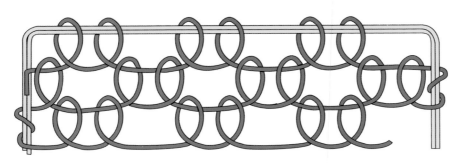

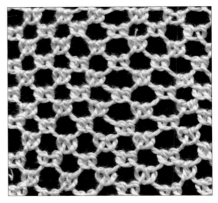

Double Brussels stitch.

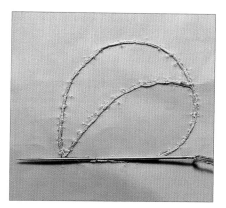

1 Secure the end of the filling stitch thread to the cordonnet by passing it under a few of the couching stitches. Take it through to a point just short of the intersection between the centre vein and the outline of the leaf.

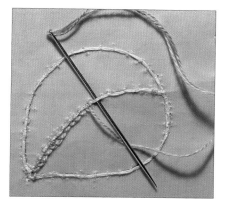

2 Work a row of evenly spaced buttonhole stitches across the central vein of the cordonnet. Do not pull the stitches too tight as you must work through their loops for the next row.

This enlarged view of the first row of buttonhole stitches shows how the loops are formed as you progress.

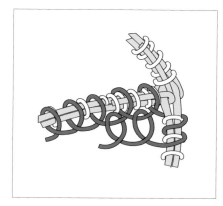

3 When you reach the end of the row attach the thread to the side of the cordonnet. Take the needle and thread under both cordonnet threads, then whip it over both threads allowing for the depth of the stitches down to the point where you want to start the next row.

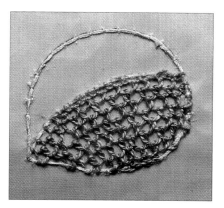

4 Work back across the shape, working one buttonhole stitch in each loop of the previous row. Whip the thread round the cordonnet again then work back across the shape. Continue until the area is filled. Always take your needle and thread straight out under the cordonnet threads; this will help to keep the rows straight. Secure the last row of stitches by whipping each loop to the cordonnet.

5 Turn the leaf shape round, attach another silk thread to the cordonnet, then work a row of buttonhole stitches, slightly tighter than those in step 2, across the central vein. At the end of the row, take the thread under, over and under the cordonnet.

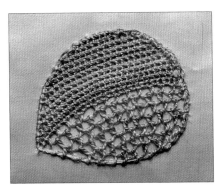

6 Lay the thread back across the space, just under the loops of the first row to form the cord. At the left-hand edge of the design whip the thread down the cordonnet to the start point for the next row of stitches.

7 Work another row of buttonhole stitches; this time, work the stitches into each loop of the previous row and under the laid cord.

8 Repeat steps 6 and 7 until the whole area is filled, then whip the last row of loops to the cordonnet as in step 4.

Top stitching and releasing the needlelace

One characteristic of needlelace is a raised outer edge. This is made by laying two threads over the cordonnet, then covering these and the cordonnet threads with a row of buttonhole stitches. Work the buttonhole stitches as close together as possible, preferably with the loops lying towards the outer edge of the shape. When the top stitching is complete, the needlelace is released from the fabric backing and assembled on the embroidery.

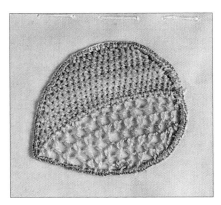

1 Cut another length of cordonnet thread long enough to go twice around the shape, with a little extra for good measure (see page 118). Fold it in half, then use the silk thread to whip the loop end to the existing cordonnet threads. Now, using the silk thread, work tight buttonhole stitches all round the shape.

2 Remove the tacking stitches around the design, fold back the bottom layer of calico, then use fine-pointed scissors to snip through all the couching stitches.

3 Remove the needlelace, then use a pair of tweezers to remove any remaining fragments of the couching threads from the back of the lace.

Flower

This first needlelace project is based on a simple flower design. The flower bud is raised on padded felt (see pages 110–111). The stalks are paper-covered wire, which is wrapped with silk thread then couched on the background fabric. The needlelace shapes are filled with single and corded single Brussels stitch (see page 120), and double Brussels stitch. The freestanding petals are only secured at the centre of the flower. The base is a calico slip, covered with French knots.

Cordonnet diagrams for petals and the parts of the bud.

Full-size pattern. The flower petals are freestanding, so use gold fabric paint to transfer just the three long stalks, the leaf and its stalk, the bud shape and the centres of the two flowers on to the base fabric.

Cordonnets

Referring to page 118, make needlelace pads for all the needlelace shapes. Use the small diagrams for all the petals and the bud, and the full-size pattern for the leaf shape (please note that this is not exactly the same shape as the leaf shape on page 118). Transfer the shape of the base on to a piece of lightweight calico in preparation for a slip.

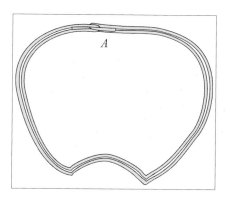

Enlarged view of the cordonnet for the flower petals. Make the join at point A.

Needlelace petals

Referring to the general instructions on pages 118–119 and the cordonnet diagram, build cordonnets for each petal. Start at point A, take the doubled thread round the shape, pass both threads through the loop, turn them back and couch down the ends.

Make five petal shapes filled with single Brussels stitch (see page 120) and ten more filled with double Brussels stitch. Top stitch round the outside of each petal as detailed on page 122.

Needlelace bud

The cordonnets for the bud parts are laid in a similar way to the petals, then each shape is filled with corded single Brussels stitch (see page 120). Do not top stitch round these shapes.

Needlelace leaf

For this project, the leaf includes a turned-over section which is worked over the top of the basic leaf shape before top stitching it. When filling curved shapes with corded needlelace, you will have more control over the cord by working with two needles.

Make a cordonnet for the leaf similar to that on page 118, then fill one half with single Brussels stitch and the other with corded single Brussels stitch (see page 120). Do not top stitch the shape yet. Work the turned-over shape with two needles and two lengths of thread as described below – for clarity, the two threads have been shown in different colours.

Attach the first thread (shown in green) to the central vein of the cordonnet, then make a row of buttonhole stitches along the outer edge of the leaf, over the previously worked needlelace. Whip the thread round the right-hand end of the cordonnet, then lay the thread back across the shape and take it under the left-hand end of the cordonnet. Do not secure this thread.

Attach the other thread (shown in pink) to the cordonnet, then start to work a second row of buttonhole stitches into the loops of the previous row and over the loose-laid cord.

When you reach the end of the second row, whip the thread round the left-hand end of the cordonnet, then lay the thread back across the row and under the right-hand end of the cordonnet. Do not secure this thread. Pick up the first needle and thread, whip it round the cordonnet, then start to work the third row of stitches.

Finish the third row of stitches, whip the thread round the right-hand end, then lay the thread back. Make a fourth row of stitches with the other thread, then, instead of laying a cord, whip the thread back across the shape, working into each loop of the last row of stitches. Fasten off both threads into the cordonnet. Top stitch round the outer edge of the whole leaf shape and along the central vein, then release from the pad as shown on page 122. Do not top stitch round the loose edge of the turnover section.

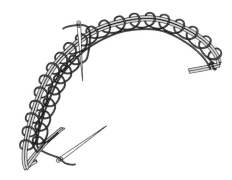

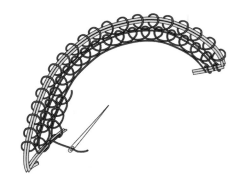

Working the needlelace leaf.

Finishing the embroidery

When all the needlelace parts of the design have been made, the embroidery can be assembled.

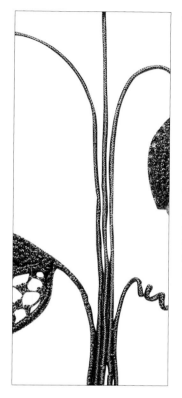

1 Measure the lengths of the three flower stalks and the leaf stalk, then cut a length of paper-covered wire for each. Dip one end of a wire into white glue then, starting 2.5cm (1in) from the tip, loosely wrap silk thread back towards the tip. At the tip, pinch the thread into the glue, then wrap the thread as closely as possible down the length of the wire. Secure the end of the thread with a touch more glue. Couch all four stalks over the outlines on the background fabric (see page 107).

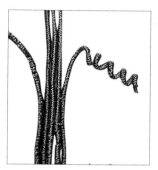

2 Make the short twisted stalk by winding a wrapped stem around a fine knitting needle or a large bodkin needle. Couch this on to the background fabric.

3 Referring to the full-size pattern on page 123, cut a piece of felt slightly smaller than the bud shape. Then, referring to pages 108–109, sew this felt shape in the gold outline on the background fabric and fill it with toy stuffing. Sew the needlelace bud pieces over the felt pad.

4 Sew the small sides of five of the double Brussels stitch petals round the gold outline of each flower centre. Overlap the petals slightly to make them look natural.

5 Sew the five single Brussels stitch petals over the double Brussels stitch petals on the top flower head.

6 Make the centres for the flowers. Cut a 20cm (8in) length of yellow thread. Thread one end of this into a needle, then wrap 15cm (6in) of the other end round a pencil. Carefully slip the wrapping from the pencil, catch the loops together with the needle and thread, then sew the loop securely in the middle of a flower head. Cut the loops and fray the ends out to resemble stamens.

7 Sew the leaf over the end of its stalk.

8 Use the base shape (see pattern on page 123) to make a small slip filled with French knots. Sew this over the bottom of the stalks.

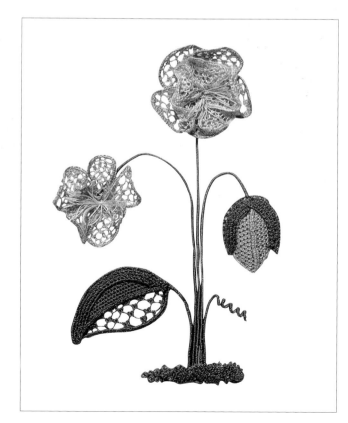

The finished embroidery.

Seaweed and fish

In this project, all the needlelace shapes are worked in corded single Brussels stitch (see page 120). The edges of the seaweed shapes are wired before they are top stitched to allow them to be entwined and stand free. The two striped fish, which are worked in two colours, are applied over layered felt (see pages 110–111). The two rocks are slips made from painted lightweight calico stretched over pieces of interfacing.

You will need

Needlelace pads (see page 118)
No. 80 crochet thread
Sewing thread
Lightweight calico for the slip and the finished embroidery
Fabric paint and brushes
No. 9 sharps needle
No. 10 ballpoint needle
100/3 silk thread
Felt
Petite bead
Fine wire
Interfacing (or card)

Full-size pattern. The bracts of seaweed are freestanding so use gold fabric paint to mark just the outlines of the two fish and the two rocks on to the background fabric.

Cordonnets

Use the exploded diagram shown opposite to make cordonnets for the four bracts of seaweed and the two fish. Remember to make the joins on one of the long edges of each shape.

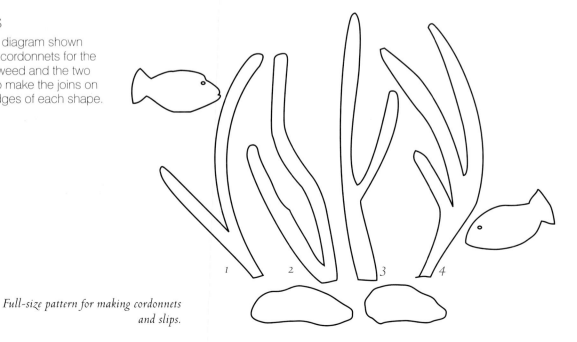

Full-size pattern for making cordonnets and slips.

Changing colours

This diagram shows corded single Brussels stitch, but the same method of changing colour works with any filling stitch.

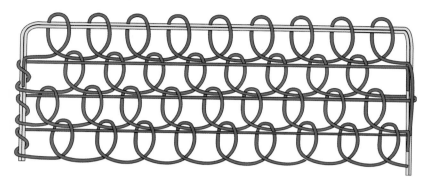

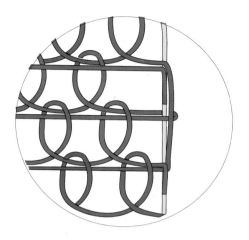

Join the first colour thread to one side of the cordonnet, then work filling stitches down to the point where you want to change colour. At the end of this row of buttonhole stitches, leave the thread to one side (do not lay the thread back across the row).

Join the new colour to the cordonnet, lay it as a cord across the shape, whip it down the other side, then work filling stitches in this colour until you want to change colour once more. If you intend using the second colour again, leave it to one side. Otherwise, run it through the couching stitches on the cordonnet and trim off the excess thread. Run the first colour thread down through the couching stitches on the cordonnet to a point level with the bottom of the last row of stitches, lay in a cord, then work filling stitches in the rest of the shape or until you want to change colour again.

Needlelace fish

The two striped fish are worked with two needles threaded with different colours as shown in the diagram above. The petite bead used for the fish's eye is threaded on to one of the laid cords, then the next row of filling stitches is worked around the bead at the required position. Alternatively, you could make the eye with a small French knot. Do not top stitch round the fish shapes, as they are applied to padded shapes on the background fabric.

Needlelace seaweed

Fill all the shapes with corded single Brussels stitch. Loosely whip a length of fine wire round each shape, then top stitch and release each shape (see page 122). Reinforcing the edges of these shapes with fine wire, instead of the usual two threads, makes the bracts stiffer and easier to mould into shape.

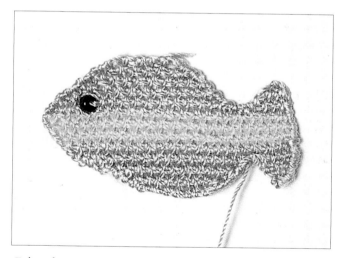

Enlarged view of one of the striped fish.

Finishing the embroidery

1 Sew the bottom edges of the seaweed bracts on to the background fabric, overlapping them so that their fronds can be entwined. Most of the left-hand side of the long stem of seaweed shape 3 (see page 126) and the right-hand side of the long stem on shape 4 are also sewn to the background fabric, leaving just their top ends free.

2 Referring to the pattern on page 126 and the layered felt instructions on pages 110–111, cut three layers of felt for each fish shape. Make the largest shape slightly smaller than the pattern, and omit the shape of the tails on all layers. Working from the smallest shape upwards, stab stitch each one to the background fabric, overlapping the sewn-down parts of the seaweed.

3 Stab stitch the needlelace fish shapes over the felt pads; secure just their bodies, leaving their tails free to give the impression that they are swimming.

4 The rock shapes are slips of lightweight calico, painted with pearlised colour to give the rocks a textured appearance. The painted area of calico should be large enough to cut out oversize shapes with an allowance of 6mm (¼in) all round. When the paint is thoroughly dry, decorate the shape with embroidery detail (if required), then cut them out.

5 Cut full-size rock shapes from a piece of interfacing (or cardboard if you want stiffer rocks). Stretch the calico over the interfacing shape and lightly glue the turned-over edges to the back of the interfacing. Stab stitch the bottom edges of the rocks over the base of the seaweed.

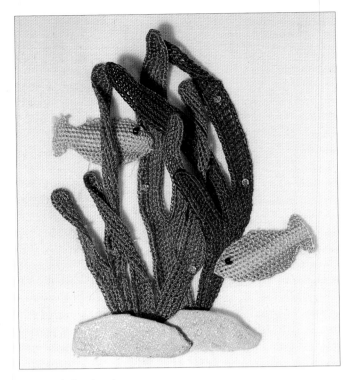

The finished embroidery.

Orange branch

This design includes five realistic oranges which are made by covering cotton moulds with single Brussels stitch. The leaves are made in much the same way as those shown previously, using both single and double Brussels stitch. However, three of the leaves are worked on the background fabric of the finished embroidery, using a cordonnet of backstitches.

Cordonnets

Use the full-size patterns to make cordonnets for leaf shapes 3, 4, 5, and 6, as described on pages 118–119. Work the cordonnets of leaf shapes 1, 2 and 7 on the background fabric by backstitching round the gold outline of each shape.

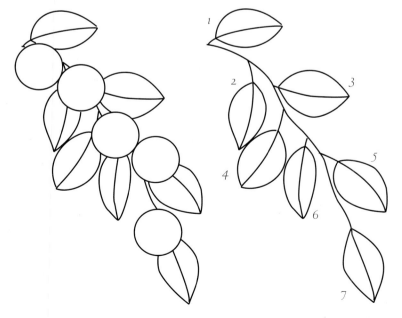

Full-size patterns for the design and the cordonnets for the leaf shapes. Use gold fabric paint to transfer the outline of the branch, the leaf stalks and leaf shapes 1, 2 and 7 on to the background fabric.

Needlelace oranges

The oranges are cotton moulds covered with needlelace. Unlike the other leaf shapes and the stalks, which are worked with silk thread, these are worked with one strand of six-stranded cotton.

Always paint cotton moulds to match the colour of the thread used to cover them. This is not essential, but a painted mould does mask any irregularities in the needlelace. However, for clarity, these step-by-step photographs have been worked on a plain, white cotton mould.

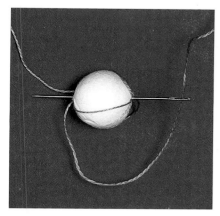

1 Using a no. 9 embroidery needle, take a long length of cotton thread down through the centre of the mould, bring the thread up round the outside of the mould, then back down through the centre to form a vertical stitch round the mould. Continue until you have made approximately ten stitches.

2 Cut a new length of cotton thread and bring the thread up through to the top of the cotton mould. Weave this thread through the vertical stitches, taking it round two or three times.

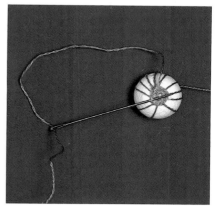

3 Now, using the same length of thread, start to work tiny single Brussels stitches, as close together as possible, over the last row of woven threads. You can disregard the vertical stitches, which have now served their purpose.

4 Continue the filling stitches round the mould, working them into the loops of the stitches immediately above. As the shape gets bigger, increase the number of stitches by working two loops into one. When the thread starts to run out, take the short end down, round the outside of the mould, to the bottom and anchor it under two or three of the vertical stitches. Attach a new length of thread under the same vertical stitches, bring it up to the needlelace and link it through the last completed loop, then continue working the filling stitches.

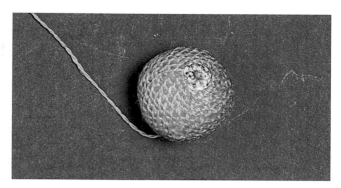

5 When you pass the widest part of the mould, decrease the stitches by missing out some of the loops in the previous row. When the whole mould is covered, trim off the excess lengths of all bar one of the loose threads. Use a cocktail stick to apply a spot of glue to the underside of the cotton mould, then push all the trimmed lengths into the recess. Finally, using one strand of green cotton thread, work a few rows of buttonhole stitches over the orange ones.

Needlelace leaves

Make leaf shapes 3, 4, 5 and 6 in needlelace, using your choice of filling stitches. Before top stitching them, lay one strand of horsehair round leaf shapes 4 and 6, and one strand of fine wire round leaf shapes 3 and 5. Leave tails of horsehair and fine wire at the base of each leaf shape to attach the shapes to the background fabric.

Fill leaf shapes 1, 2 and 7 with your choice of filling stitches, within the backstitched cordonnets on the background fabric. Do not top stitch round these shapes.

Finishing the embroidery

Work the branch and the short leaf stalks in stem stitch. Decide on the arrangement of the freestanding leaves and oranges. Use a stiletto to make small holes in the background fabric at the appropriate places, take the wire and horsehair tails on the leaves, and the cotton thread on the oranges through to the back of the work, then secure them with a few oversewn stitches. Finally, shape the freestanding leaves.

The finished embroidery.

Mushrooms

All the elements of this design are needlelace shapes except for the four small patches of grass at the base of each mushroom which are slips filled with French knots. All the padding is stuffed felt. The pads for the mushroom stalks are prepared in exactly the same way as in previous projects (see page 108), but the pads for the mushroom caps are left open along their bottom edges. The layered structure of the mushrooms means that the needlelace elements must be layered, with some pads sewn on top of needlelace shapes. A new filling stitch, crossbar stitch, is used here, and the tops of some of the mushrooms are decorated with buttonholed loops (see page 132).

You will need

Needlelace pads (see page 118)
No. 80 crochet thread
Fabric paint and brush
Sewing thread
Lightweight calico for the slips and finished embroidery
No. 9 sharps needle
No. 10 ballpoint needle
100/3 silk thread
Felt
Toy stuffing

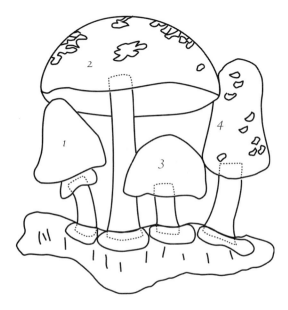

Full-size pattern. Use gold fabric paint to outline the shapes of the mushroom heads, their stalks and the large grass base on to the background fabric. The dotted lines at the top and bottom of the stalks show the size of the shapes for the felt pads.

Cordonnets

Use the exploded diagram opposite to make cordonnets for all shapes, except shapes 6a–6d, which are slips.

Slips

Prepare French knot slips for the four grass shapes 6a–6d (see page 112).

Needlelace shapes

Work the stalk shapes 1c, 2c, 3b and 4b, the mushroom cap shapes 2a, 2b, 1b and 4a, and the grass base shape 5 in corded single Brussels stitch.

Work the mushroom cap shape 1a in corded double Brussels stitch. Work the mushroom cap shape 3a in crossbar stitch.

Top stitch along just the bottom sections of cap shapes 1a, 1b, 2b, 3a and 4a. The cap shape 2a, the stalk shape 1c, 2c, 3b and 4b, and the grass shape 5 do not require top stitching as they are sewn to the background fabric.

Above: exploded diagram showing the full-size shapes for the cordonnets and slips.

Crossbar stitch

This is a variation of double Brussels stitch (see page 120). Make a foundation row of spaced pairs of stitches — the space between each pair being the width of a pair of stitches — then make a second row of stitches, looping each stitch into the stitch above. On the next row, make two stitches into the loops between the pairs of stitches in the previous row, then make another row of stitches, looping each stitch into the stitch above. Repeat until the shape is filled.

Enlarged view of crossbar stitch.

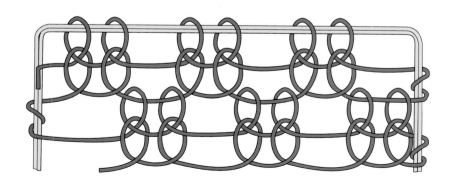

Finishing the embroidery

1 Sew the needlelace grass shape 5 to the background fabric.

2 Referring to the full-size pattern on page 130, cut slightly undersize pieces of felt for the stalk shapes of all four mushrooms.

3 Stab stitch the felt shapes for mushrooms 1, 3 and 4 to the grass base and the background fabric, then fill them with toy stuffing (see page 108).

4 Apply the needlelace stalk shapes 1c, 3b and 4b over the felt pads.

5 Apply the ring shape 1b over its stalk. Sew just the sides and top to the background fabric, leaving the bottom edge free.

6 Cut a slightly undersize piece of felt for the cap of mushroom 4, then secure its sides and top edges to the background fabric. Fill the shape with toy stuffing, then, as the bottom of the felt shape is left open, secure the stuffing with three or four loose stab stitches approximately 6mm (¼in) up from the bottom of the felt. Take these stab stitches through to the back of the background fabric, but do not pull them tight. Apply the needlelace shape 4a over its felt pad, leaving the bottom edge free.

7 Sew the needlelace cap shape 2a to the background fabric and over the edge of mushroom cap shape 4a.

8 Stab stitch the felt stalk shape for mushroom 2 to the background fabric and over the bottom needlelace section of its cap, then fill it with toy stuffing. Sew the needlelace stalk shape 2c to its pad.

9 Referring to step 6, cut, apply and fill a piece of felt for the top section of the cap of mushroom 2, then apply the needlelace shape 2b over the felt pad. Remember to leave its bottom edge free.

10 Cut and apply a piece of felt for the cap of mushroom 1, laying a small section of this over the bottom part of the cap of mushroom 2. Fill the felt with toy stuffing, then apply the needlelace shape 1a over the felt pad.

11 Repeat step 10 for the cap of mushroom 3: a small part of this fits over the stalk of mushroom 2.

12 Referring to the diagram and instructions above, decorate the caps of mushrooms 2 and 4 by overstitching them with groups of five or seven buttonholed loops, sewn through all layers.

The finished embroidery.

Buttonholed loops

Knot a silk thread, bring the needle up at point A, then back down through the work at point B – approximately 6mm (¼in) away – leaving a small loop. Repeat this stitch to make a three-stranded loop on the surface. Bring the thread back up at point A, then make a series of close buttonhole stitches over the loop. At the end of the loop, take the thread to the back of the work just above point B. Gently pull the thread to make the stitched loop twist up off the surface, then fasten off.

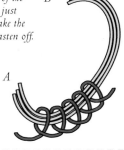

13 Apply the four French knot slips over the bottom of the mushroom stalks, sewing them along just the bottom edges.

14 Finally, make some small tufts of grass in the same way as the stamens for the flower heads on page 125, then sew these to the grass base.

Foxgloves

This design, with its tubular, bell-shaped flowers, introduces the use of a wooden embroidery shoe to make the needlelace shapes for the flower heads. Six of the flower heads are worked on normal needlelace pads, four are worked straight on cordonnets backstitched on the background fabric. All the needlelace pieces are filled with corded single Brussels stitch, then decorated with groups of French knots. The flower stalk is a slip of silk fabric stretched over a single layer of felt.

Cordonnets

Use the small diagrams below right to prepare cordonnets for the flower heads and caps. Six of the flowers are worked on needlelace pads; four are worked on the background fabric (see page 128). You only need to make eight caps, as the tops of flowers 1 and 2 are completely covered by other parts of the embroidery.

Each flower head consists of two layers of needlelace, so it is essential that the couching stitches used for the cordonnets that are made on needlelace pads are firm and close together. Use short backstitches to make the cordonnets for the flower heads 1–4 on the background fabric.

Needlelace flowers

Foxgloves are tubular in shape, and two layers of needlelace must be worked on the same cordonnet to make the shape. A wooden embroidery shoe keeps the top and bottom layers separate and helps to create a more rounded shape. Corded single Brussels stitch (see page 120) is used to fill both layers, but a slight variation is introduced on the last rows of the top piece to create a flared edge.

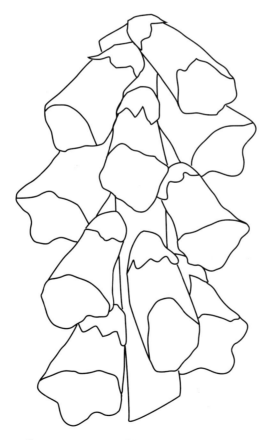

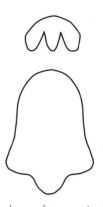

Cordonnet diagrams for the caps and flower heads.

Full-size pattern. Use gold fabric paint to outline the flower stalk and flower head shapes 1–4 on to the background fabric.

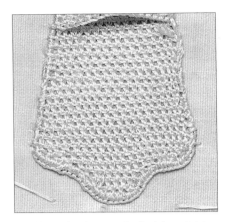

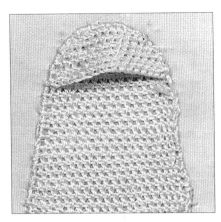

1 Make the bottom half of the eight loose flower heads on needlelace pads, filling the shape with corded single Brussels stitch.

2 Go back to the top of the cordonnet, then work five rows of corded single Brussels stitch over the bottom layer of needlelace.

3 Place the wooden embroidery shoe under the five rows of the top layer and secure it in position with three or four oversewing stitches on the neck of the shoe.

4 Continue down the shape, working rows of stitches over the shoe until you are ready to finish the shape. Refer to the full-size pattern on page 133 to determine the depth of each top layer.

5 At the end of a row of stitches, do not lay a cord across the shape. Instead, work back across the row making two stitches into the first loop of the previous row, one stitch into the next loop, two stitches into the next loop, etc.

6 Repeat step 5, lay a cord across the shape, top stitch over the cord and through each loop of the last row of filling stitches, then remove the flower and shoe from the backing pad.

7 Dab a few spots of PVA glue on a small amount of toy stuffing, then insert the stuffing between the two layers of needlelace to create a tubular shape.

8 Referring to the finished embroidery, decorate the flower head with a random group of French knots sewn into the bottom layer of needlelace.

9 Repeat steps 1–8 for the flower head shapes 1, 2, 3 and 4, over the backstitched cordonnets on the background fabric.

Needlelace caps

Work eight caps for the foxgloves (flower head shapes 1 and 2 do not require these), top stitch all round each shape, then remove them from the backing pad.

Slip

Referring to the full-size pattern, cut a piece of felt to fit the shape of the stalk. Cut a piece of silk fabric, allowing for a 6mm (¼in) turnover on each edge. Secure the turnovers to the back of the felt with a few spots of PVA.

Finishing the embroidery

Sew the flower-stalk slip to the background fabric, laying it over flower head shapes 1–4. Sew the top ends of flower head shapes 5–10 to the stalk and background fabric. Finally, sew the needlelace caps to the top of the flower heads, leaving the bottom edges free.

The finished embroidery.

Patterns

These full-size patterns are for some of the finished embroideries shown in this chapter.

Bee, page 101.

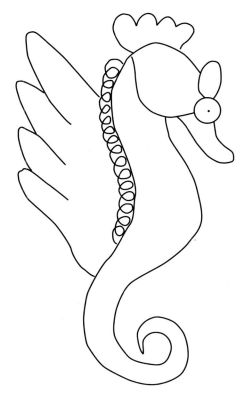

Seahorse, page 97.

Caterpillar, page 101.

Fantasy bird, page 96.

Primroses, page 101.

Snail, page 100.

HARDANGER

Hardanger embroidery is a counted thread technique incorporating drawn thread embroidery and filling stitches. The beauty of this white work technique lies in the negative and positive of the delicate openwork fillings, which contrast with the heavier surface embroidery. Thought to have its origins in the Middle East and Asia, the technique is believed to have spread to Europe during the Renaissance, where it evolved from the Italian needle-made 'lace' known as Reticella. Hardanger embroidery has developed over the years into its present form and is now associated with the Hardanger region of south-west Norway, from where it takes its name.

Hardanger embroidery can be used to decorate household items, clothes and accessories. It is an important feature of the traditional folk costume of the Hardanger region, where it is found as an inset on the apron and on the cuffs, collar and front flap of the women's blouses and on the cuffs and collar of the men's costume. The continuing popularity and ever widening interest in Hardanger embroidery, combined with pride in and appreciation of folk costume in Norway, will ensure a safe future for this traditional technique.

For an embroidery technique to survive, it is important that it continues to develop. Introducing beads into the filling stitches has produced a unique addition to the finished effect of the embroidery that does not compromise the origins and look of the technique. Similarly, a simple painted background can produce a stunning finish, or simply enjoy the clarity and freshness of white on white. Experimenting with different ideas will bring you endless hours of pleasure and fulfilment and, hopefully, a new love of this wonderfully decorative embroidery technique from Norway.

Sampler
Jill Carter

This sampler, size 18 x 24cm (7 x 9½in), shows most of the surface stitchery and decorative fillings demonstrated in this chapter. It is worked in crisp white cotton with glistening blending filament. White matt beads are added as part of the decorative fillings, to match the cotton and emphasise the effect. The sampler is designed for you to stitch as shown, using the chart and instructions on pages 160–161, or interpret with your own ideas and knowledge. Using a different-sized fabric count will alter the final measurements and is a matter of personal preference. Fillings may be worked with or without beads and the whole design could be sewn in threads of your own choice.

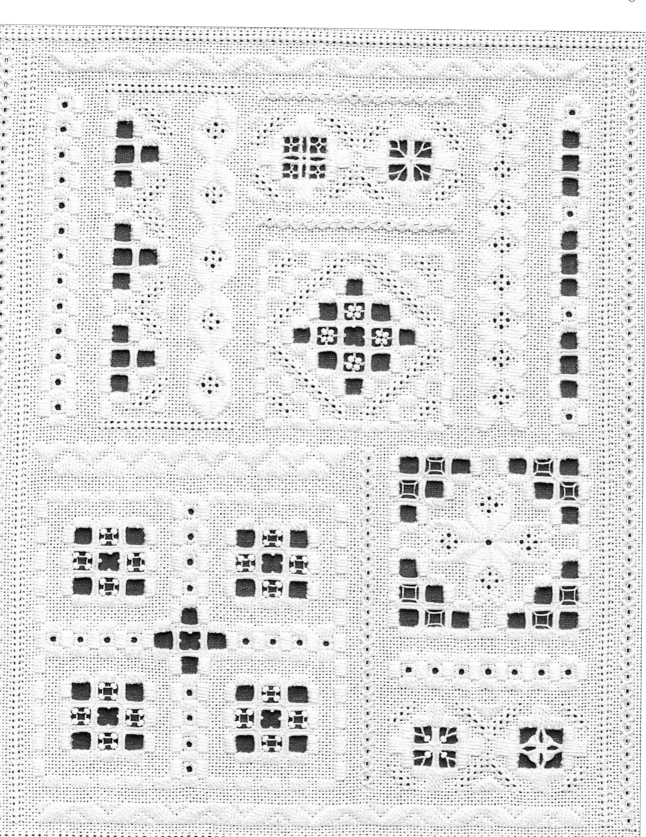

Materials

Fabric

Hardanger embroidery is worked on evenweave fabric in order for the threads to be cut, withdrawn and embellished. Fabrics have different properties and it is best to choose one to suit the use for which the embroidery is intended and of a count (threads to the inch) that you can see. The greater the number of threads to the inch, the finer and more delicate your work. Your time and work is precious, so always buy a good quality fabric. You will find suitable fabrics with counts of single threads from 18 to 32 threads to the inch in linen, linen mixes, cottons, cotton mixes, and Hardanger/Oslo fabric which has a double thread count. The decision is yours and should be governed by the final effect you want to achieve, but do not be afraid to experiment if you find a new and exciting fabric.

Linen evenweave is easy to stitch and pull, gives wonderfully fine and lacy effects and is probably the most luxurious to sew on. Cotton mix fabrics come in a wide range of colours and counts, one of the most useful being a 25 count cotton and rayon mix. This fabric will keep its shape when you are working on large areas of cut work, the end results look 'crisp' and it washes well. Twenty-five count is a good alternative for those who find the finer counts trying on the eyes but who still want delicate effects. Painted effects are also easily achievable on cotton mixes.

All the projects in this chapter may be worked on any fabric count of your choice, but the final results and dimensions will vary in size accordingly.

Threads

A thicker and a finer thread are needed for Hardanger embroidery. The thicker thread is used for kloster blocks, surface embroidery and border stitches and should be slightly thicker than the background warp and weft so that, when worked, the stitches touch each other and look slightly raised. The finer thread is used for the needleweaving, filling stitches, pulled thread embroidery (eyelets and reversed diagonal faggoting), edging and hem stitching and should be marginally thinner than the background warp and weft in order to achieve the delicate effects.

The wonderful choice of threads readily available from plain to shaded colours, from matt to shiny textures is sometimes bewildering. Using cotton perle (also called pearl cotton) is a good starting point, as it comes in a number of thicknesses and colours. The fabric count determines the thicknesses of thread you will need for your embroidery. For example, for fabrics with a 24 count or less, you will need no. 5 for the surface embroidery and no. 8 for needleweaving and pulled thread techniques. On 25/26 count fabric, you will have to choose from no. 5 to 8 for the thicker threads and 8 to 12 respectively for the finer work. Numbers 8 and 12 are used for 27 to 32 count fabric.

This selection of evenweave fabric shows the variety from which you can choose and includes one which has been painted. The rich sheen on silk makes an excellent backing fabric to offset your embroidery.

There is a variety of alternative threads which could be used for your Hardanger, such as linen, silk and metallics. When choosing a metallic thread, find one which is flexible and will lie flat when needleweaving. Iridescent blending filament is an excellent choice to combine with other threads for that subtle touch of sparkle in your finished piece. Shaded threads can 'overpower' the stitchery and do not always give the effect expected, so use them with care and choose ones which do not have sharp contrasts in them.

Needles

You will need blunt-ended tapestry needles in sizes suitable for the fabric count. Usually this is size 24 or 26. Special blunt-ended tapestry needles in size 10 will be necessary for threading and working with beads in the fillings. A crewel needle in size 10 is a useful alternative, although it has a sharp end which makes it harder to work with.

Other items

Scissors Good, sharp, fine scissors that cut 'to the point' are essential. There are various types, so-called 'specific for the technique', but simply choose ones that you like and which work well for you. Use a magnifying glass and wax if you need to. The wax will help to stiffen the end of the thread for threading through fine needles for the beaded fillings.

Bodkin A flat bodkin is useful for threading fine ribbon through blocks or stitchery.

Seed and pearl beads, ribbon and **transfer paints** are used to embellish embroideries.

Embroidery frame Using an embroidery frame is a personal choice, but not essential. If you decide to work in a frame, use it for the kloster blocks only and remember to remove the work from the frame when you have finished stitching.

Spray starch Small amounts of spray starch on the back of cut and drawn threads stabilise the threads on loosely woven fabrics, making it easier to keep the shape of the grids on which to needleweave.

Coloured or textured papers make excellent instant backgrounds to set off your Hardanger embroidery.

Aperture cards come in many colours and sizes and give an immediate frame to your work, avoiding the necessity for hemming and edging.

Cutting mat Should you decide to cut your own mounts out of card, work on a proper cutting mat. Use a craft knife with a retractable blade for safety and cut against a good metal ruler.

Spray mount or **double-sided tape** will enable you to move your embroidery if you are mounting it in a card or on paper and it is not completely straight the first time.

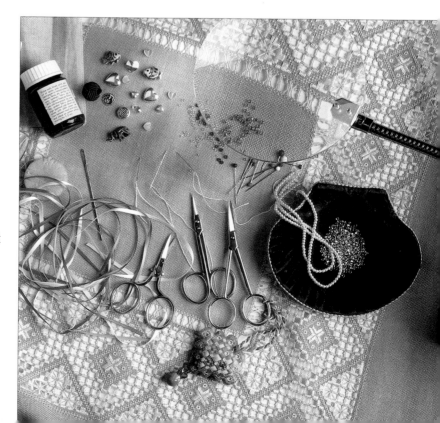

Stitches

Traditionally Hardanger is a white work technique, but all the stitch techniques shown in this chapter have been worked in a contrasting colour for clarity.

Surface stitchery

Surface stitchery and motifs are an important feature of Hardanger embroidery and create contrast and texture against the delicate openwork. As a general rule, surface stitchery requires the thicker of your two threads.

Satin stitch

This simple straight stitch requires the thicker of your two threads, which should be chosen to suit your fabric count (see page 138).

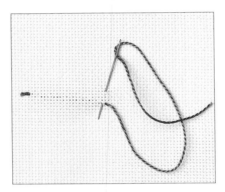

1 Bring the needle to the surface and back down again through the fabric, four threads up.

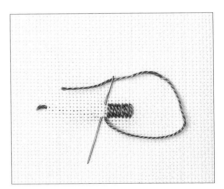

2 Continue stitching in a line to form satin stitches.

Kloster blocks

Satin stitches formed into blocks called kloster blocks are the basis for all Hardanger designs, which are geometric in form. They outline the area which will later be cut and withdrawn. Use your thicker thread. How to start and finish kloster blocks is explained on page 159.

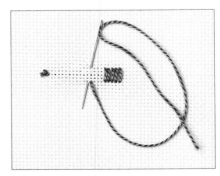

1 A kloster block is formed by working five satin stitches over four threads. Work from right to left and pull the thread so that it sits on the surface without distorting or pulling the background fabric.

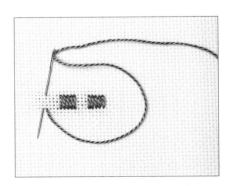

2 Kloster blocks can be sewn in a straight line, as shown.

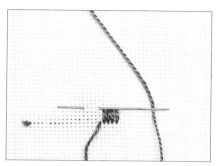

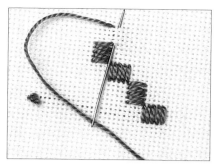

3 Kloster blocks can also be sewn on the diagonal, in this case to form a diamond. On the fifth stitch insert the needle at right angles to the last satin stitch, surfacing four threads to the left. Complete the block. To form the next, come to the front through the same hole as the last satin stitch.

4 Continue to work a diagonal line of kloster blocks. To turn the angle and stitch the second side, bring the thread to the surface at right angles and four threads up from the previous block as shown.

5 Complete the diamond, working clockwise and turning the work as necessary to stitch.

Eight-pointed star in satin stitch

Stars are probably the most commonly used motif throughout traditional Hardanger embroidery and are an important decorative feature of this technique. The dimensions of the stitch may be altered, halved or adapted in order to fit a given space.

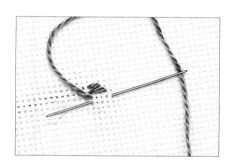

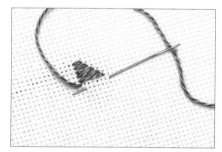

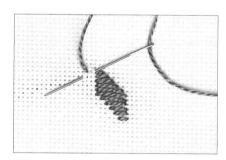

1 Bring your needle to the front two threads down from your centre point and stitch two threads across to the right. Increase the width of the next stitch to go over three threads.

2 Continue to increase the width and number of threads with each stitch on the right-hand side, up to seven, keeping the left-hand side straight.

3 Now decrease the number of threads across back to two, forming the top of the star, this time keeping the right-hand side straight. Take the thread behind and weave through the back of the stitches to the starting point, surfacing ready to begin the next star point as shown.

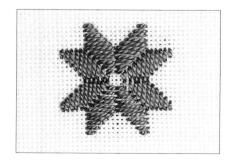

The finished star.

Tulip

Adding more stitches to the edges of a star turns it into the tulip motif.

1 Continue from the star point, stacking four more stitches in a straight line over two threads as before. Complete the shape by working three stitches on the diagonal to form the point of a 'V' shape. Work three stitches on the diagonal up the other side of the 'V'. Finish with one stitch over two threads to form the curl.

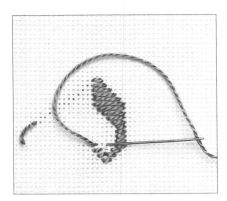

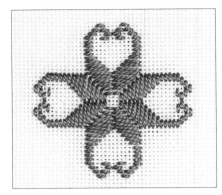

2 To complete the motif, stitch a mirror image of the first shape and then stitch three more pairs as shown.

Heart

The heart shape is another recurring motif in Norwegian embroidery. It is often seen on the embroidered square under the sleeveless jacket of the Hardanger folk costume, worked in either beads or stitchery. This small satin stitch heart variation forms an interesting single motif or a decorative border.

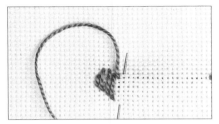

1 Make a first satin stitch over three threads. Next stitch step up one thread and down over five threads. Repeat, keeping level at the top, but going down over six threads. Step down one thread and take a stitch over six threads, repeating once more to form the centre stitch of the heart.

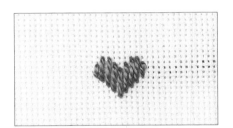

2 Complete the other half of the heart in the same way, working the stitches in reverse order. This stitch may be worked from either direction.

Twisted lattice band

This versatile braid-like decorative stitch is often seen on the edges of bands of traditional Hardanger embroidery. Ribbons or beads add an interesting dimension to the look of this stitch.

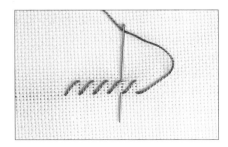

1 Form a line of half crosses over four threads.

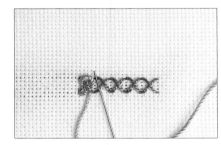

2 Complete the crosses on the return journey. Weave another thread under the legs of the crosses and over the intersections, pulling the thread gently as you go.

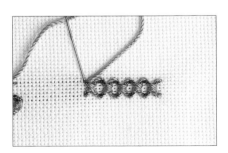

3 Complete the interlacing on the opposite side, finishing off by taking the thread to the back through the same hole as the first cross stitch.

Pulled thread techniques

Specific pulled thread stitches are a significant feature of Hardanger embroidery, used to echo or accentuate the kloster block shapes. They help to add delicacy to the finished design and are best worked in threads the same colour as your background fabric, as it is important to see the effect created by the pulled stitches. Always use the finer thread for your pulled thread stitches. How to start and finish pulled thread techniques are explained on page 159.

Square eyelets

Small stitches worked around a square are pulled to create a hole in the fabric. This technique is effective when used within a square of kloster blocks or standing alone as part of the overall design.

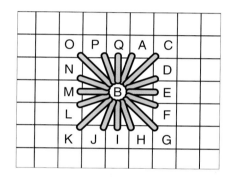

It is important to start the eyelet at A where it is shown in the diagram. The last stitch made will be vertical and so it will fit snugly between the two angled ones either side. This ensures that the finished effect will look even all the way round.

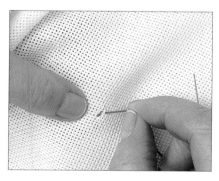

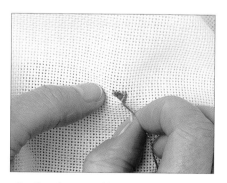

1 Bring the needle to the surface at A, two threads up from the centre and one thread to the right. Stitch back down into the middle (B) over two horizontal threads. Gently pull the sewing thread away from the centre hole before taking the next stitch (C).

2 Continue working around the square over two threads, following the diagram and pulling away from the centre between each stitch. The fabric count, type of fabric, and how hard you pull will determine the size of the finished hole.

The finished square eyelet.

Algerian eyelets on the diagonal

These can be worked around a square, but pulling and working them on the diagonal gives a more open and delicate effect, as fewer stitches are used to form the unit. 'Open' holes on the diagonal are created in solid areas, thereby outlining and lightening the overall effect of a design.

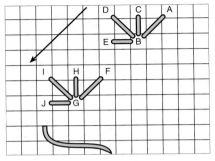

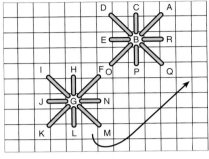

Finished Algerian eyelets on the diagonal.

1 Come to the surface at A and down into the centre diagonally over two threads to B. Pull the thread gently away from the central hole. Proceed round the outline following the lettering CB, DB, EB, FG, HG, IG, JG and pull between each stitch.

2 Turn the work to stitch the return journey. Fill in the other half of the eyelet, pulling away from the centre as before between each stitch. Continue in sequence until the other half of the stitch is completed.

Diagonal eyelets

Diagonal eyelets are extremely useful for incorporating into satin stitch motifs as they are light and open and contrast with the heavier stitchery.

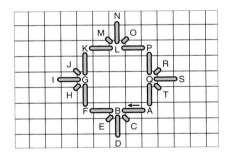

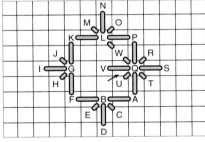

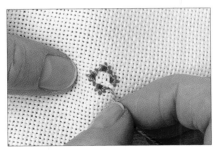

1 Work clockwise round the outer edge of the eyelets starting at A and proceeding as follows: A to B, C to B, D to B, E to B, F to B and back to F; continue as before working F to G and on through to K to G, back to K. Repeat until you reach A to Q. Gently pull the thread away from the central hole between each stitch.

2 Now reverse the direction of the stitch to work the inside of the eyelet. Proceed U to Q, V to Q, W to Q, and back to W. Carry on as before to complete the diagonal eyelet.

3 Continue to pull the thead gently away from the central hole after each stitch. Be consistent, or secondary holes will appear which will detract from the finished effect.

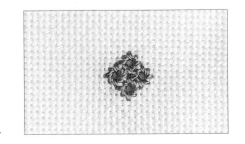

Finished diagonal eyelets.

Reversed diagonal faggoting

The slightly raised and open effect created by this diagonal line of pulled threads offsets the kloster blocks. The textural contrast with the heavier surface stitchery also provides an effective way of defining and linking designs. It is preferable to use the same colour thread as the background because the holes created by pulling stitches are the effect, not the threads.

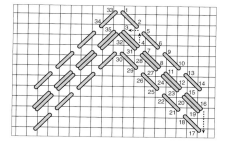

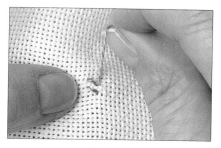

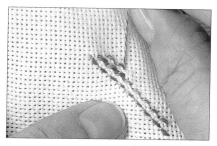

1 Follow the numbering to work the first stitch diagonally over two threads.

2 The second stitch will form the central line. Do not pull until the second stitch is made and then pull carefully away from the centre towards the next stitch. Continue to pull every other stitch, holding the stitch as you pull to prevent the fabric twisting.

3 To work the other side, turn your work upside down and you will be looking at it in the same position as when you started, which makes it easier to understand. Repeat the second line as the first and the main holes will appear down the middle line, with secondary holes on the outside.

The finished effect. You can create a mitre with this stitch, or it can be squared off to form a right angle as shown here.

Four-sided stitch

This useful and decorative technique comprising straight stitches forming a square works as a border or a filling stitch.

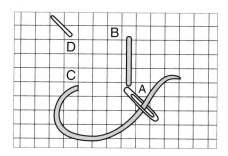

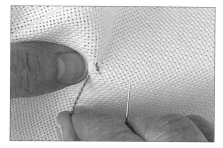

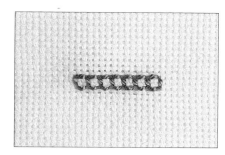

1 Follow the lettering as shown. Bring the needle to the surface at A and down through B, four threads above A, pulling firmly. Continue with the sequence to complete the square.

2 Pull the sewing thread firmly after each stitch is made, but try not to distort the fabric as you pull.

A line of completed four-sided stitch. This stitch may be worked over a different number of threads to change its dimensions and effect.

Hem stitch

This pulled thread stitch for securing a hem or bordering linen is not only decorative, but also very practical.

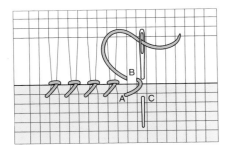

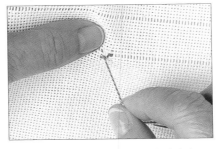

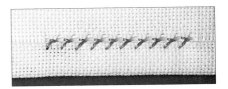

A row of hem stitch completed, showing the hem side. Hems may be folded to the front or the back as you wish. This picture shows one background thread drawn out of the hemming line for ease of sewing.

1 Following the diagram, come to the surface at A and collect the required number of fabric threads before completing the stitch, bringing the needle through at C as shown. Two, three or four threads may be gathered up if preferred.

2 Pull the wrapped threads tightly before completing the stitch. If appropriate to the design, one or more threads may be drawn out of the stitching line and hem stitch worked on the opposite side to create an open border beside the hem.

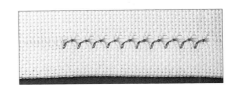

The same row of hem stitch viewed from the other side.

Pin stitch

This 'minimalist' stitch forms small holes between the wrapped bunches of threads giving hems and borders a neat, crisp and uncluttered look. A thread matching the background works best.

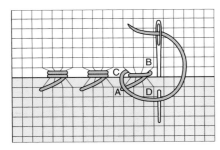

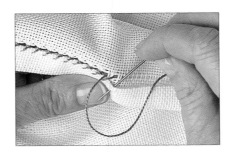

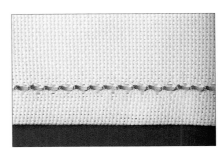

A finished row of pin stitch. The hem is always turned to the back with this stitch. A fabric thread may be withdrawn in the stitching line for ease of sewing and effect.

1 Prepare the hem in the usual way. With the wrong side facing you, bring the needle to the surface at A through the hem turnings. Gather up and wrap a cluster of threads (two, three or four) BC. Pull tightly and repeat. Bring the needle between the folded hem at D.

2 Surface with the needle two threads down from the edge of the hem and between the hem and fabric. Continue with the next stitch from this position. With a fine fabric you may prefer to wrap the clusters just once as shown above.

Edgings

Edgings are always an important element of your embroidery; they define your work with the contrast in texture and are fun to do. Traditionally, pulled thread edgings are worked in thread matching the background fabric, as the decorative effect relies on the holes which appear with the stitching. Adding beads to these traditional techniques creates a sparkling new dimension to your work.

Backstitch picot

Picots are formed with three simple backstitches worked in the fold line of the hem. Using a thicker thread gives a more prominent picot.

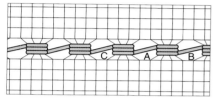

1 Leaving at least twelve threads from the outside edge of the hem, pull out a single thread to create a definite line in which to work the backstitches and form the picots. Come to the front at A and taking a backstitch to B, gather up four threads.

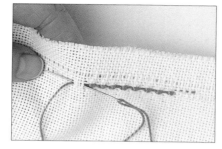

2 Gather up your clusters of four threads as shown. Repeat AB twice more, pulling tightly, ensuring the stitches are lying flat and not piled up on top of each other. Move forward to C and repeat.

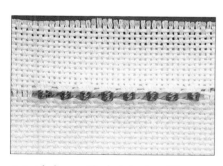

A finished row of backstitch picot. The thickness of thread defines the size of picot: the thicker the thread the more prominent the picot. To turn a corner, work to the end of the line and continue round.

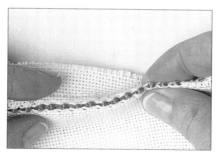

3 Once your line of triple backstitches is complete, finger press the fabric hem back on itself so that the stitches are sitting 'proud' on the top edge. Tack in place if you prefer. You are now ready to complete the hem with the open-sided square edging stitch (see page 148).

Adding beads to backstitch picot

This is an excellent way of adding interest on the edge of your finished pieces. The type of bead you choose, matt or iridescent, will determine the final effect. Use the appropriate needle and thread (e.g. waxed sewing cotton or a monofilament thread) for the size of bead you have chosen.

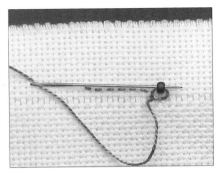

1 Follow the same process as for normal backstitch picot. Take your first backstitch over four threads, come to the surface and thread on the bead before taking the next backstitch. Work the final backstitch by going through the bead for the second time to secure it in position.

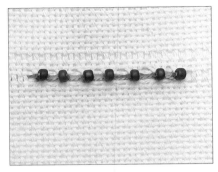

A finished row of backstitch picot with beads. Once the hem is turned over, the beads will sit proud on the edge. This picture shows a thread withdrawn on the edge side — this will make it easier to stitch the open-sided square edging stitch in the right place (see below).

Open-sided square edging stitch

This second stage of the above technique secures the hem and will create an open, lacy effect. Depending on the effect required, a single or double row of this stitch may be worked. A double row will make the hem more durable.

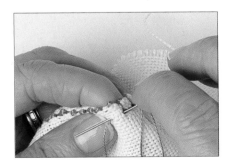

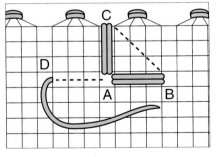

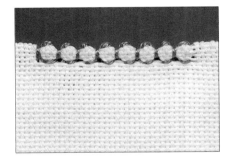

1 Working through the two layers of fabric and lined up with the picots, come to the front at A, taking a backstitch over four threads to B. Repeat the process. Follow the diagram to C and back down over four threads. Repeat. Pull firmly after each stitch to produce small holes at the base of the stitch. To turn a corner, stitch the work to within 2.5cm (1in) and mitre the corner fabric. Turn in the folds to the back and tack loosely in place. Complete the open-sided square edging stitch to the end of the line, working straight over the mitred corner and keeping the counting correct. Work the first stitch round the corner at right angles to the last stitch (over the mitre again) and you will find that it fits in to make a perfect turn.

A finished single row of open-sided square edging. To turn, simply mitre and fold the fabric on the corner and continue the edging stitch at right angles, proceeding round the corner.

Cutting

Nothing should be cut until all surface embellishment has been completed and all the kloster blocks have outlined the designs. Withdrawing the threads for embellishment is not as intimidating as it first appears; simply follow some basic rules.

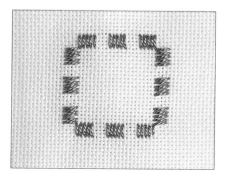

1 A square shape outlined with kloster blocks and ready for cutting. Always cut against the stitched side of a kloster block, never at the open end, and only cut four threads.

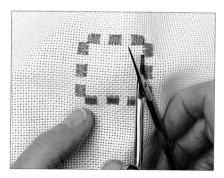

2 Place your scissors to the left-hand side of the block. Collect the four threads on your scissor blades to check you have the right number and cut all at the same time, close against the blocks.

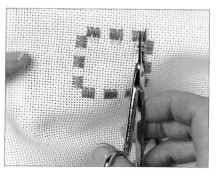

3 Cut against all the appropriate blocks on one side of the design before turning to cut the next side. Work round your shape systematically until all the opposite threads are cut.

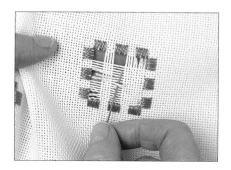

4 Once all the threads are cut, carefully loosen them with a needle and withdraw. Tweezers can be quite useful for this.

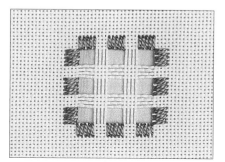

5 The finished cut square. If you cut a thread by mistake, leave it in place. Pull out a background thread from the side of the work. Follow exactly the mesh weave and darn your new thread into position ready for needleweaving. Needleweave the new and cut threads together.

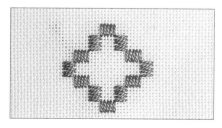

A diamond shape outlined with kloster blocks ready for cutting.

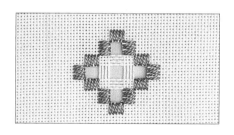

The diamond shape cut and mounted on pink fabric. Once the work is washed, the small 'whiskers' left by the cutting should disappear and be absorbed into the blocks if they have been cut closely enough. Very careful trimming will get rid of persistent visible 'whiskers'.

Needleweaving

Needleweaving uses the finer thread and forms the basis of all the open and decorative filling stitches. It is important for needleweaving to be even, tightly woven and straight, otherwise your filling stitches will look untidy. The number of needlewoven stitches to each bar depends on the fabric count. Once you have established the number on the first bar, the remaining bars should number the same to achieve uniformity throughout the design. Picots and knots may be worked on needlewoven bars.

1 To start, anchor the thread through the back of the kloster blocks, or follow the method shown above. With a waste-knot on the surface, take your thread from underneath across the open square. Place your needle in the middle of the bar threads, with the tip just over the thread.

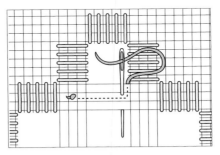

2 'Flick' or 'cast' your needle over the thread so that the thread is now lying between the two middle threads of the bar, and the tip of the needle is facing you underneath the two nearest threads. The needle is now in the right position for you to start needleweaving.

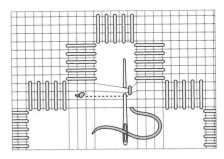

3 There will be an extra thread in this first bar to be included in the needleweaving. Once the end of the bar is reached, cut off the surface knot. This method of starting ensures that there are not so many loose ends being worked through the kloster blocks.

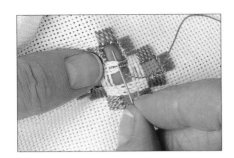

4 Bars are woven in a figure of eight. Take your needle down in between the pairs of threads, over two threads and back down into the middle. Continue weaving under and over two threads at a time until the bar is completed. Pull your stitches tightly to accomplish a neat, even tension.

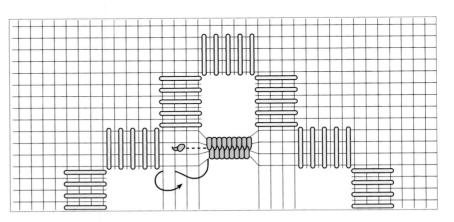

5 Move on to the next bar. Bring your needle behind the bar from the far side and down into the bar on the next 'step'. Continue needleweaving as shown by the arrow. At the end of the first diagonal row of bars, finish off the thread and re-start at the top right of the next row of steps to be worked. Working your needleweaving consistently diagonally across the design in steps from top right to left will ensure that the decorative fillings and crossed lines are all worked in the same way.

Wrapping

Wrapped bars look thinner and are harder to keep even and straight, but they are needed as the basis for some of the other decorative fillings such as Greek cross. Knots or picots cannot be worked on wrapped bars, but the threads on the bars may be divided and wrapped. As for needleweaving, the finer thread is used.

Wrapping may be worked horizontally or vertically and sometimes you may have to reverse the wrapping to suit a particular filling or design, but whichever method you use, try to be consistent.

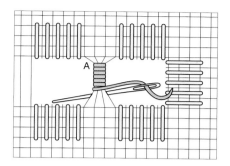

It is important to wrap without overlapping any of the stitches and to control the tension by holding each stitch as you work it. Secure a new thread in the kloster blocks and bring it to the surface from underneath the bar and wrap as shown. Finish the thread by taking it to the back and working through the kloster blocks with small backstitches as usual.

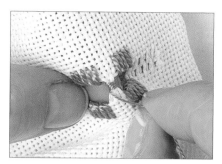

When single bars are wrapped in a line, take care, as you move from bar to bar through the back of kloster blocks, to keep straight lines and the correct wrapping method. It may be necessary to take the thread back through a kloster block which is behind the progression forwards in order to secure it. Simply take a loop stitch over a thread in the block and travel back the way you want to go, surfacing ready to start a new bar.

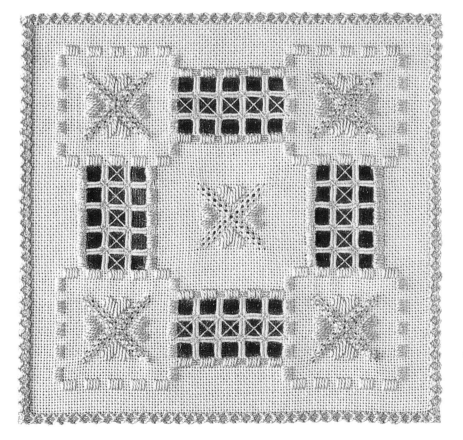

This ornate embroidery includes the heart motif from the bridal bag (see page 162). It is bordered with twisted lattice band. The heart motif is divided by reversed diagonal faggoting, with beads included in the centre stitching line for the corner motifs to create a contrast of texture. The woven bars are decorated simply with a wrapped herringbone stitch to link the theme, but cross stitches would have worked as well.

Fillings

Decorative fillings are an integral part of the needleweaving technique and soften the hard and structured cut and drawn grid lines with their delicate and lacy effects.

There is a wonderful variety of fillings, from simple to complex. The fillings in this chapter will work well with beads or stand on their own as traditional fillings. Most of the fillings in the projects are interchangeable so that you can choose whichever you like.

Introducing beads into decorative fillings is simply an extension of the basic traditional method of working the stitches, but the beads should be connected as part of the filling and not added as an afterthought. Where you place the beads as you work the stitch will alter the appearance of the filling. The beads should not be twisted in any way but left to follow the lines as the filling is formed. Using matt or iridescent beads is a personal choice and will create a different appearance. Varying the size of the beads will also change the final effect and is worth experimenting with as the results can be very unusual and interesting.

Dove's eye filling

This delightful open, lacy filling is probably the best known of all fillings and may be used with either wrapped or woven bars. There are many variations developed from this basic filling.

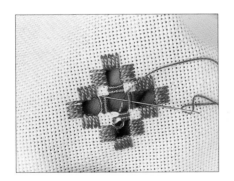

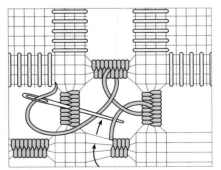

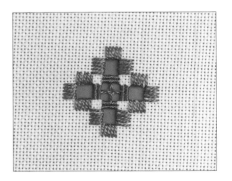

1 Needleweave (wrap or complete) three and a half bars or sides of any square in which the dove's eye is going to be worked. Bring the thread up into the middle of the square. Stitch down into the centre of the needlewoven bar to the right and make the first buttonhole loop as shown, taking the needle over the thread to form the stitch.

2 Adjust the size of the loop and shape and continue in this way round the square creating the loops which form the filling. To complete the fourth buttonhole loop, take the needle and thread behind the first loop formed, pull through to the front and adjust the shape before needleweaving the rest of the bar and continuing the design if applicable.

The finished dove's eye filling. Dove's eyes may be worked either clockwise or anticlockwise, whichever is appropriate, but all four loops of the filling should have the threads crossing in the same direction. Try to form a small, neat hole in the middle of the shape as seen in the picture.

Dove's eye filling with beads at the points

Placing and working the beads in the following manner will accentuate the little 'eye' in the middle of the filling. Larger beads may be used to crowd into the space for texture.

1 Needleweave as before to bring your thread into the middle of the square. Find a needle to fit the thread and bead. Thread two beads on to the thread and form the first loop. Bring your needle over the loop ready to progress to the next, but first go through the top bead, leaving the first bead loose on the thread as shown. Pull the thread through, thread on another bead and repeat the process to the final stitch. Come up behind the first loop as before and take the needle through that first (now last) bead before continuing with the needleweaving to finish the bar.

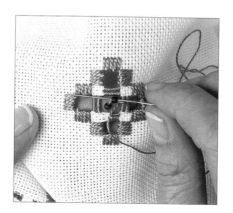

The finished dove's eye filling with beads at the points.

Dove's eye filling with beads on the loops

In this filling the beads sit on the loops between each stitch and form an attractive floret shape. Using matt beads in the same colour as the background stitching is particularly effective.

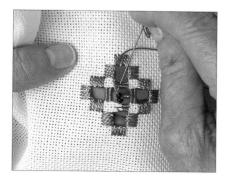

1 Needleweave as before to bring your thread into the middle of the square. This time thread only one bead on to the thread before forming the first loop. Once the loop has been formed, thread on the next bead and proceed as usual round the square. Finish off as normal.

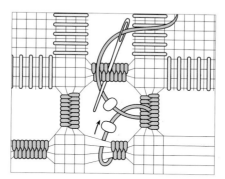

2 The beads may have to be adjusted on the loops before the filling stitch is completed.

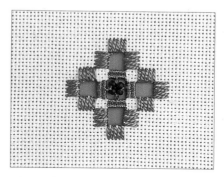

The finished dove's eye filling with beads on the loops. In this instance the needle does not go through any of the beads.

Dove's eyes with wrapped bars

The different shaped motif provides an opportunity to work a variation of dove's eye filling, in which beads could be included following the same principles as already shown.

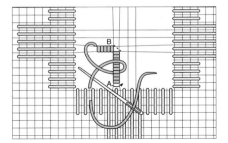

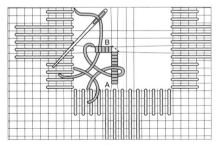

1 Secure your thread in the kloster blocks and surface at A. Wrap two threads on the first bar in the direction of the small arrow. Complete the bar, pass under the intersection to come up at B on the second bar of two threads. Continue wrapping until you reach the centre of the bar and then form the dove's eye as shown.

2 Complete the rest of the dove's eye filling in the correct progression to form the last two loops. Adjust the loops as necessary. Continue to wrap to the end of the bar. Take a backstitch under the second and third bars to pull them tightly together before moving foward to wrap bar 3 in the same way.

The finished dove's eye with wrapped bars. A small central eyelet may be included and worked before the final bar of the motif is completed.

Square filet filling

This delicate squared filling stitch may be worked on either woven or wrapped bars, and when worked over larger areas, a secondary pattern appears, effectively outlining the unfilled squares with a 'halo'.

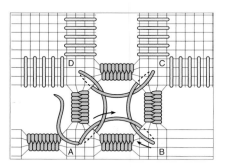

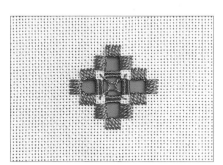

1 Complete all sides of the square. Bring your thread to the front at A and take a stitch into the first corner from underneath to surface at B, forming the first loop. Adjust and take your thread underneath the loop AB. Proceed to the next corner and repeat.

2 Make the last stitch by taking the thread over the loop AB. If working more than one filling, bring the thread up again at A and take a very small backstitch diagonally under the loop, pull tightly to hide it and then proceed with your next bar of needleweaving.

The finished square filet filling. This may be worked clockwise or anticlockwise but be consistent to ensure that the threads all cross in the same direction as the stitch is being formed.

Square filet filling with beads

The effect of the secondary pattern is changed with the inclusion of beads in this filling, making the square look as if it has textured knots in each corner.

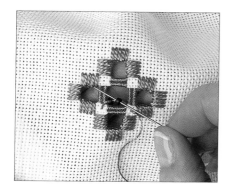

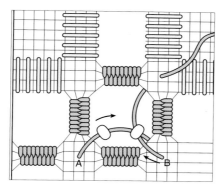

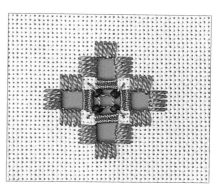

1 Come to the front in the corner as before but thread two beads on to the needle before coming from behind to surface at B. Take the needle through the nearest bead, leaving one loose on the loop. Adjust the length of the loop.

2 Continue round the square in this way until the last loop. Take the needle through the first (now the last) bead and work as before to complete the filling, or move on to do more.

The finished square filet filling with beads.

Divided branch stitch

This filling works well in a single motif to break up and lighten the definite lines of the needlewoven bars.

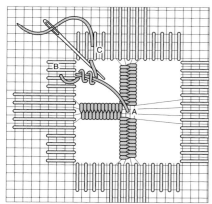

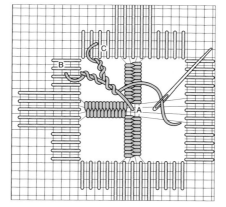

1 Anchor your thread in the kloster blocks as for starting to needleweave (see page 150). Start at the bottom of the motif and weave the two vertical middle bars. Move behind the blocks to surface and weave the left-hand horizontal bar. On completing this bar, come to the front at A in the middle of the intersection. Bring the needle up from behind at B, two threads in from the end of the kloster block motif. Go underneath the loop and make two or three wraps round the thread as shown.

2 Repeat the process to come up on the next side of the motif at C. Repeat the twists on this branch and move on to wrap the main thread. Come back up from underneath in the middle at A, ready to start the branch in the next open square. Work all four branches in this way. After the final branch is completed, come to the front and take a small diagonal backstitch on the intersection, pull tightly to hide and needleweave the last bar in the usual way.

The finished divided branch stitch. Picots could be added to the woven bars for extra decoration (see pages 147–148).

Divided branch stitch with beads

Placing the bead at the bottom of the single branch will create a focal point in the middle of the square and soften the hard lines of the bars, to give a star-like effect.

To incorporate a bead in this filling, simply thread on the bead once you have come to the front at A. Work the rest of the stitch as described on page 155. After your final twist on the main branch, go through the bead once more before surfacing from behind at A again. Work all four branches in this way.

Picot knots

Small knots formed on the sides of bars are probably the most useful of all filling stitches as they soften the lines of woven bars or, within a single square, help give the impression of rounded corners.

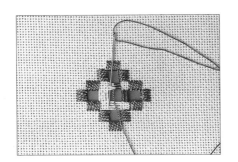

1 Weave to the middle of the bar. Follow the direction of the last stitch and turn the needle tip towards the loose thread as shown.

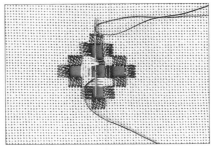

2 Take the thread under the needle and wrap it over the tip. Gently pull the needle and thread through the bar and loop. Pull tightly to form a small knot. You can place a needle in the loop as it is pulled to form an open picot if you wish.

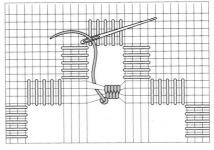

3 Take the needle into the middle of the bar to continue weaving, but first pull the thread across to the unwoven end before bringing it straight back in line. Hold the knot as you pull firmly to anchor it in position. Continue to weave as usual.

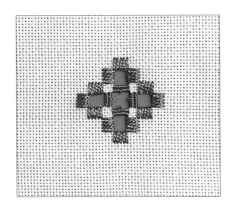

The finished picot knots. Small knots are more elegant than large ones. Try to make them all look the same and place them evenly in the middle of each bar. Knots may be worked on either side of bars, if appropriate.

Greek cross

As a filling in a single motif, this makes a strong and definite 'statement' and is fun to do. Different effects are achieved when Greek cross is used to fill larger areas or worked on the diagonal.

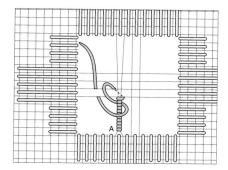

1 Secure the thread in the kloster blocks and come to the front at A to wrap (clockwise) two threads of the bar. Following the diagram, wrap to the end of the bar. Passing the thread underneath the centre intersection, work a figure of eight over these two threads and the bar already wrapped.

2 Pull the first stitches tightly and loosen gradually to form the fan shape. When the fan is the size you require, continue to wrap the rest of the bar. Remember to work the same number of wraps in each part of the stitch formation.

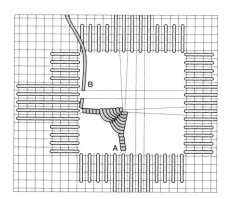

The finished Greek cross.

3 At the end of the wrapped bar, take the needle underneath the next section of two threads. At this stage one stitch may be worked over the two separate bars to pull them together at the tips. Now repeat the process of wrapping to complete the whole Greek cross filling.

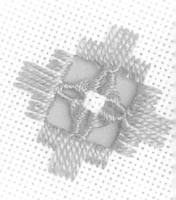

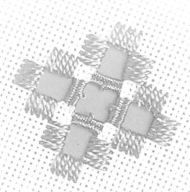

Borders

Many of the surface stitches used in Hardanger may be turned into interesting borders, from the simple to the more complex. There are various bands and borders on the Hardanger sampler on page 137 and throughout this chapter, giving you the opportunity to create your own combination of ideas. Innovative borders can be used to make an interesting traditional band sampler like those of the seventeenth century.

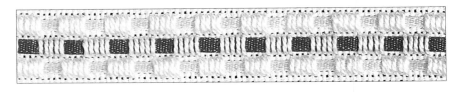

Alternating lines of kloster blocks with satin ribbon threaded through the middle.

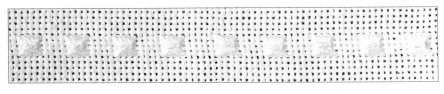

Wrapped kloster blocks give a textural outline.

Alternating lines of wrapped kloster blocks. The middle line is wrapped with a silver bead on the thread.

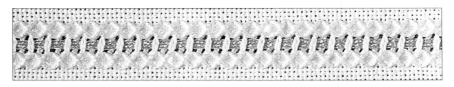

Withdrawn threads, hem stitched on both sides with twisted lattice band over the top and ribbon threaded through the clusters.

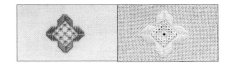

Two 'petals' of the satin stitch star reversed and formed into a diamond motif. This is then filled with Algerian eyelets or reversed diagonal faggoting and an eyelet. Motifs joined together would form an interesting border pattern.

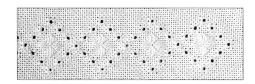

Algerian eyelets forming a diamond shape to enclose satin stitch diamonds.

Mitred reversed diagonal faggoting forming a zigzag to divide satin stitch heart motifs.

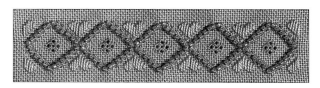

Mitred reversed diagonal faggoting, beaded down the centre line and formed into a diamond shape with diagonal eyelets in the centre and satin stitch heart motifs.

Starting and finishing

Kloster blocks

Begin with an 'away' waste-knot on the surface 7.5cm (3in) to the side of your first stitch. Always start a new thread at the beginning of a block and not in the middle as the difference between the already used and new thread is sometimes noticeable.

To finish off, go through to the back of the work, slipping the needle through the back of the kloster blocks. Come up in the middle of the second block and take a backstitch over the centre stitch. Hold the stitch as you pull tightly to set it into position. Repeat this in the next block before taking the thread through one more block to ensure it is secure. Once all the blocks are finished, cut the knot of your starting thread, rethread and take this underneath to weave through the back of the blocks as already described.

Wherever possible, try to start and finish in different directions to avoid bulk. When you are working blocks in a straight line, and if you feel confident about your counting, to save the bulk on the back you may start your thread in a different way. Come to the front with your sewing thread twenty fabric threads away from the starting point of the first kloster block and up two threads into the middle line. Weave over, under, over and under the nearest single threads and take a neat and tightly formed backstitch over the last. With the needle to the back, go behind the next four threads. Come to the surface and repeat the above process twice more before coming up at the right point to start your first kloster block. Your first three kloster blocks will cover all the weaving and backstitches and there will be a single, flat line at the back between the blocks.

Pulled thread techniques

Rules for starting and finishing the pulled thread stitches will have to be flexible depending on where the stitches will be placed. Generally, start with an 'away' waste-knot to work in once the stitch has been completed. To finish off the sewing thread, work through the back of the stitches already formed, taking the occasional backstitch to secure the thread. Make sure your thread is not visible on the surface. When eyelets are placed apart, it is best to start and finish in the individual unit and not take a long thread on the back linked to the next eyelet.

Washing finished work

Hand wash your finished piece carefully using a mild soap powder or liquid. Rinse it well and dry flat on a towel, stretching the piece carefully back into its original shape. While it is still slightly damp, iron and press it face down into the towel so as not to flatten the stitching.

The design of this decorative tassel is based on the central motif on the bridal bag project (see pages 162–164).

Using a chart

Each line represents one thread of fabric. For larger projects, a quarter or repeat chart is given, but the whole chart is usually shown for smaller projects. The centre lines are signified by small dark arrows on the edges of the chart. The lettering on the charts denotes where to start and should be used in conjunction with the text for clarification. The number of stitches shown on each bar is an average number, just to denote the procedure. The keys accompanying the charts indicate the stitches and threads to use.

Sampler

The interesting asymmetrical sampler shown on page 137, based on bands of stitch combinations and different sized 'tiles', allows you to practise and enjoy some of the ideas used in this chapter.

1 If necessary, enlarge the chart opposite so that it is easier to read.

2 Prepare the fabric by ironing it carefully and, if the edges are not straight, pull out a thread and cut straight along this line. Oversew the fabric edges to prevent fraying. Tack in the centre vertical guide line. To find the centre of your fabric, fold it in half and finger-crease the fold, then fold in half in the opposite direction and repeat. As a general rule, tack in the horizontal and vertical lines using pastel-coloured thread. If you have difficulty with the counting, you could grid up the whole piece in multiples of twelve or to suit your needs.

3 Establish the design by working the largest square with sides formed by eleven kloster blocks. Stitch the units in order as numbered 1 to 20 on the chart.

4 Using cotton perle no. 8, surface at A, 110 threads or approximately 10cm (4in) down from the centre point and six threads to the right to start square no. 1. Turn the work when necessary. Complete all the inside lines of kloster blocks.

5 Line up square no. 2 as shown, twelve threads away from square no. 1, and starting at B, work clockwise to complete a seven kloster block sided square. Fill in with the diagonal lines of kloster blocks.

6 Line up and work square no. 3 to the same size and in the same manner, stitching all the blocks to complete the design as shown.

7 Stitch the straight lines of kloster blocks (4, 5 and 6), and triangle shapes (7), followed by the motifs (8, 9 and 10).

You will need

Evenweave fabric 25 threads to the inch size: 37 x 30.5cm (14½ x 12in)

1 ball of cotton perle no. 8 white

1 ball of cotton perle no. 12 white

Silver blending filament

90 size 11 white beads (matt or shiny as you prefer)

130 silver-lined beads of the same size

Blunt-ended tapestry needle, size 24/26

Sewing or monofilament thread for threading beads

Short tapestry needle size 10 (or similar) for needleweaving and incorporating beads

8 Complete the twisted lattice bands numbered 11, 12, 13, and the heart and star band variations 16, 17 and 18.

9 Work the top and bottom star bands numbered 19 and 20.

10 Change to cotton perle no. 12, include the blending filament in the needle and follow the chart to complete all the pulled thread techniques: square and diamond eyelets, reversed diagonal faggoting and single bands of four-sided stitches over two threads both inside the design and bordering the pattern.

11 Using the cotton perle no. 8, work the two outer lines of twisted lattice band 14 and 15.

12 Continuing with cotton perle no. 12 (but no blending filament), cut the design as given in the chart, one unit at a time. Needleweave (see page 150) and incorporate beads, as shown in the pages on fillings on pages 152–157.

13 Fill all the twisted lattice bands with the silver-lined beads. Sew them on with backstitch. Using a needle and thread which will go through the bead, come to the surface, thread on a bead and take a backstitch over two threads in the middle of each cross. Progress forward to the next cross and repeat.

14 Wash and press the work carefully (see page 159), especially as there are beads in the piece. Take your finished piece to be framed by a professional, unless you prefer to lace and mount the work yourself. Coloured fabric or acid free card may be used to back the work to show up the stitchery and design.

The chart for the sampler embroidery on page 137.

Kloster blocks
Cotton perle no. 8

Satin stitch stars, border
and tulips
Cotton perle no. 8

Twisted lattice band
with beads
Cotton perle no. 8

Satin stitch triangles
Cotton perle no. 8

Satin stitch hearts
Cotton perle no. 8

Kloster block outline
Cotton perle no. 8

Needleweaving
Cotton perle no. 12

Dove's eyes with wrapped
bars
Cotton perle no. 12

Divided branches with
needleweaving and
with beads
Cotton perle no. 12

Greek cross filling
Cotton perle no. 12

Four-sided stitch over 2
threads
Cotton perle no. 12 &
blending filament

Needleweaving & dove's
eye with beads
Cotton perle no. 12

Needleweaving & square
filet filling with/without
beads
Cotton perle no. 12

Needleweaving with picot
knots
Cotton perle no. 12

Eyelets, tulip & diagonal
eyelets
Cotton perle no. 12 &
blending filament

Reversed diagonal
faggoting
Cotton perle no. 12 &
blending filament

Bridal Bag

A special bag of hearts and pearls for a special day. Decorated profusely with pearls and beaded fillings, this is a bag a bride will love to show off with her wedding dress. The design combines two of the original tile squares of eleven kloster blocks, with the side triangles opened completely to get the maximum effect of the beaded square filet filling. Algerian eyelets echo and lighten the central diamond and offset the heart motif which, in turn, is echoed as a border to the bag.

Instructions

1 Prepare the fabric and tack in the centre horizontal and vertical guide lines, as described on page 160.

2 Using cotton perle no. 8 and following the chart on page 164, come to the surface at A, 38 threads down from the centre point and two threads to the right to stitch the kloster blocks which outline the centre diamond shape.

3 Echo the kloster blocks round the central diamond and build up the rest of the kloster block pattern from this shape.

4 Stitch the outside border of kloster blocks, working round the design from the top line of blocks; this will make it easier to count and help prevent counting errors.

5 Complete all surface stitchery of hearts.

6 Change to cotton perle no. 12 and sew the Algerian eyelets before cutting and embellishing the grids.

7 Cut and withdraw the threads, then embellish and complete each triangle individually and in sequence.

8 Work the beaded square filet filling as shown or choose your own preferred filling.

9 Backstitch all the single pearls into position as shown on the chart. Embroider one or both sides of the bag as preferred.

10 Wash and press the work carefully, especially as there are beads in the piece (see page 159).

11 To complete the bag and make a small gusset, machine up the sides and bottom seams, six threads away from the outlining kloster block border. It is a good idea to tack the lines into position first to ensure accuracy. Stitch the lining in the same way to the same measurements as the inside of the bag.

Bridal Bag
Jill Carter

The bag, size 15.2 x 19cm (6 x 7½in) is an extension of the sampler design, changing the lines to give larger areas of filling stitches. The pearl beads are bigger than seed beads and take over the stitch, filling the square to give a heavily beaded look. Calming spaces are provided by the centre panel and simple border.

12 Trim away excess fabric to 13mm (½in) seam allowance and gently press open the seam. To form the gusset, place one side seam on top of the bottom seam to form a point at the corner. Tack, then machine across the point (as indicated by the pin shown in the picture below right) no more than six threads' width either side of the seam to create a gusset of twelve threads in total, when the bag is turned inside out. Repeat the process for the other side and the lining.

13 Fold over the top edge of the bag to the inside, four threads away from the top line of blocks.

14 If appropriate, buttonhole stitch round the handle ring or rings.

15 Use the satin ribbon to make a tab to hold the handle rings in place. Loop the ribbon over the ring or rings, centre and stitch to the inside lip edge of the bag. Place the lining in the bag, wrong side to wrong side of fabric, and turn the raw edge to the inside, just slightly lower than the top of the bag. Cover the raw edges of the tabs and hem the lining in position.

The chart for the Bridal Bag. Enlarge the chart so that you can see the details if necessary.

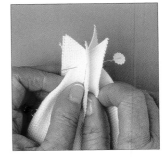

Kloster blocks
Cotton perle no. 8

Satin stitch hearts
Cotton perle no. 8

Square eyelet
Cotton perle no. 12

Algerian eyelets
Cotton perle no. 12

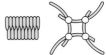

Needleweaving with beaded square filet filling
Cotton perle no. 12

Pearl beads

Cushion Cover

A mosaic of nine tiles decorates this simple concept for a cushion cover, to fit in any surrounding and to work with any colour scheme. Tied with ribbons at each side, this is a practical way of covering an old cushion or making use of a silk pad in a contrasting colour to show off the design. The understated, clean lines of the squares are embellished simply with beaded dove's eye filling for sparkle and texture and separated with four-sided stitch over two threads and square eyelets.

The design can be varied to suit other projects either by adding or reducing the number of squares or by changing the size of the background fabric. A single square could be inserted in a greetings card.

Instructions

1 Prepare the fabric and tack in the centre guide lines vertically and horizontally, as described on page 160.

2 Establish the design following the chart, starting with the centre square. To work the first kloster block, bring the needle to the surface at A, twenty-two threads down from the centre and two threads to the right. Use pearl cotton no. 8 and stitch in a clockwise direction to form the inner square.

3 Outline each square with kloster blocks and work the satin stitch stars as shown in pearl cotton no. 8.

4 Divide the squares with four-sided stitch (over two threads) and eyelets using pearl cotton no. 12 and blending filament.

5 Cut and withdraw the appropriate squares and fill with dove's eye filling with beads at the points.

6 Wash and press the work as directed on page 159, taking particular care since there are beads in the piece.

7 Leave a 5cm (2in) border round the design before turning the fabric to the back to form a 5cm (2in) hem. Turn up a seam allowance of approx 1cm (⅜in) and invisibly slip stitch the hem on the wrong side.

8 Centre the ribbons in the middle of the outside embroidered squares (on all sides of the cushion) and sew them in place on the wrong side, 2cm (¾in) down from the edge.

You will need

- 2 pieces of white evenweave 25 threads to the inch, 40.5cm (16in) square for the back and front of the cushion cover
- 1 ball of pearl cotton no. 8 white
- 1 ball of pearl cotton no. 12 white
- Iridescent blending filament
- Covered cushion pad size: 28cm (11in square) or as preferred
- Blunt-ended tapestry needle, size 24/26
- 186 size 11 seed beads to match or contrast as wished
- Short tapestry needle size 10 (or similar) for needleweaving and incorporating beads
- 2 metres of ribbon for ties (you will need more if you prefer bows)

TIP |||||||||||||||||

Put your different balls of pearl cotton into small grip closure plastic bags with just a tail of thread coming out of the top to keep them clean and controllable, and keep your Hardanger in a pillowcase or protective bag when you are not sewing.

9 Complete the back of the cushion cover in the same way. Tie ribbons in knots or bows to enclose the cushion pad. If a coloured lining is required to show up the design or hide an old cushion, cut the chosen lining fabric to fit the finished size of the cushion. Turn the hem allowance over the lining and stitch to the lining.

The chart for the cushion cover embroidery. To follow this chart, turn the book so that the A is the right way up.

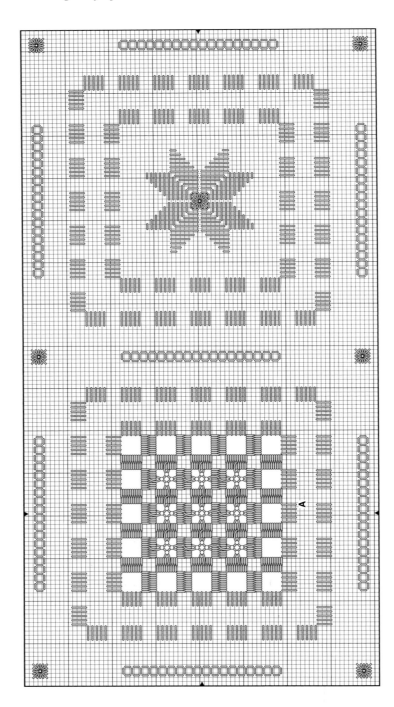

Kloster blocks
Pearl cotton no. 12

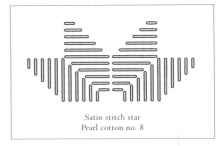

Satin stitch star
Pearl cotton no. 8

Four-sided stitch over 2 threads
White pearl cotton no. 12 with iridescent
blending filament

Square eyelets
White pearl cotton no. 12

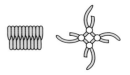

Needleweaving with beaded dove's eyes
Pearl cotton no. 12

A mosaic of tiles form the minimalist design for this cushion cover, which relies on the contrast between the decorative dove's eye filling with beads at the points and the rich satin stitch stars for its impact. Any of the fillings could be substituted in the squares and the design would work well as a repeating pattern for a bigger project. This cushion cover is 30.5cm (12in) square, but make yours to fit your chosen cushion.

BLACKWORK

Blackwork is a counted thread method of embroidery, using straight stitches in a contrasting colour worked on evenweave fabric. The true origin of this type of embroidery appears to have been the Moors and Arabs, who in the thirteenth century travelled to England with soldiers and noblemen returning from the Crusades in the Holy Lands.

In Chaucer's *Canterbury Tales*, there is a description of what seems to be blackwork in The Miller's Tale: 'Her smock was white and embroidered in front and behind with coal-black silk, and embroidered also on the inside and outside of the collar.'

It is believed that the Spanish princess, Katharine of Aragon, brought blackwork to England with her in 1501. Eight years later she married Henry VIII, and for more than twenty years she influenced the English court with her passion for embroidery. The stitch she used was known as 'Spanishwork'. It had become part of Spanish culture during the rule of the Moors. There were many portraits painted at this time showing people wearing clothes decorated with blackwork embroidery. One of the blackwork stitches was named after Henry VIII's court painter, Holbein, because so many of his sitters displayed it.

Blackwork's closely textured stitching was not only decorative – it was also used to reinforce collars and cuffs, and to disguise dirt during a time of poor hygiene. The poorer classes also stitched the delicate designs on their clothes as a cheaper alternative to lace, which was difficult to obtain due to high taxes.

After Katharine's divorce from Henry in 1533 the Spanish influence disappeared, so the term 'blackwork' replaced 'Spanishwork'. The stitches used then are very much the same as today. Patterns can look complicated, but the stitches are very simple, making it an ideal form of embroidery for beginners.

Opposite
Many blackwork patterns were inspired by Tudor knot gardens and mazes. Knot gardens featured designs of interlacing bands and ribbons made from low hedges, enclosing beds filled with flowers.

Materials

Fabric

Blackwork requires an evenweave fabric. Usually, the fabric found in good needlework stores will state the number of holes or threads to the square centimetre or inch. The fewer holes to the square centimetre, the larger a piece of embroidery will be. It is advisable not to choose a very fine fabric for your first project, as it can be very hard on your eyes, and if you are a beginner, counting the threads accurately for a first attempt may prove a little disheartening.

Aida (blockweave) This is available in various counts and in numerous colours. It is a cotton or cotton mixture fabric which is made especially for counted needlework, with two threads woven into blocks rather than single threads. The majority of the embroideries in this chapter are worked on this fabric as it gives crisp, accurate results, especially with intricate designs.

Evenweave This is a plain, single weave fabric. The number of threads for the warp and the weft are the same, and because the texture is open, the threads are easily counted. Cambric, white and coloured linens are popular evenweave fabrics.

Hardanger A good fabric for blackwork with pairs of intersecting threads which make it very easy to count. The fabric remains firm and in shape – more so than single weave.

Aida, evenweave and Hardanger fabrics. Most of the embroideries in this chapter are worked on Aida, as it is ideal for intricate designs.

Choosing fabric

When you have chosen a design, you need to work out how much fabric it will take by following the guidelines below.

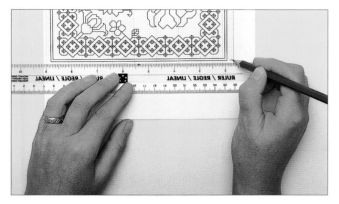

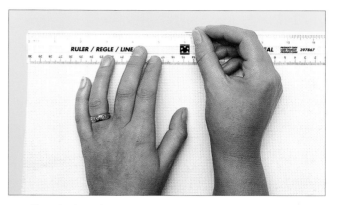

1 Take a ruler or other straight edge to the last stitch on the chart on the left, then the right, and count the squares in between, to find the width. Do the same from top to bottom, to find the height.

2 To calculate the thread or block count on the fabric, place your ruler on the material and count the number of threads or blocks there are to 2.5 cm (1in).

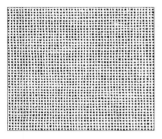

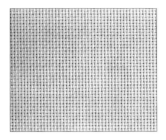

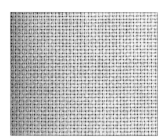

Evenweave is stitched over two threads. So, if there are 26 threads to 2.5cm (1in) and there are two threads to each stitch, that will mean 13 stitches for 2.5cm (1in). If your design has a graph count of 54 squares across and 54 squares down, divide 54 by 13 and you will require 10.5cm² (4¼in²) of fabric.

Aida is one stitch per block. So, if your design has a graph count of 54 squares across and 54 squares down, and your Aida fabric has 18 blocks to 2.5cm (1in), divide 54 by 18, and you will require a piece of fabric 7.5cm² (3in²).

Hardanger is made up of pairs of threads woven together to give a dense background, while still leaving easily visible holes between the warp and weft. It can be stitched over one or two threads. Calculate the size of material required in the same way as for Aida.

When you are happy with the measurements of the actual sewing area, remember to include extra fabric around your design. Try to leave an extra 10–15cm (4–6in) for stretching and mounting. Smaller projects do not need so much.

Threads

Today, there is a great variety of threads available for all kinds of embroidery, some specially for blackwork. The choice of threads and their thickness is of course a personal preference and depends on the type of design you are trying to achieve. It is advisable to use short lengths in the needle to avoid knotting.

Stranded cottons consist of six strands of cotton and can be separated into groups to provide different thickness and shades.

Cotton perle 5 and 8 are highly mercerised two-ply threads with a shiny finish and soft twist. They are available in many colours and are made by several well-known brands.

Coton à broder no. 16 is a single or three-strand thread which is the equivalent of two strands of cotton perle or stranded cotton. It is made in a wide range of colours.

Ordinary machine sewing cotton is harder than stranded cotton, and gives fine work a crisp effect.

Organising your threads

There are many excellent organising systems you can buy, but you can make your own cards, which are simple and cost nothing.

1 Take a piece of stiff card and punch holes down the side.

2 Cut your skeins into manageable lengths. Take a length, double it and thread the looped end through a hole in your organiser. Push the cut ends through the loop and pull tight. It is easy to remove one length of thread from the card without disturbing the rest.

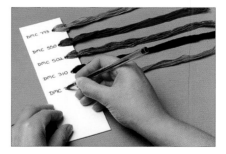

3 At the side of the thread, write the manufacturer's name and the number of the shade. When you have completed your project, any spare thread can be left on the card and used for your next embroidery.

Needles

For all counted needlework you will require a blunt needle. Sharp needles will pierce both the threads on the fabric and the stitches already worked. Also, when the needle passes through the fabric, it should not enlarge or distort the hole – if it does, then it is the wrong size. Finer needles have a larger number and thicker needles a lower number. Sizes 22–26 are usually best.

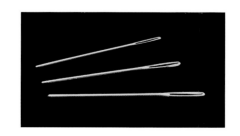

Other items

Frames There are various sizes and types to choose from, depending on the size of your work. Some are available with floor or table stands, clip-on lamps and magnifiers. So, the days of having a frame in one hand, needle and thread in the other, the chart on your knee, a magnifying glass hung around your neck and the lamp balanced dangerously on the edge of the table are over! Whichever type of frame you choose, the important rule is to keep your fabric drum tight.

Embroidery hoops It is best to use hoops only when the whole of the design fits inside the ring. Moving the hoop around your work can distort the stitches and mark some types of fabric. Place the fabric over the smaller hoop. Then force the larger hoop over it, making sure that the larger hoop is screwed fairly tightly and the fabric is taut. You will need a screwdriver to loosen the outer hoop and release the fabric.

Rectangular frames This type of frame, which is available in many sizes, can accommodate the whole width of the fabric, keeping it taut at all times. You do not need a screwdriver to release and move the fabric while you are embroidering – you just move the rollers until you reach the area you want to work on.

Dressmaker's scissors for cutting out the fabric. Follow the line of the thread when cutting, to make sure you have a straight line.

Cutting mat is useful when cutting mounting board with a craft knife.

Iron is used to press an embroidery gently on the back before mounting it.

Embroidery scissors are useful for unpicking mistakes. They should be kept sharp to prevent them from chewing the thread. The point should be fine enough to slip under the stitch to cut it.

Pins are used to mark the centre of your fabric, and to hold it in place when you are mounting an embroidery.

Measuring tape or ruler is used for measuring when choosing fabric and when mounting embroideries.

Masking tape is used to prevent fabric from fraying.

Hole punch is used for making a thread organiser.

A **craft knife, acid-free mounting board** and **double-sided tape** are used for mounting your finished work.

A variety of frames are available, from hand-held hoops to freestanding rectangular frames.

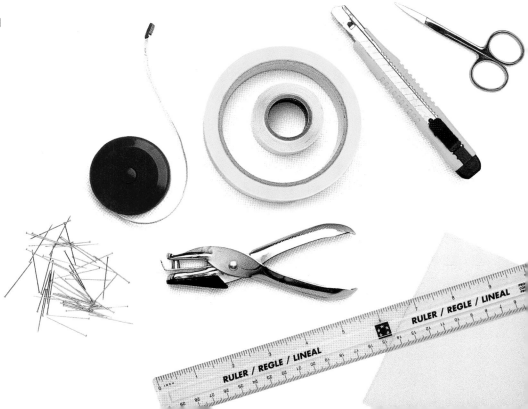

Using charts

The most important part of the chart is the point at which you will place your first stitch. Blackwork can be very intricate, so the centre point of the chart and fabric is where you should begin. Should you start sewing in the wrong place, you may find halfway through your work that you run out of space, and hours of work will be wasted.

On the chart, a grey square or black cross usually pinpoints the centre. With your fabric also marked in the centre, this is your starting point and it will ensure an adequate margin around your design.

In the chart opposite, the centre point is at the bottom of the flower, which is an excellent motif to sew first. The motif, in turn, will help to position the surrounding patterns of the flower and the centre top of the intricate border.

Once the centre motif has been completed, work the surrounding patterns in any order until you reach the outer border. One strand of thread is used throughout the design to show the intricate patterns clearly on the fabric.

Most of the designs in this chapter appear in chart form, to show the patterns clearly and to enable you to design your own band samplers.

TIP ||||||||||||||||

The easiest way to find the centre of your fabric is to fold it in half in both directions and mark the centre where the finger-creased lines cross (see page 160). A more accurate method is provided on page 14–15.

Designing your own band sampler

In an age when books were costly and rare, the sampler, which was a personal book of patterns and stitches, would have been a valuable item worth passing on to the next generation.

The motifs, patterns and borders shown in this chapter will hopefully provide you with inspiration and ideas for designing your own band samplers, which are patterns worked in long bands, enough to show the repeat, plus spot motifs such as birds, flowers and animals. You may decide to have a theme, such as flowers, and choose as many patterns and single motifs as you can find. Alternatively, you may wish to create your own patterns, which is easy and can be a great deal of fun. Experiment with simple shapes, adding lines horizontally, vertically and diagonally, and you can create your own blackwork library.

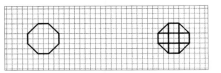

1 Take a shape such as an octagon and add a few lines horizontally and vertically.

2 Add diagonal lines. Extend the ends. What started as a plain shape has now become an intricate pattern.

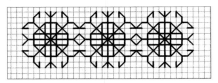

3 Repeat the pattern lengthways to make a border.

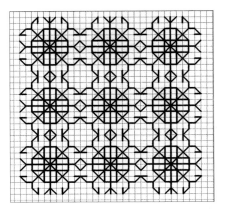

4 Alternatively, join the patterns together in a block, and they will create additional patterns.

The chart for the embroidery below. Begin working from the grey square in the centre.

TIP ||||||||||||||||

It is important to start at the centre of the chart to ensure that your finished work will be central, with sufficient surplus fabric all around it. The marker on the chart, and the pin or cross stitch you have put in your fabric indicate your starting point.

Tudor Rose, lily and pansy motifs like these were used extensively in sixteenth-century embroideries. Roses were the emblems of the Tudor kings.

Stitches

The three stitch examples given here are the most commonly used for blackwork embroidery. For intricate designs, double running stitch is favoured, and for outlining, use backstitch. Cross stitch may be found within many of the design examples in this chapter.

Double running stitch

Blackwork is traditionally worked in double running stitch, or Holbein stitch. This gives a smoother effect than backstitch, and is ideal for creating intricate geometric bands and filling patterns. Plan your route around the pattern you are working so that you work a line, then fill in the gaps on the way back.

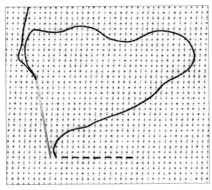

1 Work a line of stitches as shown.

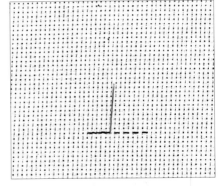

2 Fill in the spaces on the return journey. Bring the needle up at the top of the previous stitch, and then insert the needle below the start of the next stitch.

Backstitch

Backstitch is used as the basis for many other stitches, and can be used as an outline stitch.

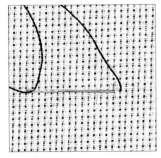

1 Bring the needle up to the right side of the material. Take it back along the line and go down to the wrong side.

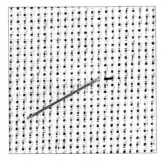

2 Bring the needle up to the right side again, in front of the first stitch, a stitch length away.

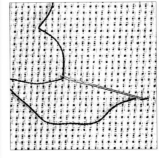

3 Always finish the stitch by inserting the needle at the point where the last stitch began.

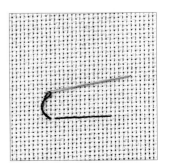

A line of backstitch.

Cross stitch

This is a very simple stitch, but it can look untidy if the direction of the top stitches differs, so always make sure they face in the same direction.

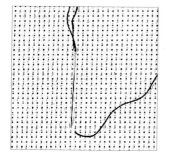

1 Start at point A. Take the needle diagonally to the left and insert it at B.

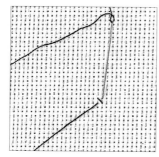

2 Bring the needle up at point C and insert down at D.

3 For the next stitch, bring the needle up at point C and repeat the procedure.

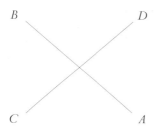

Hundreds of threads may be started and finished in a design such as this – and not just black threads; coloured threads will add another dimension to your work. The important part of any finished embroidery is to ensure that no knots are used. This will allow your work to sit flat without any bumps when mounted. Also, any loose threads left at the back may show through to the right side of the fabric if you have not woven them in correctly.

Flowers & plants

The invention of printing in the mid-fifteenth century provided a ready source of design material for the eager seamstress to sew on to fabric. Illustrations of the plants used by herbalists in their recipes, and of those found growing in Tudor knot gardens and herb gardens, such as roses, pansies, honeysuckle and comfrey, all found their way into blackwork designs decorating clothes and household furnishings.

A wide range of flower and plant motifs featured in traditional blackwork, with Tudor roses the favourite. These emblems of the Tudor kings were sewn full-face rather than in bud. Carnations, pansies, thistles, tulips, pineapples, figs, grapes and strawberries were also popular.

Figures, birds & animals

Illustrations of strange animals and birds from far-off lands, and books such as Aesop's Fables, gave additional material for motif work. Wallpaper and lining papers of the late fifteenth century depicted English birds, butterflies and floral fruits, and these motifs also appear in blackwork designs of the time.

'Boxers' were representations of the human form and were often depicted carrying hearts, acorns or flowers. The term 'boxers' is a modern interpretation, referring to their stance. One explanation for their significance is that they are lovers exchanging gifts. They have also been referred to as Renaissance Cupids, and as early representations of Adam and Eve.

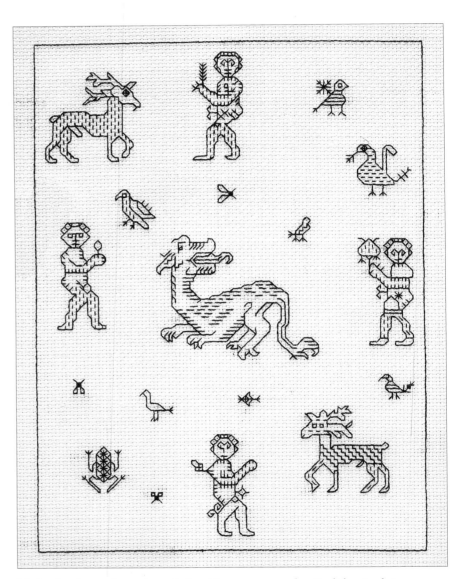

Mythical and exotic beasts featured alongside more commonplace English animals in blackwork design. The human figures are referred to as 'boxers' because of their stance, but they may have been intended as lovers bearing gifts.

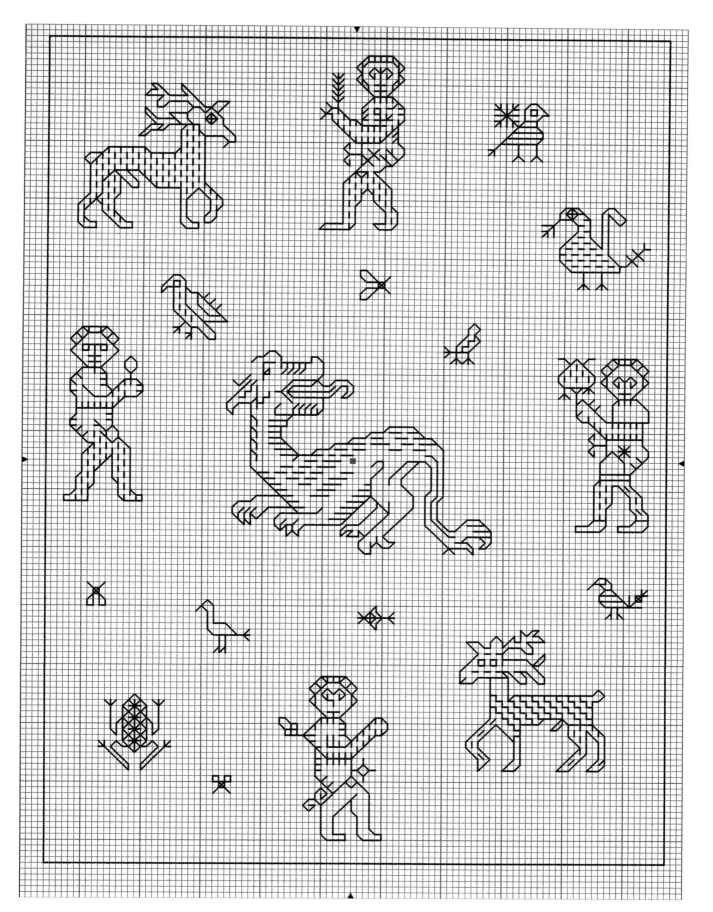

Fill-in patterns

If you have a design in mind that you would like to fill with various blackwork patterns, choose your first project carefully and do not be too ambitious. The simplest of shapes can become very impressive when finished. The following fill-in patterns are all shown in squares, but you can progress to more decorative shapes.

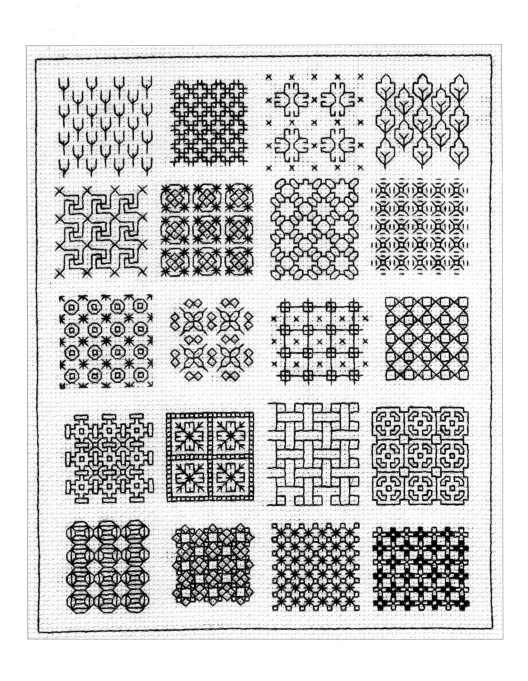

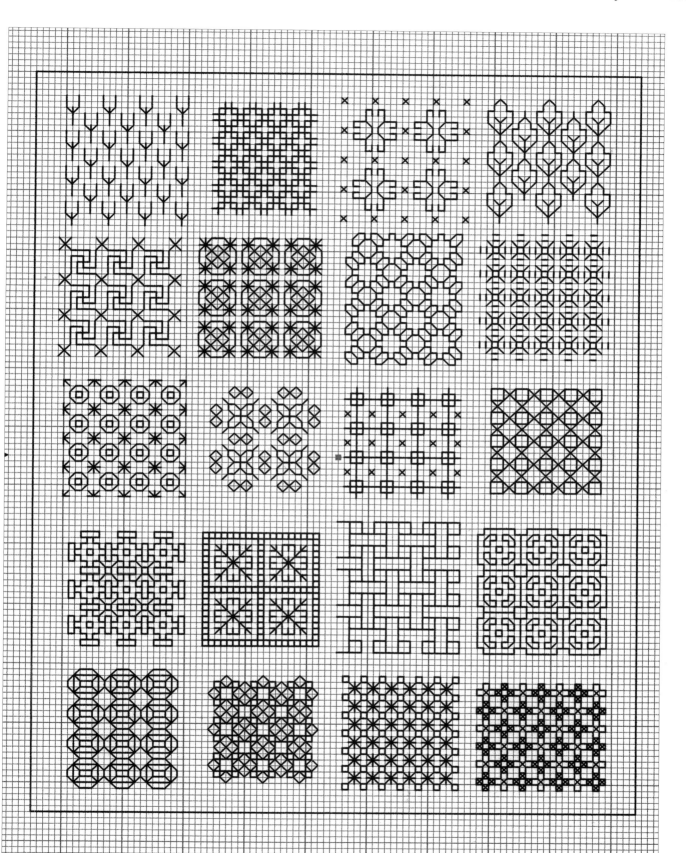

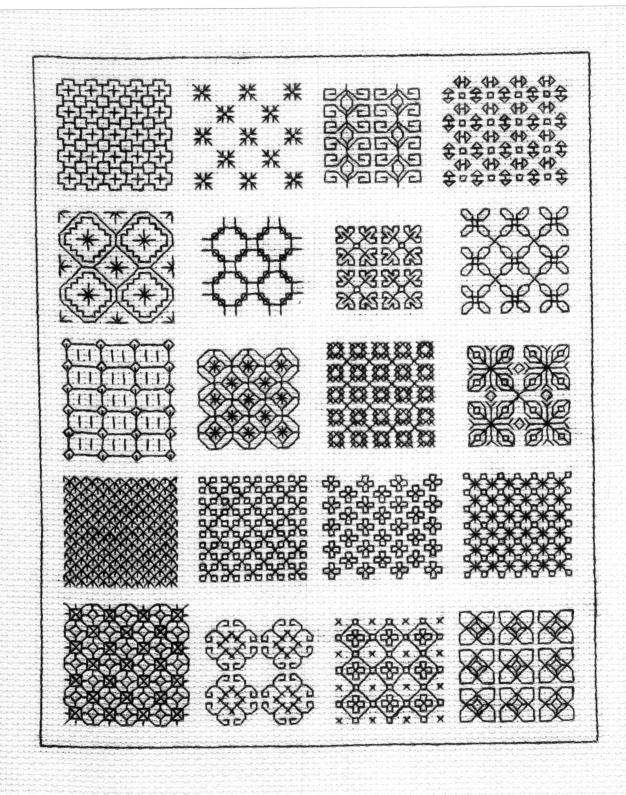

A design for a fill-in pattern may be created from one small motif, which is then multiplied, as in some of the patterns shown above. A close pattern will appear very dark, and an open pattern will look much lighter. When you need shadow in a design to create depth and form, the choice of pattern is therefore very important.

Borders

In the fifteenth and sixteenth centuries, repeating patterns were used to decorate clothing. The smaller borders were used mainly for edging garments, creating a reinforced edge to the material. Larger borders were found on household linen and furnishings.

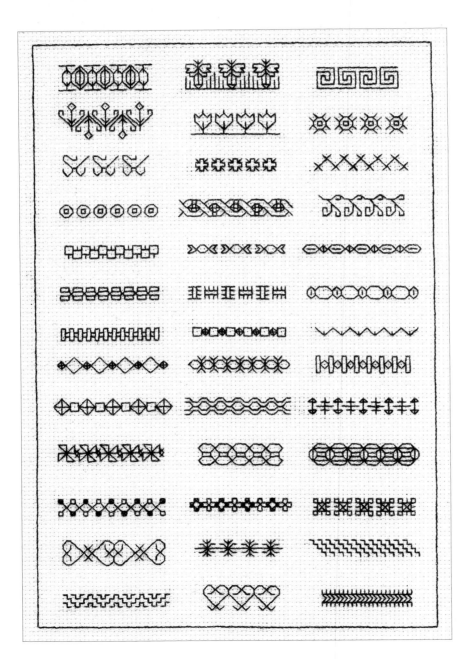

Smaller border designs like these were used to edge garments. Some of the patterns were so intricate that they resembled lace. Since lace was extremely expensive, blackwork was an ideal substitute. For the hard-working poor, it was a cheap way to reinforce the edges of cuffs and collars, while for the gentry it was a popular way to decorate caps, head-dresses and gowns.

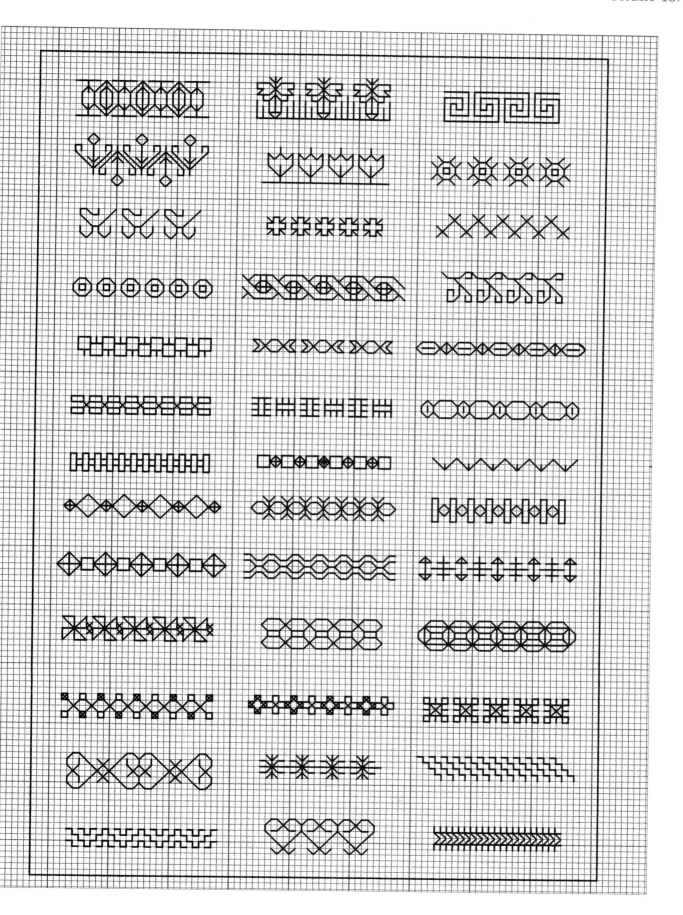

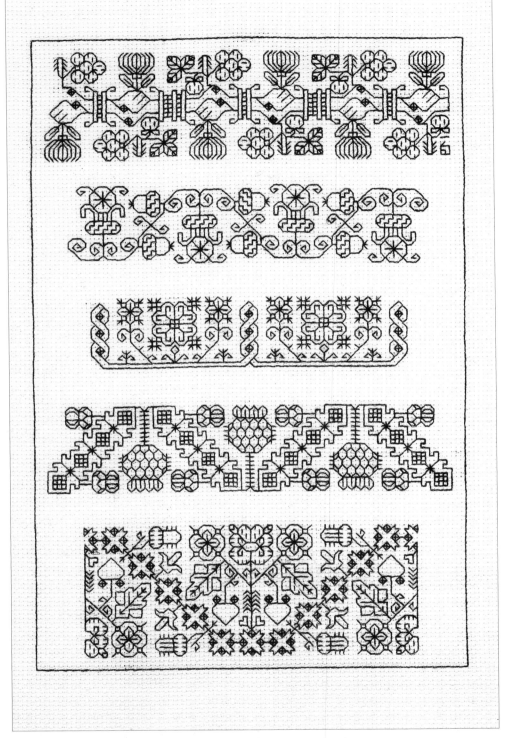

Larger borders like these were used on bed linen and other household items, and had practical as well as decorative uses. When the courts moved from place to place, a particular blackwork design would identify ownership, at a time when most people would have been unable to read written labels.

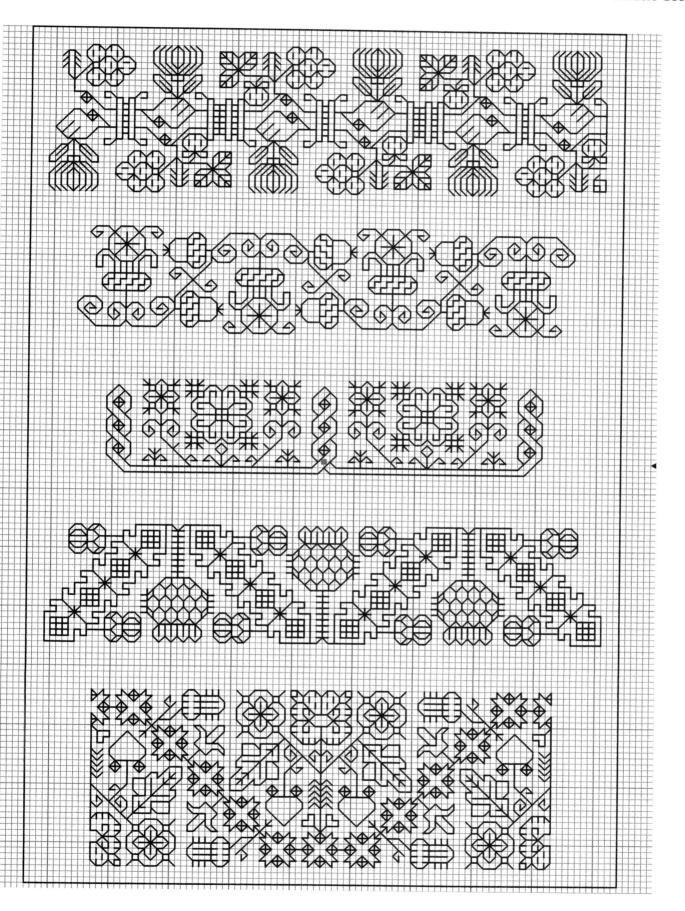

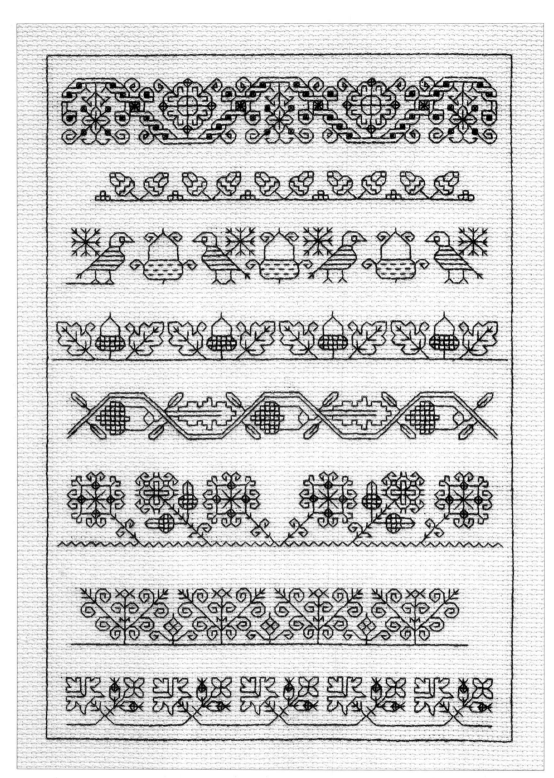

Here, bird, flower and plant motifs are repeated to create intricate borders.

DRAWN THREAD EMBROIDERY

Drawn thread work essentially involves cutting and withdrawing the fabric threads, leaving open areas in the ground fabric, which can then be embellished to create an intricate, lacy effect. Who would not be nervous the first time they cut the threads of their fabric? Even the most experienced stitcher has some trepidation before cutting their precious embroidery. This chapter will guide you through all the stages of drawn thread work, giving you the skills and confidence that will enable you to produce delicate and detailed embroideries of your own. These can then be framed, or made into decorative items such as box lids and cushions (see opposite and page 229).

Drawn thread is a counted thread technique, and one of the oldest forms of openwork embroidery. It was traditionally worked on linen. Through the centuries, many varieties of drawn thread work have evolved. In thirteenth-century Germany, drawn thread embroideries were stitched by nuns in convents to decorate altar cloths. During the Renaissance, drawn thread work became popular as a means of simulating true lace, which was expensive and painstakingly slow to produce. Garments were hemmed with ornamental hem stitching, and drawn thread work was used to trim wristbands and necklines, as well as being used to embellish household linens.

Many people confuse drawn thread work with pulled thread work, where the fabric threads are not cut but pulled to create a lacy effect. Both techniques are forms of openwork embroidery, and both can also be categorised under the term 'white work'.

The projects in this chapter are inspired by traditional band samplers of the seventeenth century. These featured counted thread embroidery stitches, and some also included areas of drawn thread work. By combining traditional stitches and techniques from the past with contemporary fibres, threads and embellishments, a modern twist can be placed on this beautiful and historical form of embroidery.

Materials

The secret to drawn thread work is a good quality, evenweave fabric and a pair of sharp scissors. You should also embellish your work with high quality threads, beads and treasures. All the materials needed for the projects in this chapter can be purchased from any good needlework shop or the internet.

Threads

Floss is a six-stranded cotton embroidery thread, and is the most common thread used for all types of embroidery. It has a natural sheen and is available in hundreds of colours. Use two strands of thread for cross stitch and speciality stitches, and one strand of thread for backstitching.

Silk thread is also a stranded thread with a natural sheen. It is stronger and smoother than standard floss and is beautiful to work with, though it is more expensive.

Overdyed thread is also a stranded thread, either silk or cotton, that has been dyed several colours to produce a variegated effect. The colours may be from the same colour family, progressing from light to dark, or may include different colours blended together. Many of these threads are dyed by hand. When stitching with overdyed threads, use two strands of thread as they come off the skein, and complete each stitch before moving on to the next one to obtain the full effect of the colour changes. Do not use the loop method (see page 200) to begin stitching.

Cotton perle is a strong thread, ideal for drawn thread work. It is a two-ply, non-separable, twisted thread that has a lustrous sheen. The largest size is 3, decreasing in order to 5, 8 and, the smallest, 12. Here, size refers to the thickness of the thread. In the projects in this chapter, sizes 5, 8 and 12 have been used.

Metallic braid gives a sparkly finish to drawn thread work. It is used as it comes off the spool, and you do not separate the strands. It is a round thread that has a bright metallic sheen. In this chapter, Very Fine Braid no. 4 and Fine Braid no. 8 have been used; it is also available in nos 12, 16 and 32. It comes in many colours, including fluorescent and luminescent colours. Other metallic threads include blending filaments, Japan threads, cords, cable and ribbon.

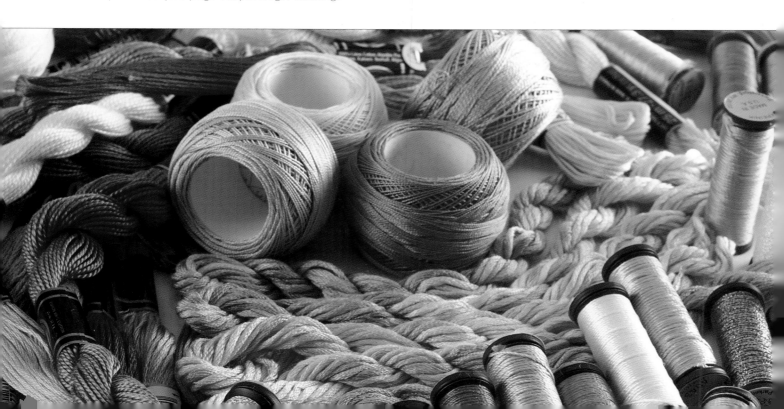

Fabric

All the projects in this chapter are stitched on evenweave linen. The term 'evenweave' means that the fabric has the same number of vertical (warp) threads as horizontal (weft) threads. Throughout the centuries, linen has been a popular choice for all types of needlework, including counted thread work and samplers. As linen is a natural fibre, the threads can vary slightly in thickness, and sometimes you will find slubs in the fabric. This adds to its authentic look. Modern speciality evenweave fabrics can be a mixture of linen and cotton. These are cheaper than pure linen and the weave of the fabric threads is uniform and without slubs.

In this chapter, linen fabrics that are either 28 count (28 threads per inch of the fabric) or 25 count (25 threads per inch) are used, though a speciality evenweave could be used if you prefer. Aida is not a suitable fabric for the projects in this chapter.

Needles

Tapestry needles are suitable for drawn thread embroidery. They have a blunt point that will not pierce the fabric, and a large eye. They are available in a variety of sizes, from no. 13 (the largest) to no. 28 (the smallest). For the projects in this chapter, use a no. 26 when stitching with floss, silk fibres and cotton perle 12, and a no. 24 when using cotton perle 8 and metallic threads.

Beading needles are useful for sewing on beads, though a no. 26 or no. 28 tapestry needle would probably be small enough unless you are using petite beads. Beading needles are very thin, and either long or short. They have a very sharp point and a very small eye so that beads can slide down them easily.

TIP ||||||||||||||||

Natural linen is very prone to creasing, so it is advisable to iron the fabric before you start stitching. To make ironing easier, first wash the linen in warm water using a very small amount of hand-wash detergent (not washing-up liquid), and afterwards rinse it thoroughly with cold water. Wrap the fabric in a clean, white, fluffy towel and gently squeeze out as much moisture as possible without twisting or wringing the fabric. Finally, place another clean, dry towel on an ironing board, lay the linen on the towel (wrong-side down if you have already started stitching), place a piece of muslin over the top and iron until the linen is dry.

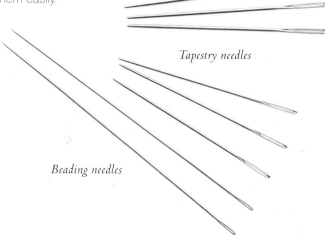

Tapestry needles

Beading needles

Other items

Frames and stands It is preferable to stitch with your fabric in a frame to ensure an even tension, though some people can stitch without a frame. It is therefore a personal choice, and depends on which method you are most comfortable with. For the projects in this chapter, a snap frame consisting of four modular plastic tubes has been used. The tubes come in a variety of lengths that you can fit together in whichever combination suits the shape and size of your embroidery. The fabric is stretched over the plastic tubes and held in place by a plastic clamp on each side. This does not mark the fabric, and keeps it really taut. You can loosen the fabric prior to cutting the fabric threads without having to remove it from the frame; just turn the clamps in towards the centre until the fabric is slack enough to allow you to comfortably cut the fabric threads. Once you have cut the fabric threads you can tighten the fabric again by turning the clamps back in the opposite direction. Unlike traditional wooden quilters' frames, you do not need to sew the fabric on to the frame.

Other popular frames are stretcher bars, hoops and scroll frames. Attaching your frame to either a table stand or a floor stand will enable you to have both hands free to work. Again, this is a personal preference. Many stands also include a light and a magnifying glass.

Scissors For drawn thread work, a good pair of embroidery scissors is essential. They need to be of good quality – sharp, with pointed blades and a good cutting edge that runs the full length of the blade. It is worth considering having a separate pair of scissors for cutting metallic threads. They are very hard on scissors and will eventually blunt the cutting edges.

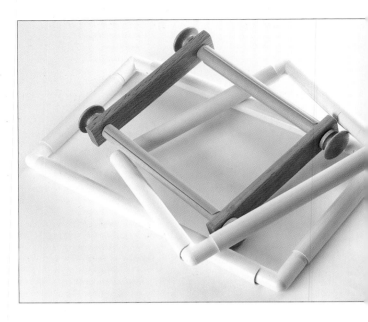

Beads, crystal and glass treasures Beads come in a variety of sizes and colours and add extra detail and sparkle to a design. Seed beads and petite beads have been used in the projects in this chapter, as well as crystal and glass treasures.

There are a number of other needlework accessories you may find useful, but which are not essential. These include a **tape measure**; a pair of **round-ended scissors** for cutting metallic threads; a **'parking lot magnet'**, which is a pair of magnets that you place either side of your fabric to provide a safe place for your needles when you are not stitching; a **'boo boo stick'**, which is a small, double-ended brush that helps you remove stitches without damaging the fabric; a pair of speciality **needlework tweezers**, which will help you remove both cut fabric threads and stitching errors; a **'bead nabber'**, used to help pick up beads; **laying tools** to keep satin stitches neat and parallel; a **needle threader**; a **magnifying glass** for detailed work; **thread conditioner**, to smooth your thread and help prevent tangling and fraying; a **thread winder**, used to keep your threads neat and tidy; a **'dololly'**, which is a useful tool for tidying up very small threads on the reverse of your stitching when they are too short for a regular needle; **counting pins**, to help you count the fabric threads accurately, which is an essential part of drawn thread work; and a **pincushion**.

To keep all of your threads neat and tidy, use a **floss storage box**, which is a lidded box divided into small sections that are large enough to hold reels and skeins of thread. Finally, drawn thread work is so precise that good light is essential. You may wish to invest in a purpose-made **stitching light** that works with a natural daylight bulb; many of these lamps are also fitted with a magnifying glass.

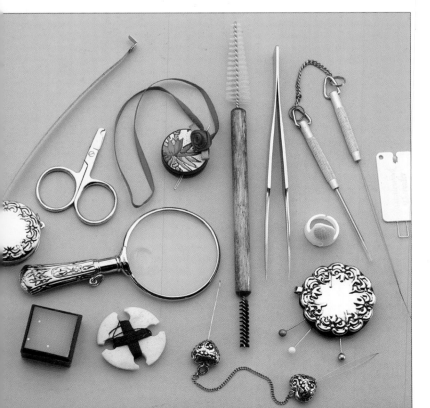

Before you stitch

The first thing you will need to do when starting an embroidery is to cut out the fabric. This needs to be 8cm (3in) wider on each side than the finished piece. Linen fabrics will fray, but do not hem the edges; if you accidentally cut the wrong thread, you will need to be able to take a thread from the edge of the fabric to repair your mistake. You are now ready to start stitching.

Marking the outline

The secret to drawn thread work on linen is careful counting, so it is advisable to mark the outline of the area to be stitched with basting stitches. These stitches will make your counting easier, and are removed once the sampler is completed.

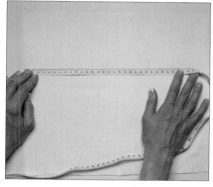

1 First, find the central vertical thread of your piece of fabric, either by folding it in half and marking the centre with a pin, or by measuring with a tape measure (as shown above).

2 Using one strand of a light-coloured floss, place two or three basting stitches (evenly worked running stitches) to mark the centre line, approximately 4cm (1½in) from one edge of the fabric. Leave the working thread on the needle.

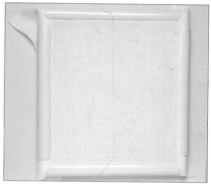

3 Secure the fabric in a frame, making sure it is taut and evenly stretched across the frame. Continue basting to the opposite edge of the frame.

4 Unclip the top of the frame, and measure 8cm (3in) down the central line from the edge of the fabric. Mark the point with a needle. This is the centre point of the top line of your embroidery.

5 Replace the frame, and carefully count the threads to the left of the centre point, so if the design is eighty threads wide, count forty threads to the left. Mark this point, and baste back to the centre line.

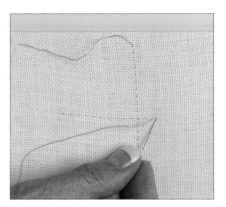

6 When you have reached the centre, count forty threads to the right and continue basting.

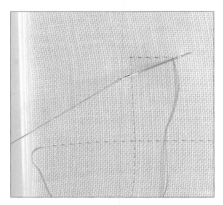

7 When you have completed the top horizontal line, turn your fabric through 90° and baste the right-hand vertical line, counting the threads as you go.

8 Complete the outline. Leave the centre line in for now, removing it later as you work. All the basting stitches can be removed once the design is completed.

Cutting the fabric threads

The first and most important tip is to always cut in a good light and when you are not tired! Everyone feels nervous about cutting their fabric threads, especially if you have already completed a large section of stitching.

There are two different methods of preparing the fabric before cutting. The first involves cutting and reweaving the fabric threads to secure them, and the second uses satin stitch blocks as security stitches. Both of these methods are described below.

Cutting and reweaving the fabric threads

When cutting and reweaving the fabric threads, only cut two fabric threads at a time. This helps with counting and prevents you from accidentally cutting the wrong thread. If you cut too many threads at one time you are more likely to make an error. If you are stitching on a frame, always loosen or remove the fabric before you begin cutting, and always work with the right side of the fabric facing up.

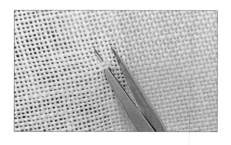

1 Place the scissors under two fabric threads in the centre of the design and cut.

2 Using the tip of a needle, carefully unweave one of the cut fabric threads. Work towards the left-hand margin.

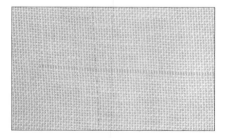

3 Unweave the thread to approximately 2.5cm (1in) past the margin, and pass the end of the thread through to the back of the fabric. Carefully start to unweave the second thread. You will be using this thread for reweaving, so it is important that it does not break.

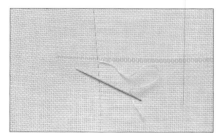

4 Stop unweaving the second cut fabric thread at the margin and thread it through a needle.

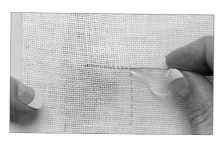

5 Reweave the thread through the gap left by the first thread to the left of the basting stitches, taking care to follow the weave of the fabric.

6 Pull the thread through, not too tightly otherwise it could break or the fabric could become puckered. Pass the thread through to the back of the fabric for a tidy finish.

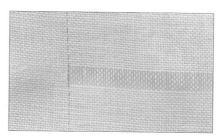

7 Continue cutting and reweaving two threads at a time for as many rows as the pattern demands, then turn your work through 180° and repeat for the right-hand side.

Satin stitch blocks

When using satin stitch blocks for securing cut threads, it is an easy mistake to misalign the satin stitch blocks, or to incorrectly count the number of satin stitches in a block. Before you begin cutting, therefore, make sure that each fabric thread that is going to be cut has a satin stitch at either end, and that there is one extra satin stitch beyond the top and bottom of the fabric threads that are to be cut. Cut and remove one pair of threads at a time. You are then less likely to make an error.

Remember: you can only cut the fabric threads along the sides of the satin stitch block where the stitches pass through the fabric; not along the sides where the stitches lie across the fabric.

1 Make a satin stitch block at each end of the threads to be cut. Check that they are in line by running a needle along the fabric from one end to the other, without crossing a horizontal thread.

2 Loosen the fabric in the frame a little, and place the lower blade of your scissors into the same hole as the last satin stitch in the right-hand block. Make sure there are two fabric threads on the blade, and manoeuvre the scissors as close as possible to the stitches.

3 Angle the cutting edge towards the satin stitches, and cut. Repeat for all the threads in the block, cutting two threads at a time.

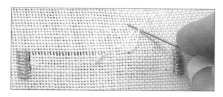

4 Rotate the fabric and cut the other ends of the fabric threads in the same way. Start to remove the cut threads using the tip of a tapestry needle, taking care not to damage the fabric.

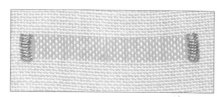

5 Continue removing all the cut threads between the two satin stitch blocks.

To hide the ends of the cut threads, take the fabric out of the frame, slide a needle under the satin stitch block and gently push the stitches towards the gap.

Stitches

Drawn thread techniques

In drawn thread work, the fabric threads are cut and withdrawn, leaving open areas in the fabric. If only the horizontal (weft) threads are cut and withdrawn, this leaves the vertical (warp) threads loose. There are various techniques for drawing the loose fabric threads into groups to produce a decorative border. When working a square design, both horizontal and vertical threads are cut and withdrawn.

Beginning a thread

Use a waste-knot to hold the thread in place while you are sewing, cutting and removing it once the stitching is complete. Make a small knot in the end of the thread, and place a single small stitch approximately 8cm (3in) from the start of your stitching. Bring the needle through to the front of the fabric to begin sewing.

To secure a working thread at the side of a block of drawn threads, make sure the waste-knot is placed level with the point at which you wish to start stitching, and about 8cm (3in) from it. As you take the working thread across the back of your work, keep it parallel with the horizontal fabric threads. Attach it carefully to a few vertical threads, at points where they cross the horizontal thread. Make sure the working thread remains invisible on the right side of the fabric. Remember that where there is a satin stitch block either side of the drawn thread area, the satin stitch blocks can be used to secure the working thread.

Another way of beginning a stitch is to use the loop method. Take a single thread, fold it in half, and thread the two ends through a needle. Make a stitch in the fabric, passing the needle through the loop on the back. This method should not be used with overdyed threads.

TIP

Always start at the bottom right-hand corner of the drawn threads and work left, unless stated otherwise.

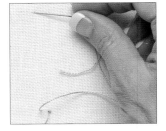

Beginning a stitch with a waste-knot.

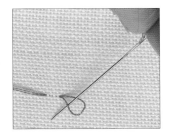

Beginning a stitch with a loop.

Ending a thread

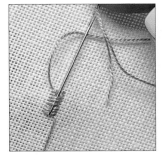

1 Take the working thread through to the back of the fabric, and pass it underneath three or four stitches.

2 Pull the thread through and pass it back under the stitches in the opposite direction.

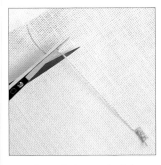

3 Cut off the end of the thread, then cut off and remove the waste-knot.

4 Weave the tail thread through the back of the embroidery and trim it off.

Hem stitch over two threads

Hem stitch has been used for centuries as a decorative hem for needlework items such as table linens, bed linens and clothing, and is featured in samplers. This simple form of hem stitch is used to gather threads into groups of two.

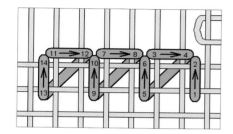

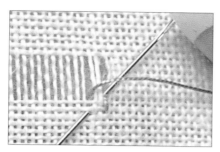

1 Come up through the fabric at 1 and go down at 2. Take the needle behind the first two vertical fabric threads and bring it up at 3, then take it back down at 4 (through the same space as 2). Bring the needle up at 5.

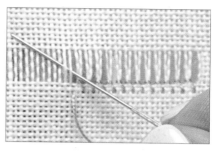

2 Pull the thread firmly to create a small backstitch that draws the two vertical fabric threads together. Continue in the same way along the row.

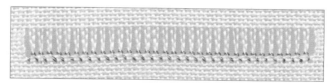

The completed stitch.

Hem stitch over four threads

This is worked in the same way as the previous stitch, but this time the fabric threads are gathered together in groups of four.

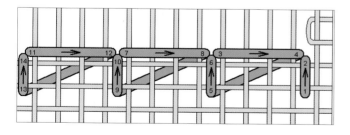

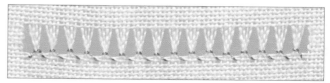

The completed stitch.

Ladder stitch

This stitch comprises two rows of hem stitch worked along the upper and lower edges of a block of drawn threads. The two rows correspond exactly so that the threads are gathered into vertical bars that resemble a ladder, which gives the stitch its name. It can be used as a decorative border, and is also the foundation stitch for a number of other stitches featured in this chapter.

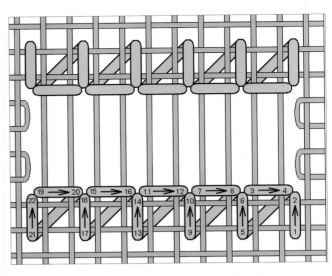

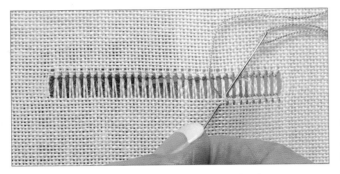

1. Work hem stitch over two vertical threads along one edge of the drawn threads, then turn the fabric through 180° and work the second row.

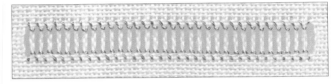

The completed ladder stitch.

Zigzag hem stitch

This stitch is also known as serpentine hem stitch or trellis hem stitch. In zigzag hem stitch, the groups of threads in the upper and lower rows do not correspond.

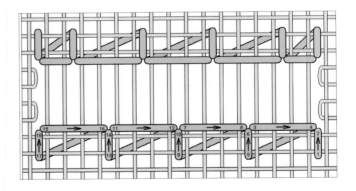

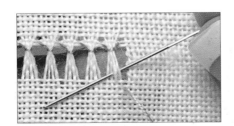

1. Work one row in hem stitch over four threads (see page 201). Turn the fabric through 180° and start the second row by working the first stitch over two threads.

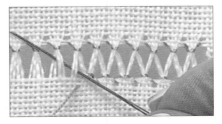

2. Work the remaining stitches in hem stitch over four threads. By gathering two vertical threads from one group and two from the next, you will produce a zigzag pattern. You will complete the row with a group of two vertical threads.

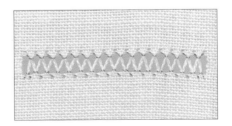

The completed stitch.

Interlaced hem stitch

This is a decorative variation of ladder stitch. Begin by following the instructions for ladder stitch on page 202.

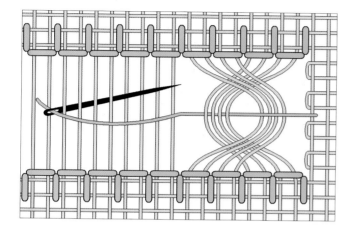

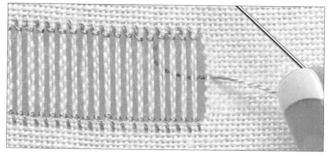

1 Work ladder stitch along the upper and lower edges of the block of drawn threads. Beginning at the right-hand side, anchor the working thread in the centre of the margin.

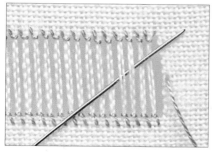

2 Count four groups of fabric threads (eight threads in total), and take the needle down after the eighth thread, then back up between the fourth and the fifth.

3 Twist the point of the needle round to the left and take it back down to the right of the first vertical thread. The group of threads will flip over each other.

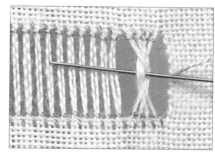

4 Continue twisting the needle to the left and bring it back up just before the ninth vertical thread.

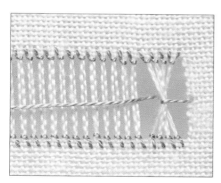

5 Pull the working thread firmly so the threads stay in position.

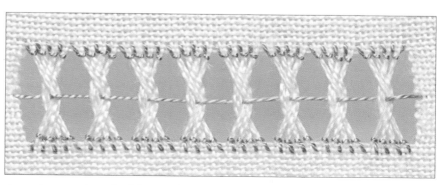

A complete row of interlaced hem stitch. At the end of the row, secure the thread at the left-hand margin.

Interlaced hem stitch with beads

This is a variation of interlaced hem stitch. First, the ladder stitch along the upper and lower edges is omitted, so the threads are not drawn into groups before interlacing, and secondly, a bead is placed between each group of interlaced threads.

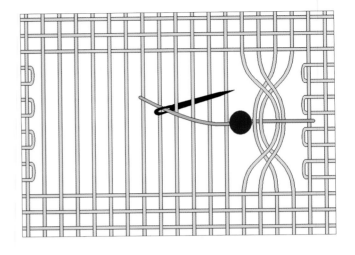

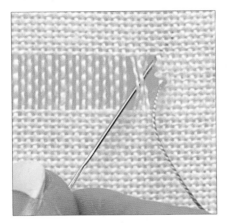

1 Anchor the working thread in the centre of the right-hand margin. Count four vertical threads along, and take the needle down after the fourth thread, then back up between the second and third.

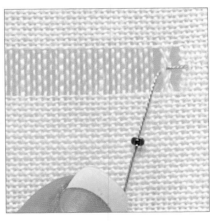

2 Twist the needle to the left as you did on page 203 steps 3 and 4, pull the working thread firmly to hold the vertical threads in place, and add a bead.

3 Push the bead down so it lies after the first stitch, and form the second stitch in the same way.

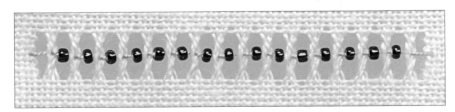

A complete row of interlaced hem stitch with beads. At the end of the row, secure the thread at the left-hand margin.

Diamond hem stitch

This stitch is worked over four horizontal fabric threads, between two bands of drawn threads. Begin by working hem stitch over two threads along the upper edge of the top band, and the lower edge of the bottom band.

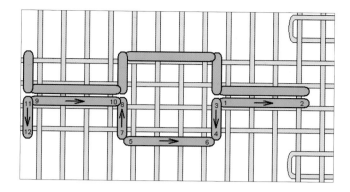

1 Begin by counting four threads in from the right-hand margin, bring the needle up at 1, down at 2, then back up at 3 (through the same hole as 1).

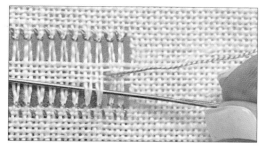

2 Pull the thread tight, and pass the needle down at 4 and back up at 5, behind four vertical threads.

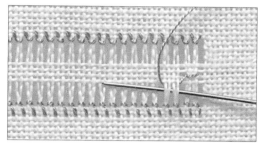

3 Take the working thread over the four vertical threads, pass the needle back through the fabric at 6 (the same space as 4), and back up at 7 (the same space as 5).

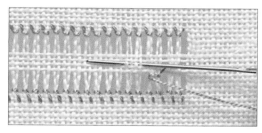

4 Draw the four vertical threads into a bundle and begin the next stitch by taking the needle down at 8 and up four threads along at 9.

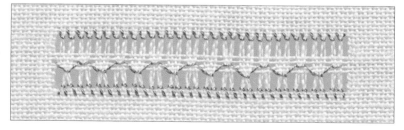

5 Complete the first row of diamond hem stitch.

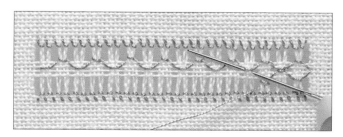

6 Turn the fabric through 180° and start the second row. Work the stitches as a mirror image of those in the first row; work the vertical stitches into the same holes as those of the first row.

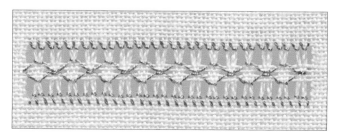

The completed diamond hem stitch.

Herringbone stitch

Herringbone stitch is also known as Russian cross or plaited stitch. It is a common feature of samplers and has many variations. Here, the stitch is used over four horizontal fabric threads between two bands of drawn threads. When working this stitch, the reverse of the fabric resembles two rows of running stitch. These stitches pull the vertical fabric threads into groups to form the pattern. Unlike the previous stitches in this section, this one is worked left to right. Begin by working hem stitch over two threads along the upper edge of the top band, and the lower edge of the bottom band of drawn threads.

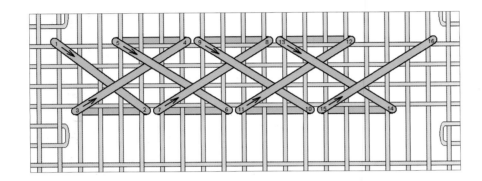

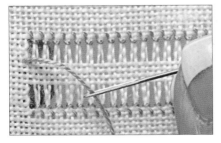

1 Starting in the top left-hand corner, bring the needle up just to the left of the first uncut vertical thread, and just below the first reweaved horizontal thread.

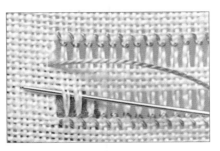

2 Take the thread diagonally across the vertical fabric threads, then pass the needle down at 2, take it behind four fabric threads and bring it up at 3.

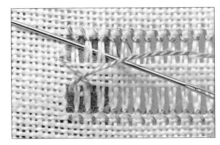

3 Gather the four threads into a bundle. Take the thread diagonally across six vertical threads, and pass the needle down at 4 and bring it up at 5.

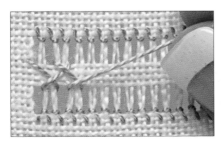

4 Gather the four threads together, and continue working in the same pattern along the row.

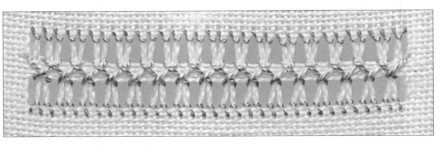

The completed herringbone stitch.

Coral knot stitch

Coral knots are used to gather groups of loose fabric threads into secondary groups, known as clusters. Begin by using a four-sided stitch (see page 216) to gather the vertical threads into groups of four. Alternatively, use ladder stitch over four threads. The first coral knot is worked over two threads and the remainder over four, two from each adjacent group, creating a diamond pattern.

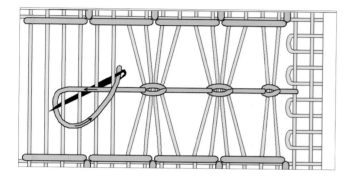

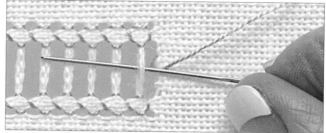

1 Anchor the working thread in the centre of the right-hand margin. Pass the needle behind the first two vertical threads.

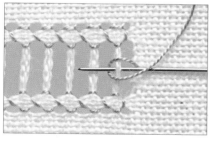

2 Loop the working thread around the needle.

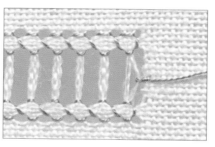

3 Pull the thread into a knot.

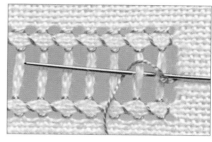

4 Work the next knot over four threads, two from the first group and two from the next.

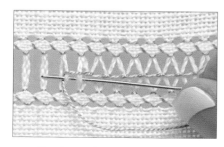

5 Continue along the row, keeping the working thread taut and gathering the threads into clusters of four. End with two threads.

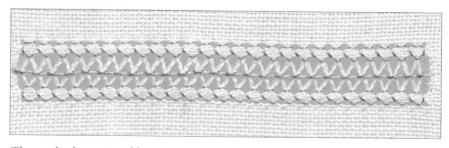

The completed row of coral knots.

Modified coral knot clusters

In this version of coral knots, ladder stitch is first worked over two threads, then coral knots are used to gather the threads into clusters. Further coral knots are then used to create a more detailed pattern.

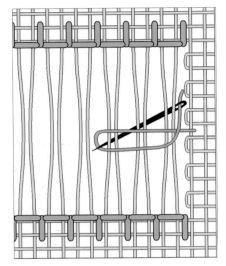

Starting modified coral knot clusters.

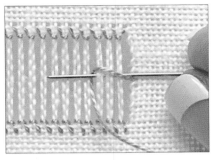

1 Anchor the working thread in the centre of the right-hand margin, pass the needle behind six vertical threads (three groups of threads) and loop the working thread under the tip of the needle.

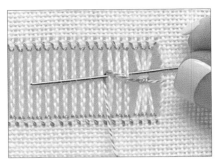

2 Pull the working thread with a medium tension, and work the next coral knot in the same way.

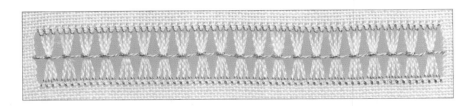

3 Continue gathering the groups of threads into clusters of three as you work along the row. Secure the thread to finish. This row is referred to as the horizontal thread.

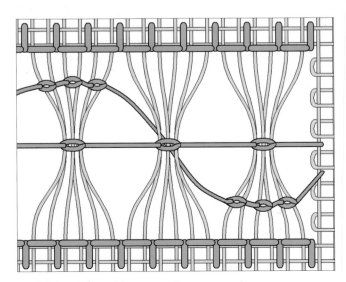

Modified coral knot clusters, second stage.

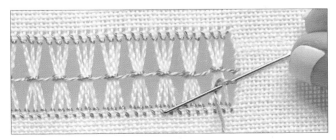

4 Start the second stage of modified coral knot stitch using a new thread. Secure it two holes below the centre of the right-hand margin. Form a coral knot over the first two vertical threads, about halfway down.

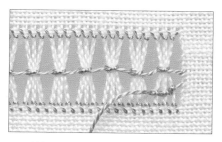

5 Work two further coral knots over the remaining two pairs of threads in the first cluster.

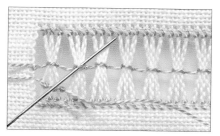

6 Take the thread through to the back of the fabric and pass the needle up through the back of the second coral knot in the horizontal thread.

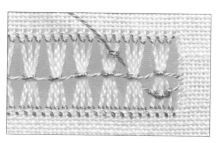

7 Bring the needle back through to the front of your work and form a coral knot over the first pair of threads in the third cluster.

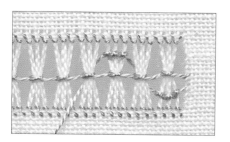

8 Make coral knots over the remaining two pairs of threads in the cluster, and pass the thread through the back of the fourth coral knot in the horizontal thread.

9 Continue working in the same pattern to the end of the row. Secure the thread to finish.

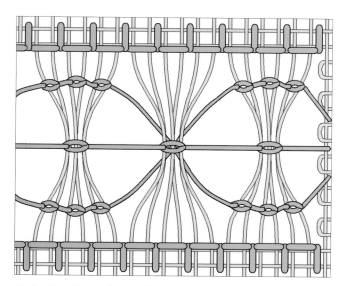

Modified coral knot clusters, third stage.

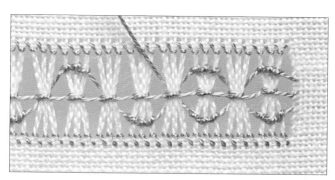

10 Start the third stage of modified coral knot stitch using a new thread. Secure it two holes above the centre of the right-hand margin and work the row as a mirror image of the previous one.

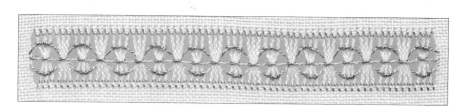

The completed modified coral knot clusters.

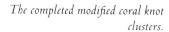

Woven wheels

To work this stitch, both the horizontal and vertical threads are cut and reweaved to create an open space. Start with interlaced hem stitch worked across the vertical and horizontal blocks of drawn threads.

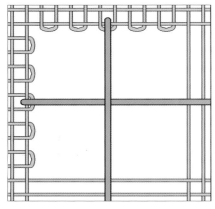

Starting a woven wheel.

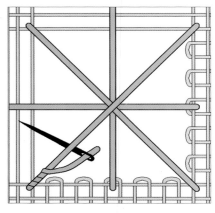

Overcasting the diagonals.

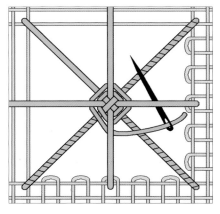

Beginning to weave the woven wheel.

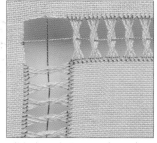

1 Work interlaced hem stitch across the horizontal and vertical blocks of drawn threads, in each case taking the working thread across the open space and securing it on the other side.

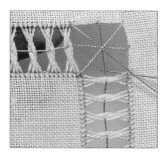

2 Turn the fabric so that the open space is positioned top right, and work a cross stitch so that a double cross is formed over it.

3 Turn the fabric so that the open space is positioned bottom right, and overcast the last diagonal you made by wrapping the working thread around it. Maintain tension on the wrapping thread using your other hand.

4 Using the same working thread, overcast the other diagonal leg to the centre only.

5 Start weaving the thread over and under the 'spokes' of the wheel. Work from the centre of the wheel outwards in an anticlockwise direction to form a circular pattern.

6 When the woven wheel is the desired size, finish by overcasting the second half of the diagonal stitch. Take the thread to the back of the fabric when you have finished, and secure it.

Embroidery stitches

Embroidery can be used to enhance any piece of drawn thread work by allowing you to add colour and texture to your design. Here is a selection of basic counted thread embroidery stitches. Many of these stitches feature in needlepoint, and as they have evolved over the years in different countries, they have been given different names. The ones demonstrated here are only a small selection of all those in existence, but with these you can produce endless varieties of patterns and designs in all different colours and using various types of thread. No embroidery stitches other than those shown here are used in the projects.

Backstitch

Backstitching is also known as point de sable. It is used to add detail, or to outline a design. Backstitches are short, even stitches that can be worked horizontally, vertically or diagonally. Rows are worked left to right, though individual stitches are worked right to left over two fabric threads. In the following demonstration, a single strand of six-stranded cotton has been used.

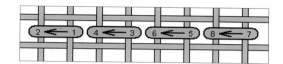

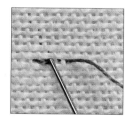

1 Make the first stitch, working right to left (1–2). Bring the needle back up at 3, two holes to the right of the first stitch, and form the second stitch by taking the needle down at 4, through the same hole as 1.

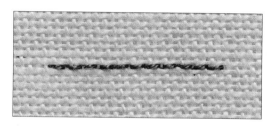

2 Continue working the rest of the row.

Running stitch

In this chapter, running stitch is used for basting the four sides of the design, and for stitching a vertical line down the centre of the fabric. Basting over and under two threads also helps with counting. Use a single strand of six-stranded cotton.

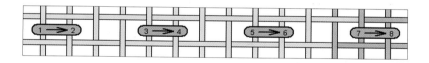

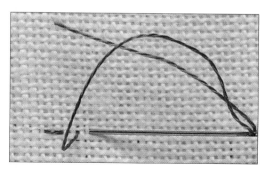

1 Take the thread over and under two fabric threads at a time to form a row of running stitch.

A row of running stitch.

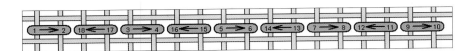

Double running stitch

Double running stitch is also known as Holbein stitch, and was commonly featured on blackwork samplers. On the front of the work it looks the same as backstitch, but on the back it looks very different; double running stitch is identical on both sides of the fabric, and therefore gives a much neater finish on the back of your work than backstitch.

Begin by working running stitch from left to right, then complete the stitch by working in the opposite direction and filling in the gaps.

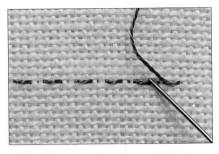

1 Work a row of running stitch, then begin to work back in the opposite direction, placing stitches in between those in the first row.

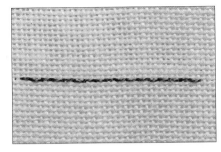

2 Continue working to the end of the row.

Cross stitch

Cross stitch is one of the oldest and most commonly used stitches. There are two possible sequences for stitching cross stitch. The first, which is recommended when using overdyed threads, is to complete each individual cross stitch before moving on to the next, working left to right. Here, two strands of six-stranded variegated cotton have been used.

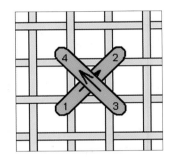

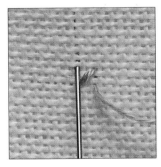

1 Work the first leg of the cross from bottom left to top right, then work the second leg over it from bottom right to top left.

2 To start the second stitch, bring the needle up at 3, through the same hole as the first stitch, and take the thread diagonally across to form the first leg of stitch two.

3 Continue the row, completing each cross stitch before moving on to the next. Notice the gradual change in colour as you progress along the row.

TIP ||||||||||||||||||||||||||||||||

For a more delicate look, cross stitch can also be worked over one thread.

An alternative method of working cross stitch is to stitch a row of half crosses, and then to complete them when working back again in the opposite direction. This method is not suitable when working with overdyed threads.

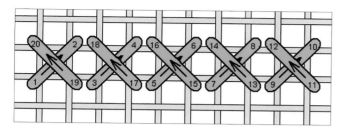

Cross stitch, working half cross stitches in one direction, and completing them in the opposite direction.

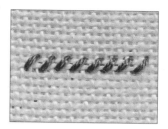

1 Working left to right, complete the first row of stitches. Work only one diagonal of each stitch, from bottom left to top right.

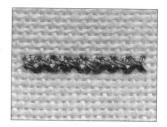

2 Work back along the row, from right to left, completing each cross stitch with the bottom right to top left diagonal.

Three-quarter cross stitch

There are four different ways of working this form of cross stitch, which can be used to add finer detail to a design.

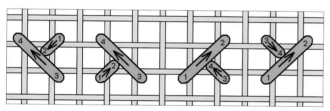

Four variations on three-quarter cross stitch.

Four completed three-quarter cross stitches, showing the different variations.

Smyrna cross

This stitch is also known as a double cross. It consists of a cross stitch with an upright cross stitch worked over the top, over either two threads or four. Being slightly raised, the stitch gives extra dimension and texture to your work. For added interest, it can be worked in two colours – one for the base cross and a second for the upright cross.

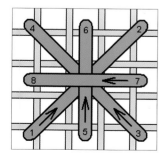

Large Smyrna cross, worked over four threads. A smaller version can be achieved by working over two threads.

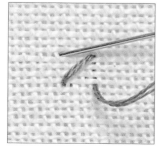

1 Work the first stitch diagonally over four threads (1–2), then work the second stitch (3–4).

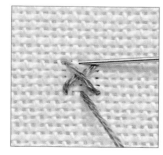

2 Work the vertical leg of the upright cross from bottom to top.

3 Complete the Smyrna cross with the horizontal leg worked right to left.

Double herringbone stitch

This stitch consists of two rows of basic herringbone stitch interlaced together. It is very effective when worked in two colours – stitch the darker colour first, and then add the second row in the lighter colour.

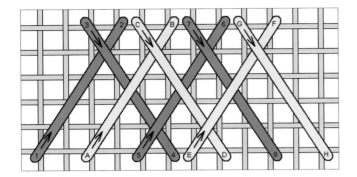

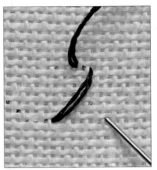

1 Work the first stitch from 1 to 2, taking the thread diagonally across four vertical and six horizontal fabric threads. Work the second stitch in the opposite direction, from 3 to 4, to create an inverted V shape.

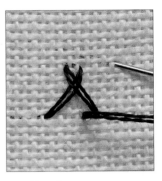

2 Keeping an even tension, bring the working thread back through the fabric two holes to the left at 5, and take the needle down at 6 to form the next stitch.

3 Complete the first row of herringbone stitch.

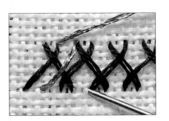

4 Change to a different coloured thread, and work the second row, placing the stitches in between those in the first row, and sharing the same fabric holes.

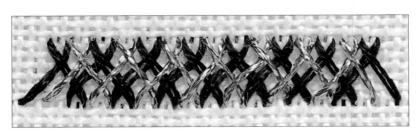

The completed double herringbone stitch.

Alternating Scotch stitch

This stitch, also known as diagonal satin stitch, flat stitch or cushion stitch, consists of solid blocks of embroidery. Each block comprises seven stitches worked over four fabric threads, all in the same diagonal direction. The second block in a row is a mirror image of the first and shares the same holes in the fabric; there are no gaps between the blocks. Rows are worked from left to right, alternating the blocks. For this demonstration, two strands of six-stranded embroidery cotton have been used.

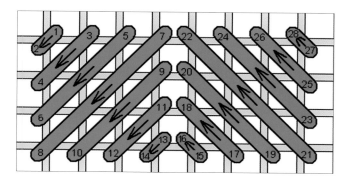

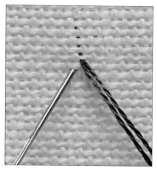

1 Bring the needle up through the fabric at 1, and take it back down the next hole along on the diagonal at 2.

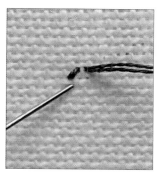

2 Pull the thread through to make the first stitch. Make the second stitch in the same way, bringing the needle up through the fabric one hole along to the right at 3, and back down one hole lower at 4.

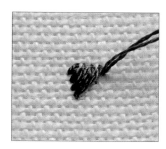

3 Make a further two stitches, moving one hole across and down each time.

4 Work the other side of the block with a further three stitches (9–14). Bring the thread up through the fabric two holes along to the right, ready to start off the second block of alternating Scotch stitch.

5 Work the second block as a mirror image of the first, taking the needle down through the same holes as the first block.

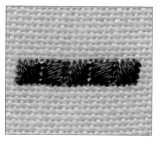

6 Continue along the row, alternating the blocks.

Four-sided stitch

This stitch is also known as square openwork. It can be worked with a normal tension or as a pulled thread stitch. When working this stitch as a pulled thread stitch, you will need to pull each leg as the needle comes up through the fabric to obtain a lacy effect; the tighter you pull the thread, the lacier the final effect will be. A cotton perle is used here, as the thread needs to be pulled quite taut.

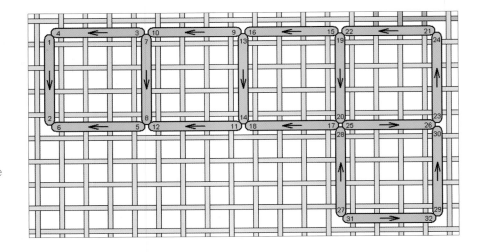

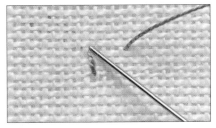

1 Work the first stitch (1–2) over four horizontal threads, pulling the stitch tight. Take the thread diagonally across the back of the fabric and bring it up at 3, then take the needle down at 4, through the same hole as 1.

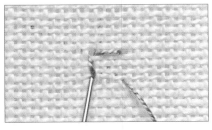

2 Tighten the thread, take the thread diagonally across the back of the fabric and bring it up at 5, then take the needle down at 6, through the same hole as 2.

3 Pull the thread tight, and complete the fourth side of the square (7–8). This forms the first side of the next square. Continue working along the row.

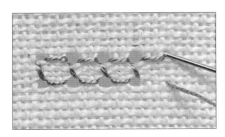

4 To turn a corner, you need to work the side of the square that will be joined to the next square last. In this case, make the stitch at the top of the square, then work the right-hand vertical stitch from bottom to top.

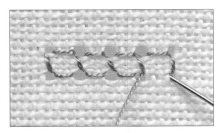

5 Take the thread across to the bottom left-hand corner, and work the stitch at the bottom of the square from left to right.

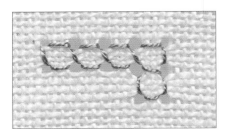

6 Form the next square below the last one following the order of the stitches shown in the diagram (27–32).

Three-sided stitch

This stitch is also known as Turkish lace. It is a triangular pulled stitch, worked from right to left. Each leg is worked twice, and the threads need to be pulled firmly to obtain the pattern. A cotton perle is used here.

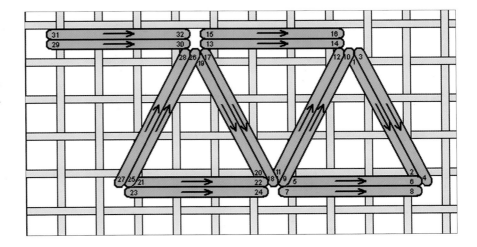

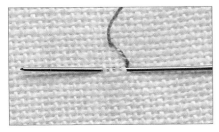

1 Begin with the right-hand side of the first triangle. Work two stitches from top to bottom (1–2 and 3–4), passing the second stitch through the same holes as the first. Tighten the thread, and bring the needle up four vertical threads to the left.

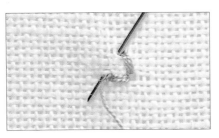

2 Work the two stitches at the base of the triangle, pulling the thread taut each time, and position the needle at the start of the next stitch.

3 Work this stitch twice, bringing the needle back through to the front of the fabric four vertical threads to the left, ready to start off the next triangle (13).

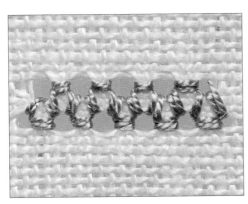

4 Continue along the row.

Satin stitch

Satin stitch is a block of straight stitches worked closely together to make a solid filling with a smooth texture. The length of each stitch, and the direction of the stitches, can vary, and the stitches can be worked horizontally, vertically or diagonally to create the desired shape. Try to keep the stitches smooth and do not let the threads twist; using a laying tool might help you keep an even tension (see page 196).

Below is a basic satin stitch, with diagrams showing some variations. Start at the dot and work each stitch in the direction of the arrow.

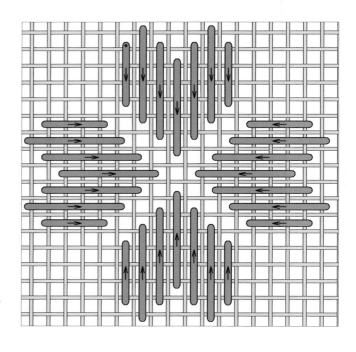

Large satin stitch flower. A smaller version can be made by reducing the number of threads over which you work each stitch.

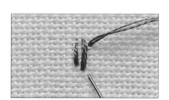

1 Sew each petal using straight stitches worked from top to bottom, following the diagram.

A completed petal.

TIP |||||||||||

Railroading = passing the needle between two threads keeps the threads parallel.

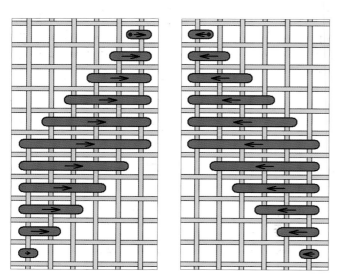

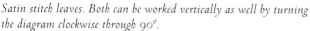

Satin stitch leaves. Both can be worked vertically as well by turning the diagram clockwise through 90°.

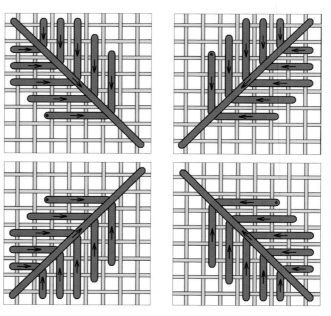

Modified satin stitch leaves. In each case, work the long diagonal stitch last.

Satin stitch blocks

These are used as security stitches worked over four fabric threads at either end of a block of drawn threads (see page 199). They wrap around the fabric threads so that they can be safely cut. The stitches are worked side by side, and all in the same direction, using either cotton perle 5 with 25 count fabric, or cotton perle 8 with 28 count fabric. You need to begin stitching with enough cotton to complete the whole block; never begin a new thread within a block of stitches.

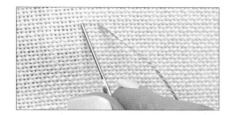

1 Bring the needle up through the fabric and pass the thread over four vertical fabric threads.

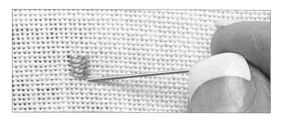

2 Pull the thread through and work the subsequent stitches in the same way, each time moving down by one fabric thread.

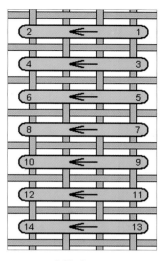

Satin stitch block.

Modified satin stitch blocks are also security stitches, consisting of four blocks of satin stitches that share fabric holes where they meet in the centre.

Right-angle satin stitch blocks are two rows of security stitches going horizontally and vertically over the fabric to form a right-angled shape.

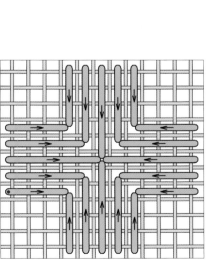

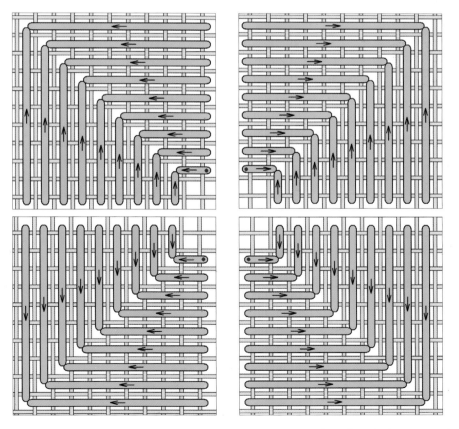

Modified satin stitch block. Start stitching at the dot and work each stitch in the direction of the arrow.

Right-angle satin stitch block. Start stitching at the dot and work each stitch in the direction of the arrow.

Rose Bud Trellis

This project can be stitched in two colourways using gorgeous metallic threads and beads mixed with traditional cotton perle and stranded cotton threads. The design features drawn thread work with counted thread embroidery stitches to create this unique sampler.

The fabric threads are not cut and reweaved in this project; instead satin stitch blocks are used as the security stitches, and the fabric threads cut and removed.

The embroidery is stitched on cream 28 count linen and measures 98 stitches horizontally and 129 stitches vertically. The finished size is 17.8 x 22.9cm (7 x 9in). Cut the linen to 33 x 38cm (13 x 15in) for framing.

Cross stitch is worked with two strands of thread unless otherwise stated; backstitch is worked with one strand of thread. Each square on the chart represents two threads of fabric.

You will need

- Cream 28 count linen
- Gold fine braid no. 8
- Shell pink stranded cotton
- Green stranded cotton
- Cream cotton perle no. 8
- Cream cotton perle no. 12
- Gold petite beads
- Cream seed beads
- Stranded cotton for sewing on the beads

Colour is an important aspect of any design. The richness of this embroidery is enhanced by the use of both gold threads and gold beads.

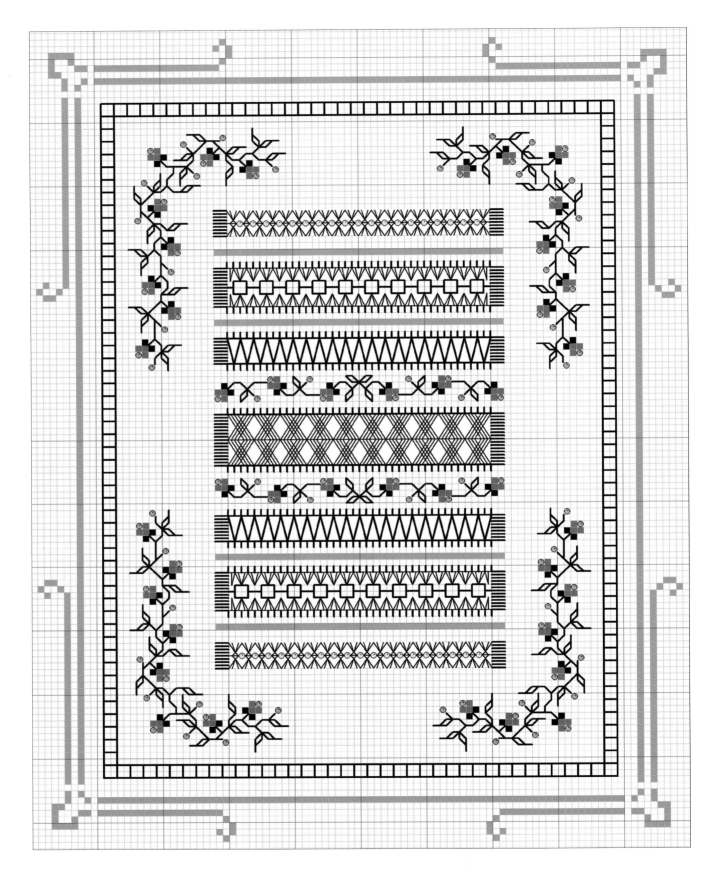

Border

1 Cross stitch the gold border (see page 212) as indicated on the chart using gold fine braid no. 8.

2 Work the four-sided stitch border (see page 216) with one strand of cotton perle no. 12.

3 Backstitch (see page 211) the stems and leaves with one strand of stranded cotton. Work the flowers using shell pink and green thread in cross stitch.

4 Attach the gold petite beads as indicated on the chart (see page 224).

Band 1

Work interlaced hem stitch with beads (see page 204) over eight horizontal threads. For clarity, these horizontal threads are now numbered 1 to 8 from top to bottom.

1 Work two blocks of satin stitches (see page 219) with one strand of cream cotton perle no. 8. These each consist of nine satin stitches covering eight fabric threads, as indicated on the chart. Double check that there are eighty vertical threads and eight horizontal threads between the two satin stitch blocks before you cut the fabric threads. Cut and remove the eight horizontal threads (see page 199).

2 Work interlaced hem stitch with beads (see page 204) with one strand of cream cotton perle no. 12, placing a cream seed bead between each group of four threads.

Band 2

Cross stitch (see page 212) using gold fine braid no. 8 as indicated on the chart.

Band 3

This band is stitched in diamond hem stitch (see page 205) over sixteen horizontal threads. For clarity, these horizontal threads are now numbered 1 to 16 from top to bottom.

1 Work two satin stitch blocks (see page 219) with one strand of cream cotton perle no. 8. These each consist of thirteen satin stitches covering twelve fabric threads, as indicated on the chart. Double check that between these two satin stitch blocks there are eighty vertical threads and twelve horizontal threads before you cut any fabric threads. Cut the first four horizontal threads (threads 3–6) on the right-hand side first. Leave threads 7, 8, 9 and 10 uncut. Cut the next four horizontal threads (threads 11–14). Turn the fabric 180° to complete the left-hand side to match. Carefully remove the loose fabric threads.

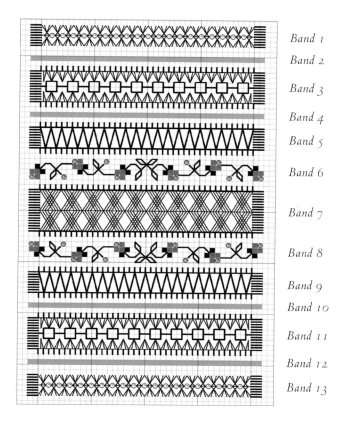

Band 1
Band 2
Band 3
Band 4
Band 5
Band 6
Band 7
Band 8
Band 9
Band 10
Band 11
Band 12
Band 13

2 Work hem stitching over threads 15 and 16 (see page 201) with one strand of cream cotton perle no. 12. Turn the fabric 180° and work a second row over threads 1 and 2.

3 The centre four uncut threads (7–10) are completed by stitching diamond hem stitch (see page 205) with one strand of cream cotton perle no. 12. Begin the diamond hem stitch at the right-hand side. Note that the first and last stitches in this band are modified and stitched over two threads not four, as shown in the stitch diagram. Work along the row to the left-hand side and finish the thread into the satin stitches.

4 Turn the fabric 180° to work the second row. The stitches are a mirror image of the first row.

Band 4

As for Band 2.

Band 5

This band is zigzag hem stitch (see page 202) worked over twelve horizontal threads. For clarity, these horizontal threads are now numbered 1 to 12, from top to bottom.

1 Work two blocks of satin stitches (see page 219) with one strand of cream cotton perle no. 8. These each consist of nine satin stitches covering eight fabric threads, as indicated on the chart. Double check that there are eighty vertical threads and eight horizontal threads between the two satin stitch blocks before you cut the fabric threads. Cut and remove the eight horizontal threads.

2 Work zigzag hem stitch (see page 202) over threads 11 and 12 with one strand of cream cotton perle no. 12. Turn the fabric 180° and work the second row over threads 1 and 2.

Band 6

Cross stitch the flowers (see page 212) as indicated on the chart using shell pink and green stranded cotton. Backstitch the stems and leaves (see page 211) with one strand of green stranded cotton. Attach gold petite beads (see below) as indicated on the chart.

Band 7

This band is worked in interlaced hem stitch (see page 204) over twenty horizontal threads. For clarity, these horizontal threads are now numbered 1 to 20, from top to bottom.

1 Work two satin stitch blocks (see page 219) with one strand of cream cotton perle no. 8. These each consist of seventeen satin stitches covering sixteen fabric threads, as indicated on the chart. Double check that between these two satin stitch blocks there are eighty vertical threads and sixteen horizontal threads before you cut the fabric. Cut and carefully remove the threads.

2 Work hem stitch over threads 19 and 20 (see page 201) with one strand of cream cotton perle no. 12. Turn the fabric 180° and work a second row over threads 1 and 2.

3 Work interlaced hem stitch (see page 204) with one strand of cream cotton perle no. 8.

Band 8

As for Band 6.

Band 9

As for Band 5.

Band 10

As for Band 2.

Band 11

As for Band 3.

Band 12

As for Band 2.

Band 13

As for Band 1.

Beadwork

Beads and treasures can add extra texture, detail and sparkle to a design. Attach them with a single strand of floss that matches the colour of the fabric, though if you are using transparent beads their colour may change depending on the colour of the thread used.

Beading needles have a very sharp point and a small eye, which can make them difficult to thread. A no. 26 tapestry needle is small enough for sewing on seed beads, but if you are using petite beads you will have to use a beading needle.

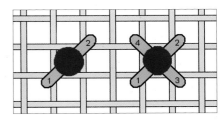

Beads attached using a half cross stitch and a full cross stitch (see page 212).

1 Bring the needle up through the fabric (1), pick up a bead and push it to the end of the thread, then take the needle back down on the diagonal, at 2.

2 Tighten the thread.

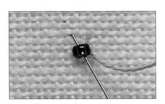

3 For a full cross stitch, work a second stitch across the other diagonal (3–4).

4 Pull the thread tight.

To stitch this design in the second colourway, use pink fine braid no. 8 instead of gold; antique mauve stranded cotton instead of shell pink and dark green stranded cotton instead of green; and use pink cotton perle nos 8 and 12 instead of cream. Replace the gold petite beads with pink petite beads, and the cream seed beads with pale pink seed beads. For sewing on the beads use pink stranded cotton. The fabric used is lavender mist 28 count linen.

Flower Garland

This design is worked in silk threads, which are gorgeous to work with. It can be framed, stitched into a decorative cushion, or used to decorate a box top. For this project, the blue and green colourway is used as a box top and the pink and green variation (see page 229) has been stitched into a cushion.

The embroidery is stitched on antique white 25 count Dublin linen and measures 88 stitches horizontally by 88 stitches vertically. The finished size is 17.9 x 17.9cm (7 x 7in), and the linen should be cut to 33 x 33cm (13 x 13in) for framing.

All the stitches are worked with one strand of thread. Work the cross-stitched borders after the cutting and reweaving of the fabric threads has been completed; add the treasures once the sampler is finished. Each square on the chart represents two threads of fabric.

You will need

- Antique white 25 count linen
- Gold fine braid no. 8
- Cream cotton perle no. 5
- Cream cotton perle no. 8
- Cream cotton perle no. 12
- Stranded cotton for attaching the treasures
- Blue Silk Serica
- Dark green Silk Serica
- Two packets of blue crystal treasures

Purpose-made boxes with an aperture lid in which to mount your embroidery are widely available in a range of shapes and sizes. The one used for this project measures 22.5cm (9in) square with an 18cm (7in) square aperture. It comes with a piece of card on which to mount your embroidery. Add a layer of wadding or interlining and then a piece of lining fabric on top of the card to give the embroidery a soft and slightly raised finish. Place this backing underneath the embroidery and pin it in place. Make sure you centre the design on the backing and that the sides of the embroidery and the backing fabric are turned in neatly, particularly the corners. Stitch the backing fabric in place using a matching silk or cotton thread.

The centre square

Begin stitching at the centre of the design. Work the four sets of modified satin stitch blocks (see page 219) with one strand of cream cotton perle no. 5. Before you start to cut the fabric threads, double check that there are sixteen threads between the modified satin stitch blocks both vertically and horizontally. Cut and remove the four vertical threads between the top and bottom modified satin stitch blocks. Cut and remove the four horizontal threads between the right and left modified satin stitch blocks. Work ladder stitch (see page 202) with one strand of cream cotton perle no. 12. The centre square is now completed.

The flower garland

Work the satin stitch leaves (see page 218) and backstitch the stems (see page 211) with one strand of green Silk Serica. Work the satin stitch flowers, including the centre flower (see page 218), with one strand of blue Silk Serica.

Four-sided stitch border

Work the four-sided stitch border (see page 216) with one strand of cream cotton perle no. 12.

Outer drawn thread area

1 This area is over twenty threads. With careful counting, begin to cut and reweave the threads. As this is a square design, you will be cutting both horizontal and vertical threads. Once the preparation work is finished, you will have four square holes in between the fabric threads.

2 Work hem stitching (see page 201) with one strand of cream cotton perle no. 12. Work both the outside and inside edge. Work each side individually and do not take the thread across the corners.

3 Work the interlaced hem stitch (see page 203) with one strand of cream cotton perle no. 8. Secure the working threads in the margin. These threads will form a cross in the square holes and become part of the woven corner.

4 Work the woven wheels in each of the four corners (see page 210) with one strand of cream cotton perle no. 8.

Gold borders

Finally, work the gold borders in cross stitch (see page 212) with one strand of gold fine braid no. 8, as indicated on the chart.

To finish

Add the crystal treasures as indicated on the chart with one strand of stranded cotton.

Cushion

To stitch the design for the cushion, use pearl fine braid no. 8 instead of gold; white cotton perle no. 8 instead of cream cotton perle no. 8 and white cotton perle no. 12 instead of cream cotton perle no. 12; pink Silk Serica instead of blue and pale green Silk Serica instead of dark green; and white Silk Serica instead of cream cotton perle no. 5. Replace the blue crystal treasures with pink crystal treasures and replace the centre flower and blue crystal treasure with a pink heart glass treasure. To sew on the treasures, use white stranded cotton.

To make the cushion, you need an inner pad measuring 20.5cm (8in) square and two pieces of satin or silk each measuring 23.5cm (9in) square. This allows 1.5cm (½in) all round for seams. Cut around the embroidery to within 2cm (1in) of the stitching, and gently press the seams under to form a neat square. Pin the embroidery on to one of the pieces of satin or silk, making sure it is centred all the way round. Stitch it in place using a small blind stitch. With the wrong sides together, pin and sew around the outside of the cushion, 1.5cm (½in) in from the edge. Leave a gap in the bottom large enough to push the pad through. Turn the cushion in the right way and insert the pad. Pin and hand stitch the gap at the bottom. Sew a row of beading around the outside of the cushion to cover the seams.

GOLDWORK

Goldwork is a traditional form of embroidery using predominantly gold threads and enhanced by the use of coloured silk threads. Its roots can be traced back to the Opus Anglicanum – the name given to English embroidery during the thirteenth and fourteenth centuries. The work at this time was of a tremendously high standard, much sought after by church officials, and costly because of the use of silver, silver gilt threads and precious stones and pearls. It is thought that the design for a lot of the work of this period was taken from the illuminated manuscripts and was drawn by the artists who worked on them.

The embroidery itself was often referred to as 'acupicture' (painting with a needle) and was carried out by highly trained and skilled professional embroiderers who were employed in workshops in London.

As goldwork has evolved, so too have the materials available. In the early days of ecclesiastical embroidery, silver gilt threads were used frequently: they were easily obtainable but costly. Nowadays there are many and varied gold threads available. Jap gold is the most precious and is glorious to use. It is made in Japan of pure gold leaf bound around a pure silk thread. The threads vary in thickness from very fine to thick, and they are bought in hanks (shown in the picture opposite). Jap gold has a wondrous quality and comes in various gold colours, from pinky gold to a more lustrous gold colour. There are also numerous coloured metallic threads on the market, adding yet another dimension to this richly decorative form of embroidery.

All the basic techniques of goldwork are explained in this chapter, and were used to create the sampler shown opposite. Once mastered, there is nothing to prevent you from using the same methods to design a sampler of your own.

The sampler

Ruth Chamberlin

This sampler is worked on a cream brocade called St Nicholas. Silk of this sort enhances the richness of the piece and gives it lustre.

Materials

As with any new technique, you have first to consider the materials and equipment you need. There are those items you must have, of course, but gold threads and embroidery silks can be bought gradually as your work dictates.

Gold threads

There are many gold threads available nowadays. Jap gold, made in Japan of pure gold leaf bound around a pure silk thread, is the most precious and is wonderful to use. The threads vary in thickness from very fine to thick, and come in various gold colours from pinky gold to a more lustrous gold colour. They are bought in hanks (shown on page 230).

There is an extremely good imitation gold thread on the market which is used extensively. It is called imitation Jap gold. Like Jap gold, it comes in various thicknesses and colours. It is lovely to use, is much less expensive than Jap gold and will never tarnish. Sold on reels, there is a huge variety of imitation gold threads and cords available, some of which are shown opposite. As you progress it is exciting to experiment and see how they can be incorporated into your embroidery to give many different effects and textures. This is where the joy of using these gorgeous threads comes in!

When starting a piece of goldwork embroidery, begin with two imitation Jap threads known at T69 and T70 (one thick and one finer). These threads are easier to manipulate when you are a relative beginner: they do not slip too much and will make a sharp corner when required!

As a general rule, the correct way to use gold thread is to use two threads together. It is therefore important to be able to use the appropriate thickness. If the design is very large and bold, a thicker gold thread is used. If a small and delicate shape is to be either filled or surrounded, a finer thread is required.

When using Jap gold or imitation Jap gold, it is always advisable to handle the gold thread as little as possible (hands can become hot however careful you are!). When using Jap gold, some people prefer to make a roll of felt and then to wind the thread on to it. Others prefer to shake the hank to obtain two threads with which to work, making sure that enough has been undone to enable you to work comfortably. You then lay the hank at the side of your work. When using imitation Jap gold, use two reels and take a thread from each, making sure that the reels are in a safe position on the frame.

Real silver thread will tarnish quickly but there are various aluminium threads on the market. These can look cold when used on their own, but mixing threads can be very exciting and can help the tonal effect enormously. When storing gold and silver threads, line the box with black acid-free tissue paper.

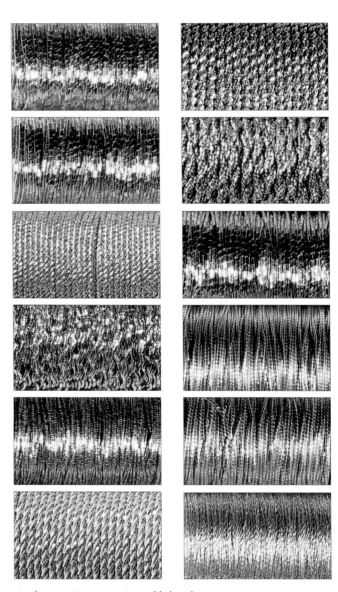

A selection of imitation Jap gold threads.

The other imitation gold threads to mention here are pearl purl, check purl, bright check purl, rough purl, smooth purl, gold coloured twist, rococo thread and gold plate. Some of these are shown opposite. They come in gold, silver, copper and numerous other colours, and some pearl purl is made with a quantity of real gold in it.

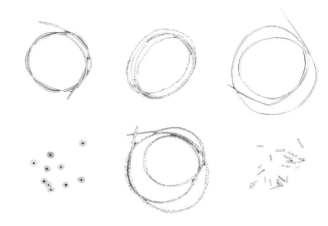

Coloured threads

A silk thread is usually used when couching gold threads down, but if you cannot find the colour needed in a silk thread use a synthetic thread instead: colour is all important to the finished piece! Threads come in varying thicknesses and so it is important to find the right thickness for the work being undertaken.

To embroider the different stitches shown on the sampler, both pure silk floss and twisted embroidery silks have been used. Floss comes in skeins packaged on card. The finished thread is made up of six fine threads and one or two threads are used as required. Pure silk twisted thread is also packaged in skeins. In this case, you might find it helpful to undo the skein and cut it in half (this gives the right length of thread to use in your needle) and then to plait it together loosely, tying each end with a contrasting thread. (It is always advisable to keep the number of the thread used as a reference.) You are then able to pull the appropriate number of threads required for the work being undertaken: always pull your threads from the same end. The range of colours obtainable is magnificent.

These threads can be cut to form beads of different lengths. Pearl purl can be pulled and, when sewn, used as a border. Plate can be sewn on the surface of the fabric, and usually a rough purl or perhaps a bright purl (cut like a bead) sewn at intervals over the top. This method is called Burden stitch.

Silk threads used for couching.

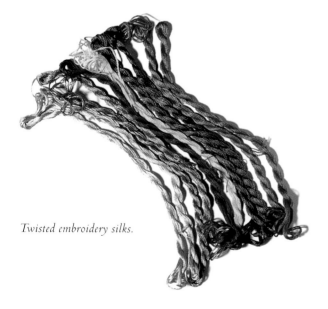

Twisted embroidery silks.

Pure silk floss.

Kid

Kid is made of real leather and comes in different colours: bronze, silver, and a variety of gold colours and textures. Use it sparingly. It comes in varying thicknesses – always choose the thinnest you can sensibly use.

Needles and pins

Use a no. 9 or 8 sharps needle for couching, depending upon the type of thread used, and a no. 10, 9 or 8 sharps needle for the floss work depending upon the level of fineness required. Embroidery needles have a larger eye and can be used if preferred. Nos 14, 16, 18 and 20 chenille needles are used for passing gold threads through the surface of your work. Steel pins which are fine and strong can be used; also pins with coloured heads are useful as they can be seen easily. They also come in differing lengths and strengths. When sewing kid you will need a fine needle, for example a sharps no. 10. (Use a no. 10 embroidery needle if you find a sharps no. 10 too fine to thread.) For lacing your embroidery frame, you will need a tapestry needle or a strong rug needle.

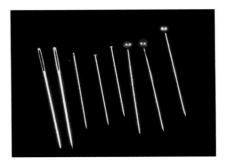

Fabrics

The fabrics that can be used for goldwork are extremely varied. Traditionally, pure silk damask is used with this technique. Some silk damask designs have been woven for many years and are still being woven today. They are all named and are very beautiful to look at and to use. It is important, when placing a design on to a fabric of this sort, that you use the background design to the best advantage: the silk can enhance the embroidery design enormously.

Shown here, from left to right, are a tapestry needle, a chenille needle, a fine sharps needle, two steel pins and three pins with coloured heads.

Linen

When working a very solid piece, you should consider the weight of gold being placed upon the background fabric and choose the appropriate weight of cloth, such as a fine linen or a heavy calico.

A selection of pure silk damasks.

Other items

Various types of linen and calico suitable for supporting goldwork.

Slate frames come in various sizes and are ideal for goldwork because of the weight of the fabrics and threads used (see pages 232–234)

Thimbles Wear two thimbles (as you use both hands when working on your frame), one on each of your middle fingers. This helps your needle slide through the fabric and of course protects your fingers!

Felt, string, soft cotton thread, and firm card are used for padding, as shown on pages 243–244.

Embroidery scissors, goldwork scissors and large scissors for cutting fabrics and threads.

Ruler and tape measure for measuring accurately.

Marker pens and pencils for transferring your designs to your fabric.

Masking tape for attaching your design to the fabric before tracing over it.

Set square or protractor to enable you to set your fabric straight on the grain, and on your frame.

Strong thread for sewing linen on to your frame.

Magnifying glass if needed for detailed work.

PVA glue for finishing off work.

White tissue paper for use when sealing work once it has been finished off.

Stiletto for making holes in linen when making up a frame.

Beeswax for passing silk thread through when working with gold thread – thread slides through the fabric better, stops knotting and gives the thread strength.

String for threading the sides of your frame.

Greaseproof paper and tracing paper are used to transfer your design to the fabric, and for making templates for padding, kid and so on. Greaseproof paper is softer and more malleable than tracing paper and therefore preferable when creating templates from three-dimensional shapes.

Stitches

On the following pages, all of the embroidery and goldwork stitches used on the sampler on page 231 are described. An enlarged section of the sampler is shown opposite. All have been worked into simple shapes on a linen ground, with the occasional small project in the form of a design to consolidate what you have learnt, and to give you the opportunity of applying your knowledge in a more interesting and creative way.

Goldwork is a beautiful art form, and one which requires a certain amount of skill and concentration, but the satisfaction that can be gained from mastering the skills involved and producing designs of your own is enormous. Coloured silks are used to complement and enhance the richness of the gold. Raised embroidery, worked over a padding, is a wonderful way of giving your work a three-dimensional feel and really makes the gold threads shine out. There is therefore a section on padding, and a number of stitches are worked over a raised base.

One of the skills you will learn is how to pass gold threads through the fabric as you work (see pages 240–241). Never pass the threads all together when you have finished the piece in hand, for you will have missed the opportunity to make a beautiful shape with your gold thread. On page 247, for example, there is a leaf worked in satin and laid stitch. You will see clearly that the gold threads have been passed one at a time at the top and bottom of the leaf, and dovetailed. The result is a beautifully shaped leaf with a sharp point.

This attention to detail is essential – always keep the shapes of your stitches neat and consistent and, when working in straight lines, keep your lines evenly spaced and parallel. Take time to practise the techniques and perfect them – they will equip you with everything you need to know to design and produce a piece of work of your own, and to try out the numerous gold and metallic threads, coloured silks and background fabrics that are available.

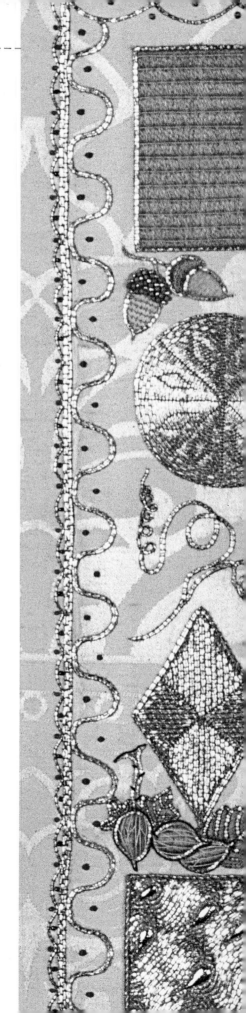

Laid stitch

Laid stitch is a very old form of embroidery. It is used as a filling stitch and considered a far quicker form of embroidery than long and short stitch (see pages 248–249).When filling a shape with a solid area of embroidery, always take the needle to the outer edge of the shape, so that the pencil outline is hidden beneath the embroidery.

Laid stitch is a surface stitch, as its name implies. The first stitch is worked from the top of the required shape to the bottom, and the next stitch from the bottom to the top, with no gap in between. This procedure continues until the shape is filled. Always use a substantial thread for this purpose: a floss is ideal. Work with 46cm (18in) lengths of floss – any longer and the floss becomes worn with use. In the example shown here, two threads are used together so that the linen is well covered.

Having finished this first stage you will see that these long stitches would be completely useless and would catch with the slightest touch, so the tying-down stitch is essential and is worked to complete the whole. This tying-down stitch is worked from the left side of the shape to the right, with the sewing thread travelling under the surface of the linen (see step 2). The silk used for tying down can vary in thickness; here a fine silk thread in a contrasting colour is used.

Begin by drawing out a rectangular shape on the linen. The rectangle should measure 5 x 2.5cm (2 x 1in).

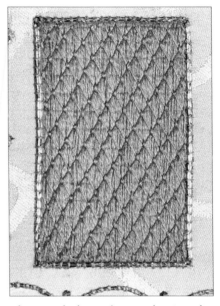

The rectangle shown above is taken from the sampler. It is worked in laid stitch that has been couched down with trellis stitch, and given a gold border.

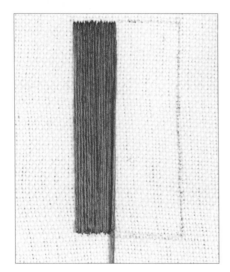

1 Using two threads of silk floss and a no. 8 sharps needle, use a knot and small stitch to secure the threads. Bring your needle up at the top left-hand corner of the rectangle and take it down through the fabric at the bottom left-hand corner, ensuring that the thread lies perfectly parallel to the vertical edge. Bring the needle up as close as possible to the first stitch and continue laying even, close stitches until the shape is filled.

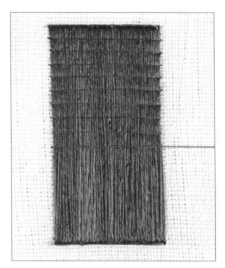

2 Change to a no. 9 sharps needle and a fine silk thread, and lay parallel tying-down stitches going from left to right across the shape, approximately 3mm (⅛in) apart. Lay the first stitch along the top edge of the rectangle, and work down to the bottom edge, with the thread travelling beneath the linen. Note: to achieve a neater finish, lay a silk thread in the same colour as your embroidery along the top and bottom edges.

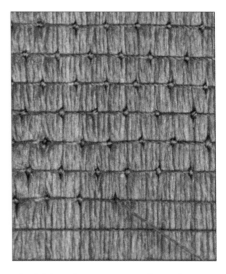

3 Using the same needle and thread, use brick stitch (see pages 250–251) to secure the tying-down threads. Take each stitch just above the tying-down thread and just below it, keeping the stitches as small and as neat as possible. Leave approximately 3mm (⅛in) between stitches. Start at the top left-hand corner of the rectangle and work down to the bottom right.

Bees' Delight

Ruth Chamberlin

This design is based on a patio garden. The laid stitch in the corners has been tied down at intervals to give an impression of garden paving, while the beaded sections are raised to suggest hedges dividing the main areas. In each 'gravel' section there are flowers: convolvulus, antirrhinum, foxgloves and nasturtium, and on each pink section vegetables have been embroidered: peas, beans, a courgette and a marrow. All these have flowers that the bees delight in. The calico behind the skep (the beehive) is painted with watercolour, the bees are embroidered, and the skep itself is worked in brick stitch interspersed with lines of cord.

Couching

Couching is a means of stitching gold threads to a background fabric using a different thread. In this case imitation Jap gold is used to surround the rectangle on page 238 and a pure silk thread for the couching.

Traditionally, gold threads are couched down in pairs as this gives a finished and more substantial look. It will also enable you to pass the two threads at slightly different points at the corner to obtain a good shape. The procedure for turning corners is shown below. Always try to work either one or both of the gold threads from the reel, rather than cutting off lengths as required. This is a more economical method of working, and the threads are less likely to be damaged.

The distance between the couching stitches depends upon the style and texture you wish to achieve in your finished design. It is important always to keep your stitches straight and even, firm but not so tight that they pinch the gold.

Couching stitches are usually worked at right angles to the gold thread, but if you need to place a diagonal stitch when turning a corner, make sure you hold the silk firmly beneath the frame, then keep the gold threads taut while you turn them to form a really sharp bend. (See steps 3 and 4.) Always twist the gold thread slightly as you work to ensure that the core of the thread remains evenly covered. You would do this if you were using real Jap gold as well.

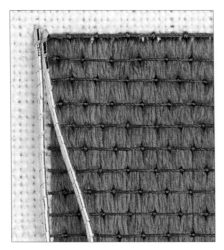 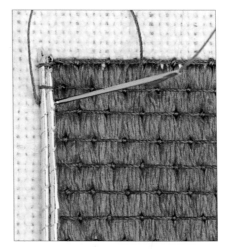 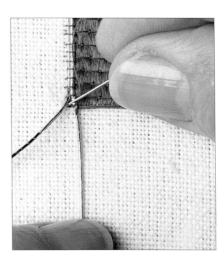

1 Cut a length of gold thread that is long enough to go round the perimeter of the rectangle, plus an additional 1cm (½in). Thread a chenille needle with the gold thread and pass it through the fabric at a point just above the top of the rectangle so that it lies adjacent to the left edge of the shape. Pass a second gold thread through just to the left of the first thread and at a point just above it. Keep this thread on the reel. There is no need to secure the threads at the back of the embroidery, as they will be held in place by the couching.

2 Using contrasting silk thread and a no. 9 sharps needle, couch down the two gold threads. Remember to keep your couching stitches straight and evenly spaced. Hold down the gold threads firmly while you work. Remember to twist them slightly as you work so that the core of the gold does not show.

3 When you reach the first corner, hold the inner gold thread taut and secure it with a small diagonal stitch, worked from right to left.

4 To ensure a sharp corner, turn the inner gold thread tightly back on itself.

5 Lay the inner gold thread along the horizontal edge of the rectangle.

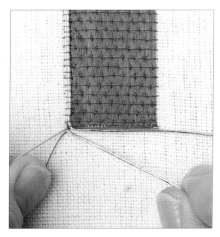

6 Secure the corner of the outer gold thread with a small diagonal stitch, worked from the outside edge to the inside. Hold the thread taut while you make the stitch, in the direction in which it will be laid.

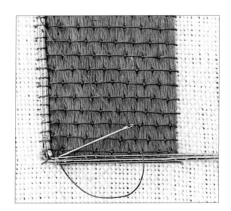

7 Lay the two gold threads together along the bottom edge of the rectangle. Hold them taut and make sure the corner is sharp and square. Couch down the two gold threads.

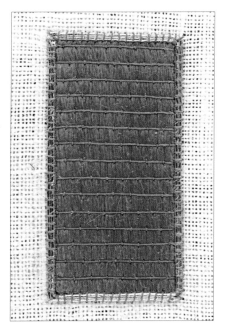

8 Continue round the rectangle and complete the couched edging by passing the two gold threads back through the fabric at the point where they started (the top left-hand corner), making sure that they 'dovetail'. Finish off by couching down each gold thread separately at the corner using a diagonal stitch. First secure the inner gold thread working from the inside outwards, and then secure the outer gold thread working from the outside in.

TIP

To pass a gold thread through fabric, always use a chenille needle. Place the needle vertically halfway through the fabric. Thread it with the gold thread, then pull the thread through the fabric. Leave a tail of about 1cm (½in) on the back of the fabric.

Trellis stitch

This is an alternative, more decorative tying-down stitch and an easier one to work, although it doesn't look it! Here, the process of working the stitch is shown in its simplest form, but when used within an embroidery it can be embellished with beads or gold threads. It is important that the stitches are evenly spaced.

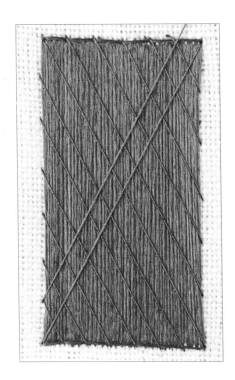

1 Using contrasting silk thread and a no. 9 sharps needle, begin in the top left-hand corner of the rectangle, and take the first tying-down stitch across diagonally to the bottom right-hand corner. Take the thread back up beneath the linen, and repeat. Complete all the stitches going in this direction, filling first one side of the rectangle and then the other, before starting those going in the other direction. Keep the stitches parallel and evenly spaced by placing the thread in the correct position and holding it taut while you make each stitch.

2 Continue to build up the trellis pattern, passing the needle through the same holes as the previous stitches to ensure a neat finish to your work.

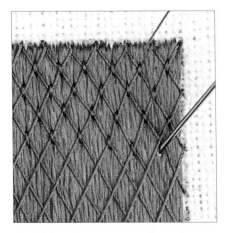

3 Using the same needle and thread, lay small securing stitches at the intersections of the diagonal threads. Keep these as small, neat and even as possible.

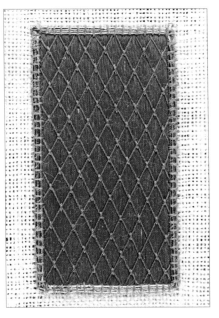

4 Complete the design by couching down a gold border (see pages 240–241).

Padding

You can introduce different levels to your design by working parts of it over a padded base. Adding depth in this way gives a beautifully rich, textured feel to your work. Four different types of padding can be used, each producing a very different effect. The floss and cotton paddings shown below give a more rounded finish, whereas the card padding shown on page 244 produces a sharper edge. Floss gives a finer padding than cotton.

Felt padding should be used if you require more height than can be achieved with a stitched or card padding. It also gives a more rounded finish to your embroidery. Here, felt padding with only two layers is shown, but if you require more height to your design you can add more layers as needed. Planning the height of your work before you start is important so that you can graduate the felt (always place the largest piece on top).

Floss padding

This type of padding is made using long stitches running the length of the shape you wish to fill. Use two strands of silk floss, and alternate long and shorter stitches. Leave a narrow 2mm (1/8in) unpadded border around the edge of the design to give a smoothly rounded shape to the finished piece.

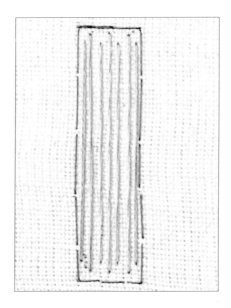

Floss padding.

TIP

When using a stitched padding, always make sure that the padding is sewn in the opposite direction to your embroidery stitch or gold threads.

Cotton padding

This is created in the same way as floss padding, but using thick, soft padding cotton. It gives a more raised effect.

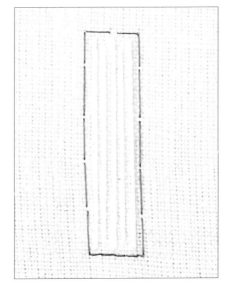

Cotton padding.

Card padding

Card padding is used when a sharper edge is needed. The card is cut to fit just within the shape and tied down in place with large, slanting stitches worked across the card. Smaller stitches are then worked at a slant around the edge, bringing the needle up through the fabric and taking it down through the card. A no. 8 needle and a fine thread are used.

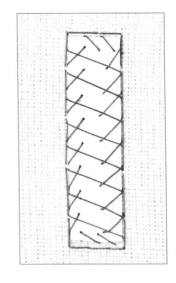

Card padding.

TIP |||||||||

Always pass the needle down into the card when sewing; never bring it up through, as this is more likely to cause damage.

Felt padding

To pad a rectangular shape with two layers of felt, begin by cutting out the first layer of felt, approximately 2mm (⅛in) smaller all round than the shape you wish to pad. Secure it using stab stitches placed along its length.

Cut out the second layer of felt, this time approximately 1mm (¹⁄₁₆in) smaller all round than the shape. This ensures that it fits comfortably over the first layer, and lies just within the shape you wish to pad. Hold the felt in position using diagonal holding stitches (shown far right). Finally, stitch it into place around the edge using slanting stitches. These are less likely to damage the felt than stitches placed at right angles to the edge as these may cut into it. Always come up with your needle through the fabric and go down into your felt – never come up into your felt as this could easily displace it.

To pad a circular shape, follow a similar technique. Hold the second layer of felt in position using long stitches that cross in the centre of the circle, like the spokes of a wheel, and secure the felt using slanting stitches placed around the edge.

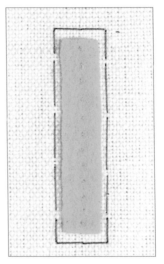

Securing the first layer of felt using stab stitches.

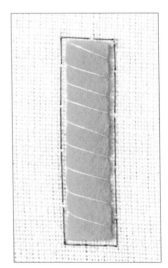

Holding the second layer of felt in position using diagonal holding stitches.

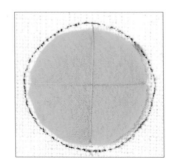
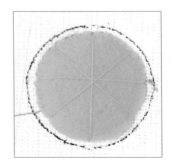

Padding a circle.

Satin stitch

Satin stitch is a very beautiful stitch, enhancing any embroidery and giving it lustre. It is nearly always worked over a padding to lift it from the background (see pages 243–244). The stitch itself is a continuous one worked from one side of the shape to the other. Go over the surface of the padding with your thread and back underneath the fabric so that your needle comes up on the same side of your shape every time. This gives the stitch a tautness which will enhance the floss and, when the floss is stroked, give a wonderful lustre to your work. To stroke the floss, lay a chenille needle across the surface of the floss and stroke it firmly (not using the point of the needle). This helps the threads lay evenly, and gives them a beautiful sheen.

Satin stitch cannot be used to fill very wide areas as the surface would not remain taut and the floss would wear. You will see below that a floss padding has been used: this is ideal if you do not need too much height. You would use a felt padding for more height and a card padding if a sharp edge were needed.

Begin by drawing a rectangle measuring 1 x 5cm (½ x 2in) and filling it with floss padding in the same colour as the satin stitch (see page 243).

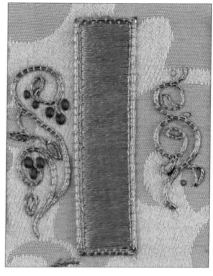

A detail from the sampler, showing satin stitch worked over a floss padding.

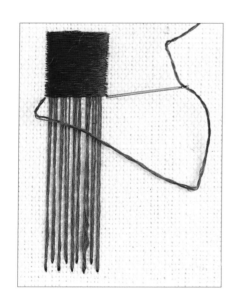
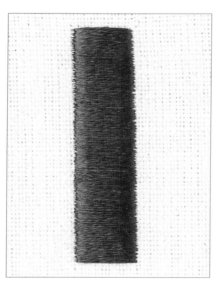
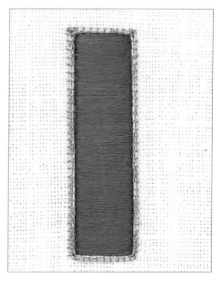

1 Using a 46cm (18in) length of thread, create the first stitch by bringing the needle up through the fabric in the top left-hand corner of the shape, and taking it back down on the other side. Make sure the stitch runs parallel to the top edge of the shape. Make the next stitch by bringing the needle back up just below the start of the first stitch, and as close as possible to it. Take the thread across the shape so that it runs parallel to the first stitch. The two stitches should be as close as possible to each other without overlapping and with no gap between the two. Continue down until the shape is completely filled.

2 To complete the design, add a gold border (see pages 240–241) couched down using a silk thread in a contrasting colour to the satin stitch.

Decorative Leaf

This project is to allow you to put into practice the stitches learnt in the previous sections. Here laid stitch and satin stitch have been put together to form a leaf shape. The leaf is worked in two different coloured flosses, but in step 3 a variegated cotton thread is used to show the effect it can give.

You will need a no. 8 sharps or embroidery needle, soft cotton thread for padding, silk floss for embroidering, K2 imitation gold thread for the surrounding edge and silk thread for couching down.

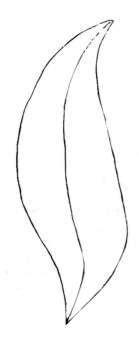

The template for the leaf design, reproduced actual size.

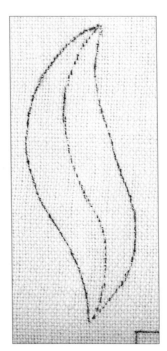

1 Transfer the leaf design on to the fabric using one of the methods described on pages 14–15.

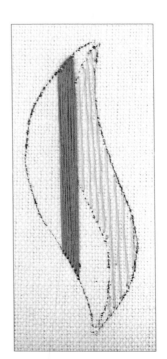

2 Begin by padding the right-hand side of the leaf with long, vertical stitches. In this case a soft cotton padding thread has been used (see page 243). When completed, fill the left-hand side of the leaf with laid stitch worked in dark green floss (see page 238).

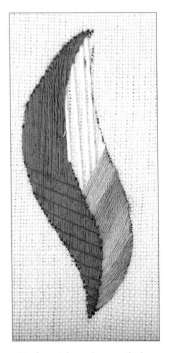

3 Lay tying-down stitches diagonally across the laid stitch on the left-hand side of the leaf using a no. 9 sharps needle and silk thread in a matching colour. These stitches imitate the veins of the leaf. Fill the right-hand side with satin stitch, mirroring the angle of the tying-down stitches on the left (see page 245). Here a variegated cotton thread has been used to show the effect that can be achieved.

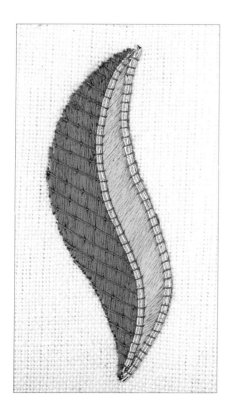

4 Complete both sides of the leaf, securing the tying-down stitches on the left-hand side using small stitches (see page 238). Couch down two gold threads to form the central vein, first passing through the two threads, the outer one above the inner, at the top of the leaf (see page 241). Work down the vein with couching stitches until you reach the bottom of the leaf and then pass through one thread above the other to finish off.

Surround the leaf with gold thread, working one side at a time. Pass the gold threads through at the top, placing the inner thread lower than the outer thread to form a point. Work down the outside of the leaf with couching stitches, taking your needle from the outside into your work. When you reach the bottom of the leaf, pass through the inner gold thread first to the back of the work, and then pass through the outer thread at a slightly higher position. To outline the other side of your leaf, place the gold threads in between those already there when passing them through top and bottom. This is called dovetailing, and will make a beautiful shape.

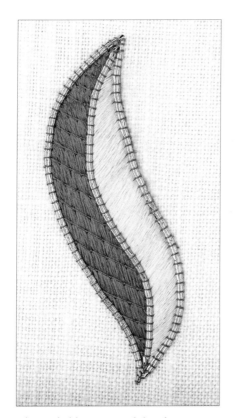

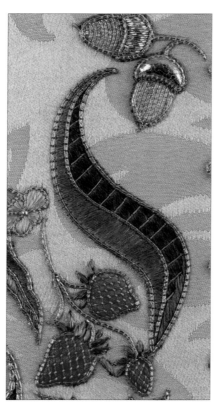

TIP ||||||||||||||||

When filling a shape with vertical stitches, in this case with either laid stitch or cotton padding, begin by placing the first stitch down the centre of the shape. Work from here outwards to one side, then return to the centre and work outwards to the other side. This helps to keep your stitches straight and parallel.

The finished leaf surrounded with gold thread.

A detail from the sampler, showing a leaf worked in a similar design.

Long and short stitch

This is an ancient form of embroidery stitch, one that is extremely beautiful to look at but can be difficult to achieve. It is a filling stitch and can be used with different thicknesses of silk embroidery thread. In ecclesiastical embroidery it is a stitch that is 'split' when worked (which means that the needle pierces the thread when it comes up into the floss). It is also a stitch that goes back upon itself a little in the second and subsequent rows: this ensures the work is well covered, and when only one colour is used gives a wonderful richness and sheen. As you become more accomplished, you should use either a single thread of floss, or two threads of fine twisted silk. When shading is needed, different tones of the same colour can be incorporated. The size of the needle varies with the thickness of the thread, but usually a no. 9 sharps needle is used. The first and most important thing to remember is that after the first row of long and short has been completed all the stitches in the subsequent rows are the same length. It is only the lengths of the stitches in the first row that give the stitch its name!

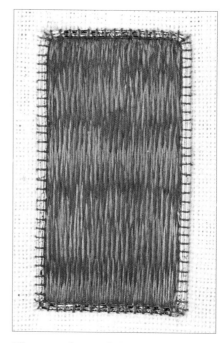

This rectangle is worked in two shades of colour so that the positions of the stitches can be seen clearly, and to show how two similar colours can merge.

The rose at the centre of the sampler is worked in long and short stitch using a paler colour towards the outside than at the centre of the flower. On to this are worked rays of fine gold thread.

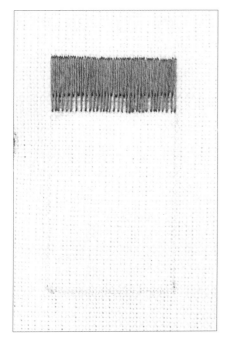

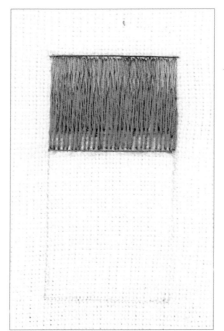

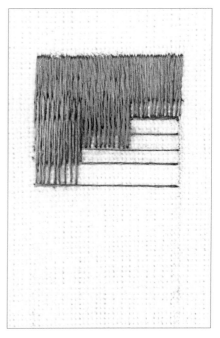

1 Begin by drawing a rectangle on to your linen. It should measure 2.5 x 5cm (1 x 2in). Using one thread of floss and a no. 9 sharps needle begin by sewing the first long stitch in the top left-hand corner of the rectangle. The length of the stitch depends on the size of the shape to be filled, but in this case it should be approximately 1.5cm (¾in) in length. Bring the needle back through at the top of the rectangle as close as possible to the first stitch and lay the second stitch, which is the short stitch. The length of this stitch should be slightly more than half the length of the long stitch. Lay alternate long and short stitches until the first row is completed.

2 To illustrate the second row clearly a contrasting colour has been used. Place your needle underneath the linen and bring it up through the first long stitch just above the end of the short stitch in the previous row. Take your needle down into the linen making this stitch the same length as a long stitch in the previous row (1.5cm or ¾in). Start the second stitch 6mm (¼in) below the top edge of the shape and bring your needle up through the first short stitch of the first row. Make this stitch the same length as the first stitch, so that it ends just below the long stitch in the first row. Repeat this process until the second row of stitching is completed.

3 Work the third row (shown here in the same colour as the first row) following the same method as the second row. The straight, horizontal lines in this picture show the positioning of the stitches more clearly.

TIP

Remember that each stitch you work splits the stitch in the previous row, and after the first row all the stitches are the same length.

Brick stitch

Brick stitch is a surface stitch in which the gold threads (which are always worked in pairs) lie on top of the fabric and are held down by couching stitches worked in a finer silk thread. The couching stitches are sewn in the form of bricks in a wall, hence the name brick stitch. It is essential to work brick stitch carefully, making sure that the stitches are straight and evenly spaced. Colour and pattern can be introduced into your design by working the couching in one or two contrasting colours.

   Brick stitch can be used to fill large areas very satisfactorily. When the gold threads are passed through the fabric, there is no need to secure them at the back of your work as they will be held in place by the couching stitches. Make sure, though, that they are not lying over your work, otherwise they may become entangled in subsequent stitching. If necessary, turn them away from the work and hold them in place. When a section is finished, turn the frame over and cut off all the gold ends, leaving a tail approximately 1cm (½in) long.

Winter

Ruth Chamberlin. Reproduced here by kind permission of Mr and Mrs Julian Amey.

The tree is worked on a calico background that has been painted using watercolour. The trunk is raised slightly in the middle. The trunk and the branches are worked in brick stitch, and where the moon's rays rest, a silver thread has been added.

The example below uses a method called 'turning and passing'. It enables you to fill a shape without passing in both gold threads at the top and bottom every time.

1 Begin by marking out the shape you wish to fill on your fabric: in this case a rectangle measuring 5 x 2.5cm (2 x 1in). Pass the first gold thread through the fabric in the top left-hand corner of the shape. Cut off the length required for the first line of gold, equal to the depth of the rectangle (5cm or 2in) plus an additional 1cm (½in) for passing through.

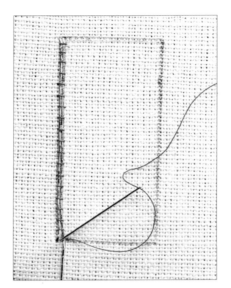

2 Pass a second gold thread to the right of the first, keeping this thread on the reel. Couch down the two threads all the way to the bottom left-hand corner, working the stitches from right to left (this ensures that no space is formed in between the pairs of threads). As you work, keep the second gold thread taut and hold it as close as possible to the first gold thread to create an even line. Pass the first thread in at the corner, and take a stitch over the second gold thread to secure it at the bottom.

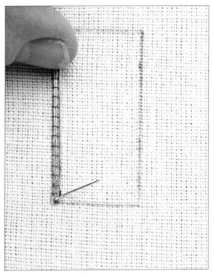

3 Bring the needle up halfway, just to the right of the second gold thread, and turn this thread sharply upwards to form the third line of gold thread.

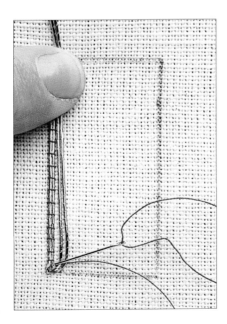

4 Cut off the gold thread from the reel, ensuring it is as long as the rectangle plus 1cm (½in). Pass a fourth gold thread at the bottom of the rectangle next to the third, leaving it attached to the reel. Couch down these last two threads.

5 Continue using the turning and passing method, working your way up and down the shape until all of it is filled. Couch a gold border around the rectangle to finish (see pages 240–241).

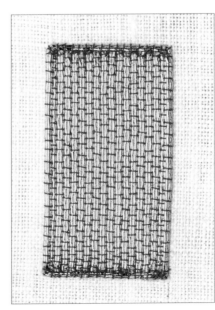

Golden Diamond

In this project, you will be using brick stitch in a more interesting and decorative manner. It uses a K3 imitation Jap gold thread, and a no. 9 sharps needle and a red silk thread for the couching to make the stitchery clearer.

There is quite a lot to think about when working this shape; not only are there the corners to consider, but also the passing in of the two gold threads has to be very sharp on both the horizontal and vertical lines and also on the edge of each segment. The turning and passing method, described on page 251, is not appropriate to this shape, or indeed any shape that requires a very sharp outline – this can only be achieved by passing both threads through each time. At the corners, each gold thread has to be stitched separately to form a sharp bend. This is explained in the following instructions.

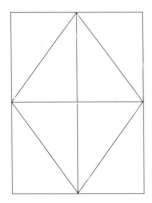

The template for the diamond design, reproduced actual size.

TIP

When working with pairs of gold threads, remember to cut one to the correct length, allowing 1cm (½in) for passing through, and leave the other attached to the reel.

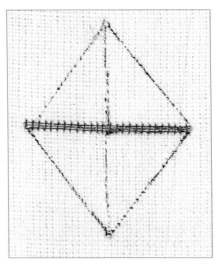

1 First transfer the design on to the background fabric using the template (see pages 14–15). On the right-hand side, pass two gold threads either side of the centre line running horizontally. Starting on the right, couch down the two threads, taking the stitches from above the gold threads to below them. When you reach the left-hand edge of the shape, pass the two gold threads through.

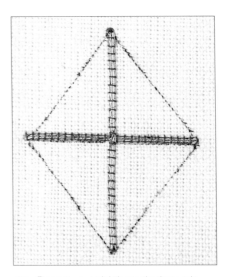

2 Pass two gold threads through at the top point of the diamond, one either side of the centre line, and couch them down to the bottom point. Make sure one gold thread is placed either side of the centre line. The vertical line is more important than the horizontal in this design, which is why it must be worked over the top. Pass the gold threads in at the bottom.

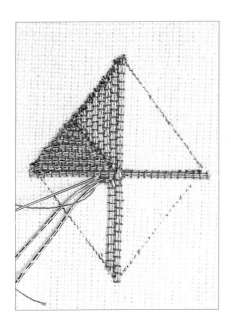

3 Fill in each segment of the diamond with L-shaped lines. Begin by passing through two gold threads on the sloping line (the outline), exactly next to the vertical line, and couching to the centre. Work the stitches from the outside into the shape. At the centre, turn the inner gold thread sharply (as explained on page 241), and place a couching stitch worked from the outside into the corner at an angle. Turn the second thread in the same way. Continue couching, keeping the needle on the outside of the gold as you come up so that there is no gap created between the gold threads. Pass the two threads in through the fabric on the sloping line.

The diamond design, couched using green silk, on the sampler.

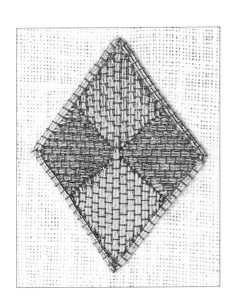

4 Complete the diamond by couching a gold border around the outside edge of the shape (see pages 240–241). Notice how the variation in the colour of the gold thread is achieved by the direction of the threads, adding depth and richness to the design.

Golden Circle

There are so many ways of using gold, and in this project the threads are laid on the surface of the fabric in order to make a circular form. It shows very clearly the malleability of the gold thread. The circle is embellished with simple, straight lines of couching in a contrasting colour. A more intricate design worked within the same shape is also shown.

For working gold into a circular shape it is best to use a fine thread (K4 imitation Jap gold is ideal) as a thick thread would not turn so well. Use a silk thread for couching down the gold, and a no. 9 sharps needle.

First draw a circle measuring 4.5cm (1¾in) diameter on to your fabric. Using a pencil or marker pen, draw within this shape eight diagonal lines, as shown in step 1. If a sharper line is required, these can be tacked in, as shown in the first two steps.

Gold will not sit neatly around a curve without being held in position with a stitch. You will see, therefore, when you arrive at step 4 that more lines have been drawn in between those already worked to mark the positions of the additional stitches required as the circle widens.

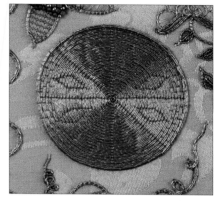

A detail from the sampler showing surface stitch worked in a circle. The securing stitches have been worked in a pattern using silk thread in a contrasting colour.

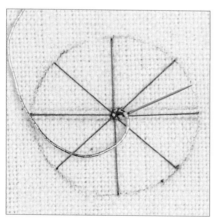

1 Pass through a single gold thread at the centre of the circle. Keep this thread on the reel. Secure it with a small stitch placed on one of the diagonals. Curve the gold thread round to form a tight inner circle, positioning the securing stitches so that they lie on the diagonals.

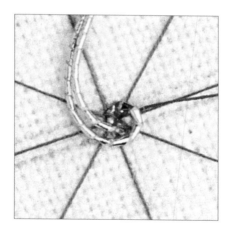

2 Continue round once more, and then pass through a second gold thread, just inside the first. This second gold thread should be cut from the reel and must be long enough to finish the whole shape (to pass a new thread at any point within the circle would be very difficult to hide).

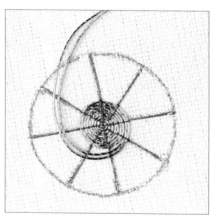

3 Continue forming the circle, placing securing stitches over the two threads on the four diagonals to create the pattern. Work the securing stitches from the outside in towards the centre of the circle. This helps keep the circle as neat and tight as possible.

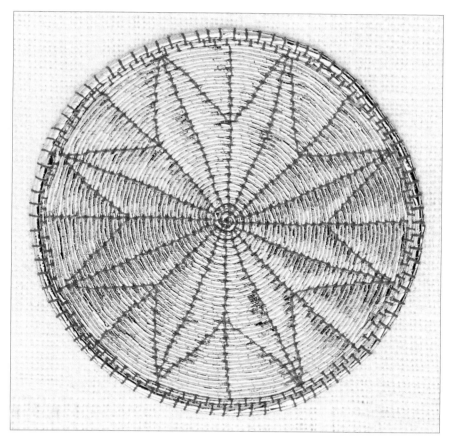

This circle has a more decorative finish than the one in the demonstration, created by placing securing stitches in a pattern. For the gold border, pass the inside thread first, just within the worked shape, and the second thread, offset slightly, just outside it. Work around the circumference of the circle, sewing equally spaced couching stitches. Take the needle from the outside and work inwards to ensure the edge of the work is completely covered and to create a perfect circle. When you arrive at the point where the two outline threads meet, pass the inside thread first and then the outer thread, dovetailing the two ends together in each case.

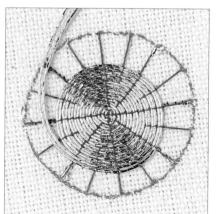

4 When you have worked approximately one-third of the circle, draw in four more diagonals, halfway between the first, and place securing stitches on these also.

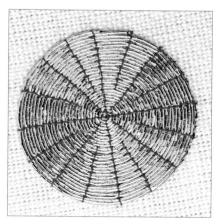

The completed circle.

TIP ||||||||||||||

Be firm with your gold threads – place them exactly where you want them to go, and remember to always work the securing stitches from the outside in towards the centre of the shape. This helps to hold the circle together and to maintain a regular shape.

Kid

Introducing kid into your design will help give it a wonderful liveliness, though it should be used sparingly and thoughtfully: it can look inartistic when used in slabs. Kid should always be used so that it merges into the design and it is nearly always padded. The area to be filled with kid should always be worked with a solid area of goldwork around it so that the finished design looks well balanced.

Slanting stitches are used to edge fragile materials such as felt and kid. This is because they 'bind' the edge and do not cut into it, as might shorter stitches placed at right angles to the edge.

Always sew downwards into kid, not up through it – this gives you more control over the positioning of the stitches, and is less likely to cause damage to the kid as you pass the needle through.

Begin by drawing a circle measuring 4cm (1½in) in diameter on to your linen, and adding two layers of felt padding following the technique shown on page 244. To achieve the right sized circle of kid, place a piece of greaseproof paper (it is softer than tracing paper) over the two thicknesses of felt and pencil around the shape. This will allow for the fullness of the felt. Place the greaseproof template on to the wrong side of the kid and draw around the shape. Cut it out using sharp scissors on the pencil line.

The acorns on the sampler are worked in brick stitch. The cups have been worked in raised gold and kid.

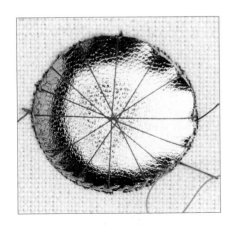

1 Secure the kid over the felt by using long tacking stitches that cross the shape like the spokes of a wheel. These long stitches should be done with a fine silk thread as this will not mark the kid as would a thicker thread. Sew around the edge of the kid using slanting stitches taken from the outside and going down into the kid. Use a fine no. 10 sharps needle and a silk thread. This is a vulnerable edge, so your slanting stitches should wrap the edge and not pull it.

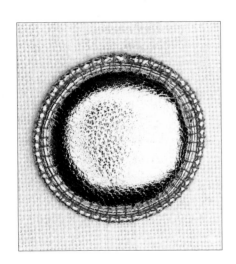

2 Once the kid is sewn securely to the background, remove the tying-down stitches and complete the design with a gold border. In this case, two pairs of gold threads have been couched down using brick stitch. (See page 255 for instructions on adding a border to a circle.)

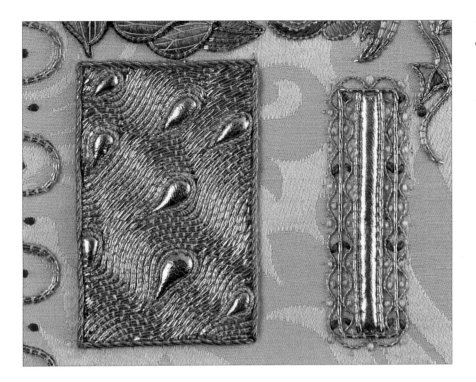

Two details from the sampler, showing different ways in which kid can be used.

To add kid to an oblong shape, first draw an oblong on to your fabric – the one shown here measures 1.5 x 6.5cm (¾ x 2½in). Add two layers of felt padding following the technique shown on page 244.

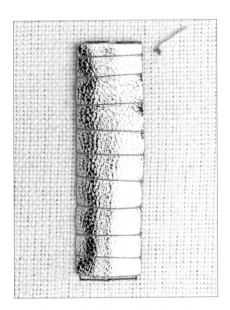

1 Secure the kid over the two layers of felt padding using long, parallel tying-down stitches.

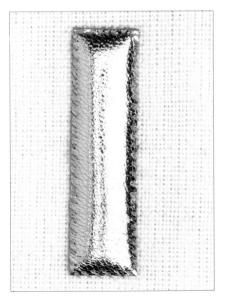

2 Sew the kid in place with a fine needle using slanting stitches, then remove the tying-down stitches. Do not leave in the tying-down stitches longer than necessary, as they can mark the kid.

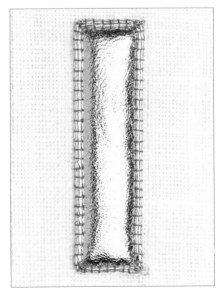

3 Complete the shape with two threads of gold couched down around the edge (see pages 240–241).

Teardrops

This small, more advanced project is an excellent way to gain valuable practice in working with kid and gold thread in a more fluid way. One of the beauties of goldwork is the sense of movement and freedom that can be gained from working the gold threads into gentle curves and shapes. The changing patterns of shadow and light that this creates can be truly breathtaking.

The kid used here is fairly light in weight, and the colour works well with the K3 imitation Jap gold chosen. The teardrop shapes are very small, so it is better to use only a single layer of felt for padding. When one layer of felt is used it is important that a good shape is cut with sharp scissors (making sure it is a little smaller than the shape drawn on your linen), and that it is secured to the background by tacking it in position first and then sewing around the edge (see page 244).

Use a no. 9 sharps needle for sewing the kid, and a no. 8 or 9 for the brick stitch. For the couching, use a fine silk thread in a contrasting colour.

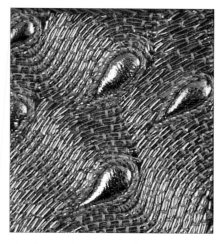

Detail taken from the sampler.

The template for the teardrop design, reproduced actual size.

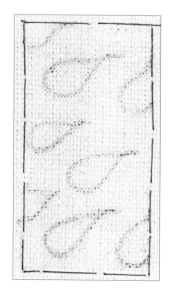

1 First, transfer the design to your background fabric and outline the rectangle using tacking stitches to give it a sharp defining edge.

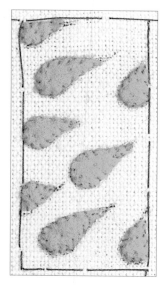

2 Add a single layer of felt padding to each teardrop, secured using small, slanting stitches (see page 244).

3 Attach a layer of kid to each teardrop. Sew it on carefully, ensuring that the stitches are sufficiently slanted to avoid them cutting into and damaging the edges.

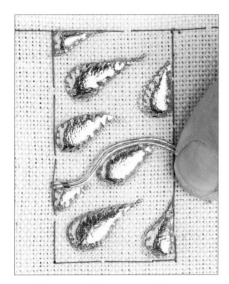

4 Starting in the centre of the design, build up the background by laying lines of gold couched in pairs across the shape, working them closely around the teardrops.

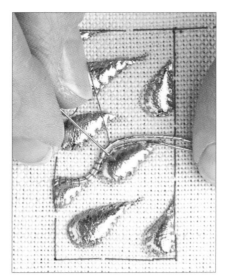

5 The first line of gold is important as it defines the shape of the subsequent ones. Hold the two gold threads firmly in position while you couch them down, working the stitches from the outside in. It is important that you actually attach the couching to the kid to obtain a snug fit around the teardrops.

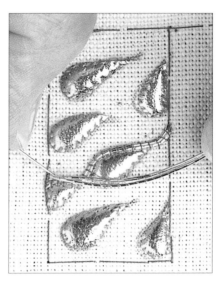

6 At the end of the line pass the two gold threads back through the fabric. Start the second line of gold, which will lie adjacent to the first line and just above it.

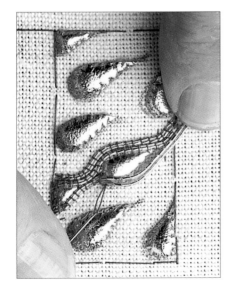

7 Work the third row just below the first one. Gradually build up the background by moving outwards from the central line.

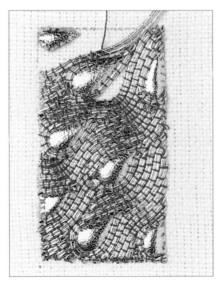

8 Remove the tacking stitches and continue building up the background. Fill any small spaces left in the background at the end.

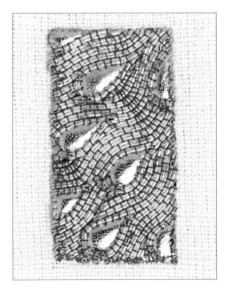

The completed design.

Raised gold

Raised gold involves laying gold threads over a raised surface. It is a wonderful form of embroidery for it can bring so much light to any design. The thickness of padding can vary according to the depth required in your design, but the width of raised gold cannot exceed 1cm (½in) – if wider than this, the gold would become worn and the threads would not stay firmly in place. Here, K4 imitation Jap gold is used and a no. 9 sharps needle for the couching.

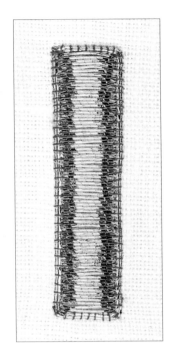

The completed embroidery with a gold border
(see pages 240–241).

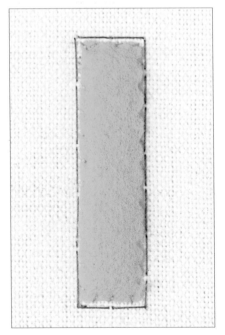

1 Transfer the outline of the shape on to your fabric, using either a pencil line or tacking stitches (as done here). Build up two layers of felt padding, as described on page 244.

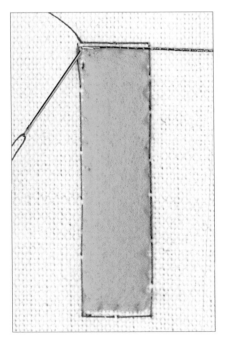

2 Working straight from the reel, pass a single gold thread through the top left-hand corner of the shape. Hold the thread firmly in place across the top of the felt and harness the thread using a single couching stitch, worked from top to bottom.

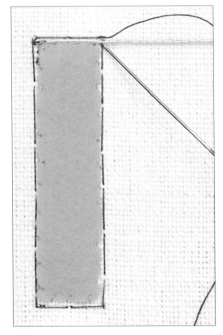

3 With the thread across the felt, (allowing for the fullness of the raised shape), from the top right-hand corner take a tiny stitch over the gold thread. Make sure the gold thread is lying parallel with the edge of the rectangle, and as close as possible to it.

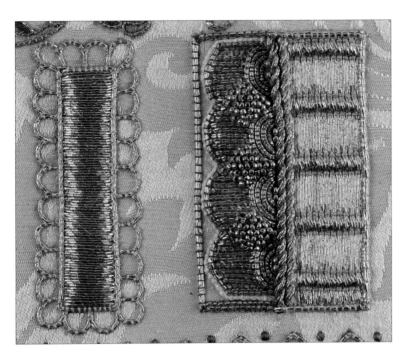

Two details from the sampler, showing raised gold worked over felt on the left-hand side, and raised gold worked over string on the right-hand side of the oblong on the right.

TIP |||||||||||||||||||||||||

You may get a small gap between the first two threads where they lie over the edge of the felt. This can easily be adjusted later.

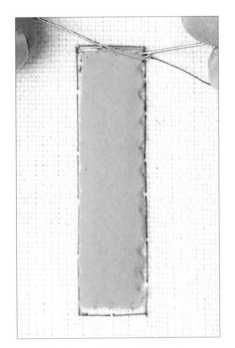

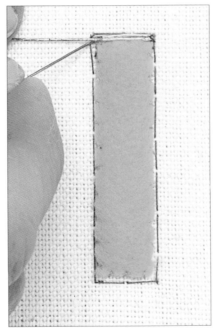

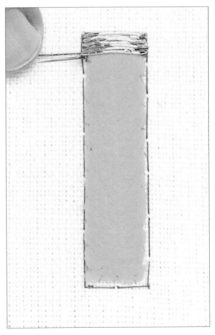

4 Turn the gold thread sharply around your needle, and harness it on the bend with a tiny stitch placed snugly beside the first. Take a tiny securing stitch by the edge of the felt to secure it.

5 Lay the gold thread back across the shape. Take your needle across the back of the work and bring it up on the left-hand side. Keeping the gold thread as close as possible to the one above, take a stitch over the gold thread (worked from bottom to top) and turn the gold sharply. Sew a securing stitch by the edge of the felt.

6 Continue working backwards and forwards across the shape, keeping the gold threads as straight and as close to each other as possible, and allowing for the fullness of the felt. Work each stitch from bottom to top, and harness each one with a small holding stitch placed just below it by the edge of the felt.

Basket stitch

Basket stitch is a surface stitch that can give height and texture to any goldwork design. It is worked over string, which can vary in thickness according to the thickness of the gold thread used. Here, a white-coloured string is used, but very often gold-coloured string is used for this purpose. The thickness of string used here is suitable for use with K3 imitation Jap gold.

Basket stitch can be worked with alternate gold threads, as in the centre of the rose on the sampler. Here, a fine K5 Jap gold thread has been used. In the demonstration below, three pairs of gold threads are used (remembering that it is always correct to work gold threads in pairs).

It is very important when using this stitch that the foundation is worked extremely carefully – the string must be placed evenly on the background, and each piece of string must be carefully shaped and sewn firmly in position – for the gold basketwork will not stay in place if not.

Detail from the sampler, showing the centre of the rose worked in basket stitch using alternate threads of K5 Jap gold.

1 Begin by drawing a rectangle measuring 2.5 x 5cm (1 x 2in) on to your background fabric. Cut lengths of string measured accurately to fit just within the outlined shape: in this case just under 2.5cm (1in). Twelve pieces will be required. Trim the ends of the string at an angle to create a smooth edge.

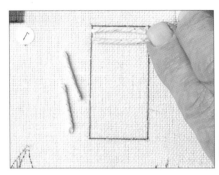

2 Lay the string across the shape, placing it just within the outline. Space out the string evenly leaving gaps between the strings equal to the width of the string, and make sure that the cut edge is facing upwards.

3 Attach each piece of string to the fabric using matching thread and evenly spaced overstitches. Pass the needle up through the fabric at a slant from underneath the string, take the thread over the string, and pass the needle back through at a slant on the other side. This closeness of stitch to the string will ensure a firm hold. Hold the string in place with a pin if necessary, but be careful not to break the twist of the string.

Detail taken from the sampler, showing basket stitch worked into two rectangles. The left-hand shape has been worked with two pairs of K4 Jap gold threads in each section (remembering that you always use two threads together), and the right-hand shape has been worked using three pairs of K3 Jap gold threads per section.

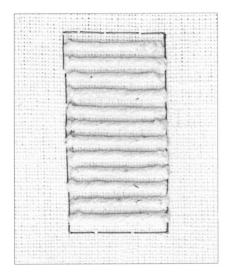

The rectangle with all the string in place.

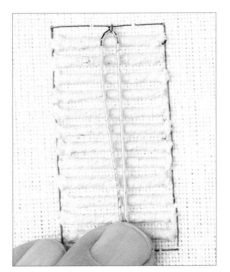

4 Starting in the centre at the top of the shape, make a loop in the gold thread and harness it to the fabric with a single stitch worked from the edge of the shape in. Leave the right-hand thread attached to the reel; the left-hand thread should be twice the length of the rectangle plus 2cm (¾in).

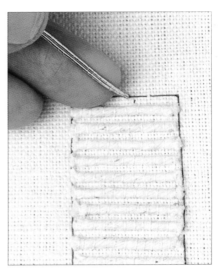

5 Place a small holding stitch just within the shape. Pull the gold threads back firmly whilst holding the sewing thread tightly underneath the frame. This helps to straighten the gold thread in readiness for laying it down in position on the linen.

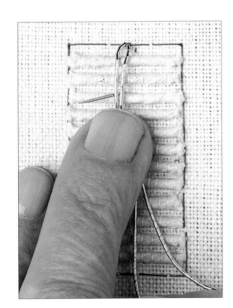

6 Holding the two threads of gold in place, bring the needle up at a slight angle from underneath the gold threads and just to their left, and between the second and third pieces of string.

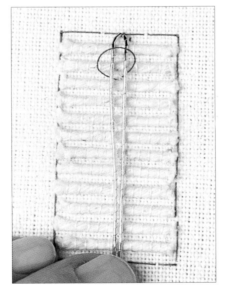

7 Take the needle back down on the other side of the gold threads, again at a slight angle, to form a stitch. Take another tiny stitch by the side of this stitch to harness it. Make sure that the gold thread is raised slightly over the string to give the embroidery depth. If you pull the gold too tightly it will lie too flat and the three-dimensional quality of the work will be lost.

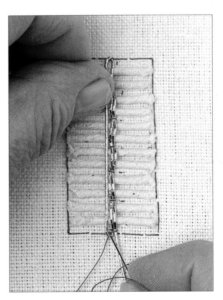

8 Continue to the bottom of the shape, then turn the left-hand gold thread sharply upwards (see page 241). Bring your needle up through the linen and take a stitch over the thread at the base of the turn.

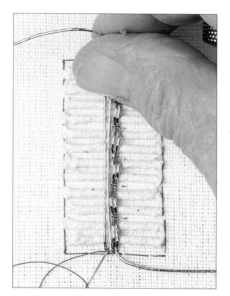

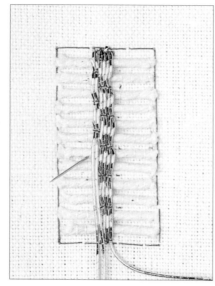

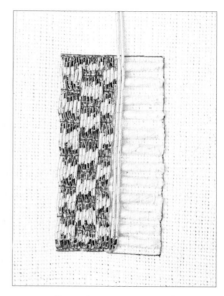

9 Cut the gold thread from the reel, leaving a tail equal to the length of the rectangle plus an extra 2cm (¾in). Working again from the reel, pass a gold thread exactly next to the turned thread and work your way back up the shape, placing your couching stitches as in the first row.

10 At the top of the rectangle, pass the right-hand gold thread through and turn the left-hand thread down sharply. Cut this thread from the reel as before, and pass through another gold thread next to the previous one, again working from the reel. Couch down the two left-hand threads, this time placing your stitches between the first and second strings, the third and fourth strings and so on, thus creating the basketweave effect.

11 Complete the left-hand side of the rectangle, changing the position of the securing stitches every third pair of gold threads. Start the right-hand side of the shape at the bottom, turning the thread left on the reel at the start of the first line of gold, and passing through a second gold thread just to its right. Place the securing stitches for these first two gold threads in the same positions as those just to their left. Change the positions of the securing stitches every sixth line, as before.

TIP ||||||||||||||||

Always work your securing stitches from the outside of the design inwards. This helps to draw the gold threads together.

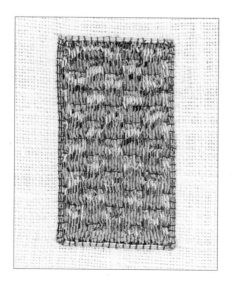

The completed design, with a gold border.

Acorns

The acorn lends itself perfectly to interpretation using a number of the techniques described in this chapter. Below is a small design which you should be able to complete fairly quickly. It has been worked twice, using different techniques in each case. By working through these two projects, you will consolidate much of what you have learned and, in the process, gain the inspiration and confidence to move forward with your goldwork and create designs of your own.

For each project you will need nos 8, 9 or 10 embroidery needles and a chenille needle. The materials required are listed separately under each project.

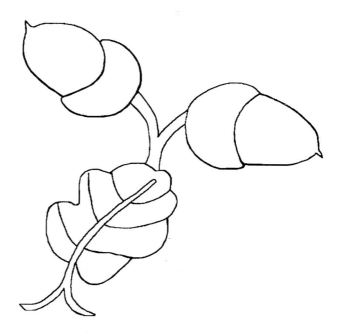

Template for the design, shown actual size.

Golden acorns

In this design, the acorns are worked predominantly in gold. For the brick stitch on the two nuts, the raised gold on the right-hand cup and the veining on the leaf, K4 imitation Jap gold thread has been used, and for the gold border around the acorns and leaf and for the stems, K3 imitation Jap gold. All the couching is worked using gold-coloured sewing silk, though green is used in the example below so that the stitching is clearer. The leaf is filled using laid stitch worked in a variegated green floss. A small piece of felt is required for padding the acorn cups, and greaseproof paper for covering the raised felt in preparation for cutting the kid. The finished acorns and stems have been edged with a light green silk floss couched down with green sewing silk.

In both this and the following design, the stems have been given a raised edge by working two layers of couched gold threads. Having laid and couched down the first two threads, lay another pair over the first, placing one thread on top of them down the centre of the stem and the second alongside them, just to the left of the left-hand thread. Couch down the second pair by working the stitches from the outer edge inwards, passing the needle back through the fabric in between the first two threads laid.

The completed embroidery, shown actual size.

The nuts

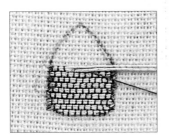  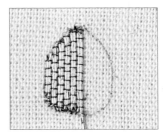 

1 Starting at the base of the shape, work the right-hand acorn in brick stitch using the K4 imitation Jap gold thread. Lay the gold threads horizontally, passing the first two one above the other on the left-hand edge of the nut. Continue up the nut, passing the threads in at the sides to retain a good shape. Make sure that your couching stitches are worked from the top to the bottom of the gold threads so that there are no gaps between the rows. Add a gold border to finish.

2 Create the left-hand acorn also using brick stitch, but working vertically with the threads. Always start in the centre of the shape and work outwards, first to the left and then to the right.

TIP

Because the nut is slightly rounded, begin and end the gold threads of the first row within the nut shape.

The leaf

The leaf is worked in laid stitch using two shades of green floss. Combining two different shades of green creates an interesting variegated effect. Twist together two strands of silk floss as you work. When you transfer your design, draw in the curving central vein to divide your leaf in two.

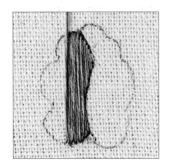   

1 Place the first laid stitch down the centre of the left-hand side of the leaf and work first towards the vein on the right, and then towards the left.

2 Complete the right-hand side in a similar fashion, working first towards the vein and then towards the right.

The completed laid stitch.

3 Couch down two gold threads for each vein, and complete the leaf with a central vein, stem and border couched down using green silk thread.

The cups

1 Begin by applying three layers of felt padding to each cup as shown. The sizes of the pads need to be made progressively larger to achieve a smooth, domed shape.

The first layer of felt, stab stitched in place.

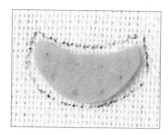

The second layer of felt, stab stitched in place.

The third layer of felt, secured with slanting stitches worked around the edge.

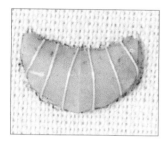

2 You now need to measure the fullness of the left-hand cup so that when the kid is cut it is the correct size. Place a small piece of greaseproof paper over the felt shape, and draw around it with a marker pen or pencil. Cut this shape out with sharp scissors and tie it down over the felt to see that it fits perfectly. Release the paper shape and place it on the wrong side of the kid. Mark around the shape with a marker pen or pencil and cut this out with sharp scissors. Now you have a perfectly shaped piece of kid to cover the raised felt.

3 Tie the kid in position with a fine silk thread (this will not mark the kid as would a thicker thread), then sew around the edge of the kid using a silk thread and a fine needle. Remember to use slanting stitches worked from the outside of the shape into the kid (never come up with your needle into the kid). Remove the positioning threads.

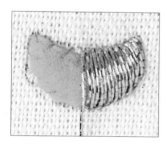

4 Complete the right-hand cup using raised gold over the felt padding. Start at the top in the middle as this helps you maintain a good, symmetrical shape. Take a loop of gold thread over the shape and make a stitch over the gold loop at the bottom, working from right to left, using a fine silk thread in a matching colour. Let the single gold thread lie with some fullness over the felt shape. Harness with a tiny stitch just under the felt shape so that it doesn't show. Turn the gold thread up firmly, laying it over the raised felt. Continue to fill the right-hand side of the shape, turning the gold on each edge of the shape and working the securing stitches from the outside in. Pass the gold thread in at the point and with a firm stitch secure the end. Repeat this process on the left-hand side of the cup.

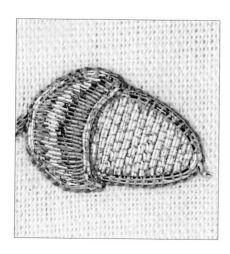

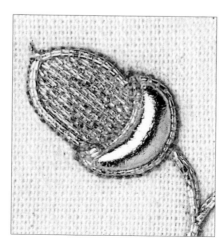

5 When you have completed both the acorns, add a gold border first to the cups and then the nuts, turning a single gold thread up at the top of the nut to finish.

Green acorns

This design is a mirror image of the previous one. The right-hand nut is worked in laid stitch using a light green silk floss with a decorative lattice tying-down stitch worked in gold sewing silk. The cup is worked with variegated green beads sewn over a felt-padded base. The left-hand nut is worked in vertical satin stitch (using the same light green floss) over a silk padding, and the cup is worked in variegated fine green ribbon which is tied down over a felt-padded base (this is worked following the same method as raised gold). For the leaf use the same method as for the previous design. The gold outline, the veining on the leaf and the stems are all worked using K3 imitation Jap gold.

Attaching beads

Beads are always sewn securely using a waxed thread, and it is often advisable to use a fine bead needle as the eye of an ordinary sewing needle may not be small enough to allow the beads to pass over easily. Beads can be used singly, as in borders like the one on the sampler, but very often they are used in groups to achieve some lovely textural effects.

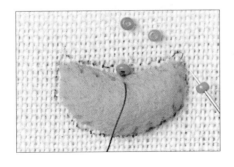

1 To sew on the beads, thread a fine needle with a length of waxed thread. Knot the end of the thread and pass it through to the front of the fabric. Pick up a bead with the point of your needle and push it down to the end of the thread. Secure the bead with a single small stitch, taking the needle through the fabric at a slight angle underneath the bead. If the hole is big enough, take a second stitch through it. Bring the needle back up through the felt leaving a small space just large enough for the next bead.

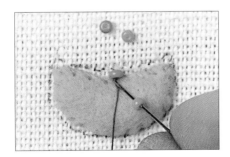

2 Secure the second bead adjacent to the first and continue in this manner until the shape is filled.

Spring

Ruth Chamberlin

This tree is worked in exactly the same way as Winter on page 250. To indicate Spring, blossom has been created using beads in various shades of pink, and leaves cut from green felt.

Index

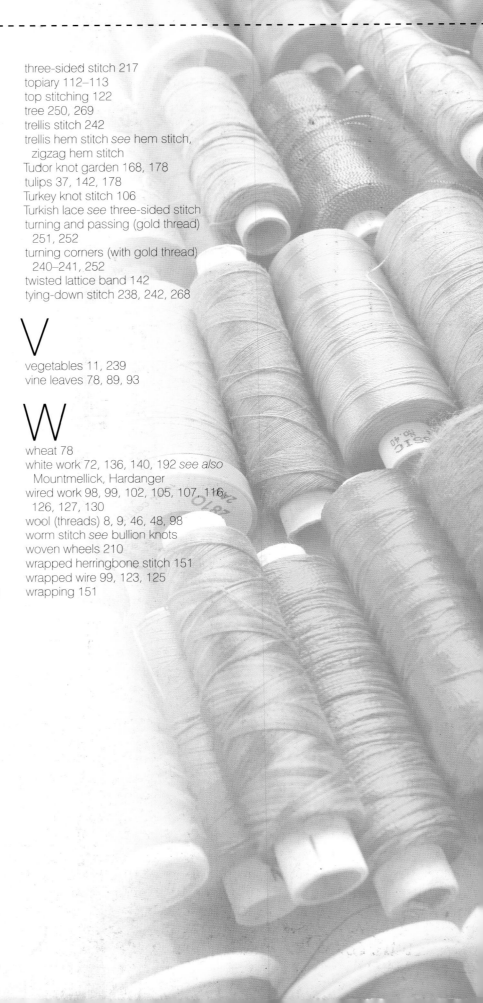